Learning MCollective

Jo Rhett

Beijing · Cambridge · Farnham · Köln · Sebastopol · Tokyo

Learning MCollective

by Jo Rhett

Copyright © 2014 Jo Rhett. All rights reserved.

Printed in the United States of America.

Published by O'Reilly Media, Inc., 1005 Gravenstein Highway North, Sebastopol, CA 95472.

O'Reilly books may be purchased for educational, business, or sales promotional use. Online editions are also available for most titles (*http://safaribooksonline.com* (*http://safaribooksonline.com/?portal=oreilly*)). For more information, contact our corporate/institutional sales department: 800-998-9938 or corporate@oreilly.com.

Editors: Courtney Nash and Brian Anderson	**Proofreader:** Amanda Kersey
Production Editor: Kara Ebrahim	**Indexer:** Judy McConville
Copyeditor: Jasmine Kwityn	**Interior Designer:** David Futato
	Cover Designer: Ellie Volckhausen
	Illustrator: Rebecca Demarest

August 2014:   First Edition

Revision History for the First Edition

2014-08-11:   First Release

See *http://oreilly.com/catalog/errata.csp?isbn=9781491945674* for release details.

Nutshell Handbook, the Nutshell Handbook logo, and the O'Reilly logo are registered trademarks of O'Reilly Media, Inc. *Learning MCollective*, the image of English Leicester sheep, and related trade dress are trademarks of O'Reilly Media, Inc.

Many of the designations used by manufacturers and sellers to distinguish their products are claimed as trademarks. Where those designations appear in this book, and O'Reilly Media, Inc., was aware of a trademark claim, the designations have been printed in caps or initial caps.

While every precaution has been taken in the preparation of this book, the publisher and author assume no responsibility for errors or omissions, or for damages resulting from the use of the information contained herein.

978-1-491-94567-4

[LSI]

Table of Contents

Part II.   Complex Installations

Part IV. Putting It All Together

Preface

This book will teach you to install and use the Marionette Collective, hereafter referred to as MCollective. It will outline how MCollective works and how MCollective's design provides value to you. You'll learn how to seamlessly orchestrate change on thousands of nodes worldwide or on a handful of nodes with a specific characteristic just as easily.

This book provides specific instruction on how to use configuration management tools like Puppet and Chef to deploy MCollective. It covers how MCollective can manipulate the Puppet and Chef agents and use data provided by them.

Who This Book Is For

This book is primarily aimed at system administrators and operations or DevOps engineers. If you are responsible for development or production nodes, this book will provide you with useful tools to make your job easier than ever before. If you are using Puppet or Chef to manage your nodes, you're going to learn how MCollective snaps into your existing configuration management to give you instant control of your managed nodes. Within a month, you'll wonder how you ever got along without it.

No matter what you call yourself, if you feel that you spend too much time managing computers, then this book is for you. You'd like to get it done faster so you can focus on something else. You'd like to do it more consistently, so that you don't have to chase down one-off problems in your reports. Or you've got some new demands that you're looking for a way to solve. If any of these statements fit, you will find MCollective to be one of the best tools in your toolbox.

What to Expect from Me

This book will not be a tome filled with reference material irrelevant to the day-to-day system administrator—exactly the opposite. Throughout this book, we will never stray from one simple goal: we focus all our efforts on how MCollective can help you do something faster or better than ever before.

This book will never tell you to run a script and not tell you what it does, or why. I hate modeling systems to determine what an installation script did, and I won't do this to you. In this book, you will build up the entire installation by hand. You'll know where every configuration file lives. You'll learn every configuration parameter and what it means.

And yes, then you will learn the Puppet modules and Chef cookbooks you can use to automate deployment seamlessly throughout your environment.

What You Will Need

You may use any modern Linux, Unix, Mac, or Windows system and successfully follow the hands-on tutorials in this book.

Although we'll introduce a web client for MCollective, the majority of the process of configuring and enabling MCollective and utilization of client apps will be performed through the command line.

A beginner to system administration can follow every tutorial in this book. Any experience with scripts, coding, or configuration management will enhance what you can get out of this book, as we will spend some time documenting how MCollective can utilize and enhance each of those.

Part III documents how to build custom plugins for MCollective in the Ruby language. Ruby programmers will be able to utilize this immediately, while others may need reference materials—such as Michael Fitzgerald's *Learning Ruby* (O'Reilly)—as they add more features to the working examples provided here.

What You'll Find in This Book

Chapter 1 discusses what MCollective does, how it works, and how it can be used to orchestrate change on your systems faster and easier than you could have imagined. Learn how MCollective is different from control systems that loop through each target and how true parallel execution can benefit your environment.

The remainder of Part I will focus on getting you up and running with a working MCollective installation. You will learn the components that make up the MCollective infrastructure. You'll install and configure each in a manner suitable for your specific environment.

This won't be a test environment for training that doesn't match your real concerns; instead, you'll perform real operations on hosts that match your production environment. You'll see how easy it is to deploy MCollective and exactly how powerful the tools it provides are.

Part II takes you on a nuts-and-bolts tour inside MCollective's architecture, backbone, transport, and security controls. You'll learn about using a *network of brokers* to resolve multisite or redundancy requirements. You'll learn how to create and use collectives to handle thousands of MCollective agents spread around the world. After finishing this section, you'll be able to fine-tune MCollective for your exact environment: small but globally diverse, immense in scale but localized, or a combination of both.

MCollective has an active developer and user community. "Finding Community Plugins" on page 53 directs you to online repositories of clients and agents built by others, as well as concrete examples of how to use others' plugins in your environment.

In Part III, you will create your own *server* and *client* plugins to perform any action you can conceive of. You'll learn how to create application clients and how to create listeners to collect registration details from the agent systems. Best of all, the secrets of collecting and processing responses using a directed reply will allow you to create self-healing systems.

How to Use This Book

This book provides explicit instructions for configuring and using MCollective from the command line without the use of an external tools.

The book documents and utilizes a Puppet module that can implement and control every feature of MCollective documented in this book. In Part II, every configuration option is documented for both standalone and Puppet configuration.

The book documents a Chef cookbook that can be used to maintain MCollective and gives MCollective the ability to manage the Chef agent.

If you use Salt, Cfengine, or any other configuration-management system, the instructions here can be used to deploy MCollective. You will find it easy to create configuration policies from the examples in this book. The server plugin provided in Part III, along with the section about how to interact with external commands, could be easily adjusted to control the management agent on each node.

IPv6 Ready

Every example with IP addresses will include both IPv4 and IPv6 statements. If you're only using one of these protocols, you can ignore the other. MCollective will happily use any combination of them. More details about complex IPv6 setups will be covered in "IPv6 Dual-Stack Environments" on page 100.

Conventions Used in This Book

The following typographical conventions are used in this book:

Italic
> Indicates new terms, URLs, email addresses, filenames, and file extensions.

`Constant width`
> Used for program listings, as well as within paragraphs to refer to program elements such as variable or function names, databases, data types, environment variables, statements, and keywords.

`Constant width bold`
> Shows commands or other text that should be typed literally by the user.

`Constant width italic`
> Shows text that should be replaced with user-supplied values or by values determined by context.

 This element signifies a tip or suggestion.

 This element signifies a general note.

 This element indicates a warning or caution.

Using Code Examples

Supplemental material (code examples, exercises, etc.) is available for download at *https://github.com/jorhett/learning-mcollective*.

This book is here to help you get your job done. In general, if example code is offered with this book, you may use it in your programs and documentation. You do not need to contact us for permission unless you're reproducing a significant portion of the code. For example, writing a program that uses several chunks of code from this book does not require permission. Selling or distributing a CD-ROM of examples from O'Reilly books does require permission. Answering a question by citing this book and quoting example code does not require permission. Incorporating a significant amount of example code from this book into your product's documentation does require permission.

We appreciate, but do not require, attribution. An attribution usually includes the title, author, publisher, and ISBN. For example: "*Learning MCollective* by Jo Rhett (O'Reilly). Copyright 2014 Jo Rhett, 978-1-491-94567-4."

If you feel your use of code examples falls outside fair use or the permission given above, feel free to contact us at *permissions@oreilly.com*.

Safari® Books Online

 Safari Books Online is an on-demand digital library that delivers expert content in both book and video form from the world's leading authors in technology and business.

Technology professionals, software developers, web designers, and business and creative professionals use Safari Books Online as their primary resource for research, problem solving, learning, and certification training.

Safari Books Online offers a range of plans and pricing for enterprise, government, education, and individuals.

Members have access to thousands of books, training videos, and prepublication manuscripts in one fully searchable database from publishers like O'Reilly Media, Prentice Hall Professional, Addison-Wesley Professional, Microsoft Press, Sams, Que, Peachpit Press, Focal Press, Cisco Press, John Wiley & Sons, Syngress, Morgan Kaufmann, IBM Redbooks, Packt, Adobe Press, FT Press, Apress, Manning, New Riders, McGraw-Hill, Jones & Bartlett, Course Technology, and hundreds more. For more information about Safari Books Online, please visit us online.

How to Contact Us

Please address comments and questions concerning this book to the publisher:

O'Reilly Media, Inc.
1005 Gravenstein Highway North
Sebastopol, CA 95472
800-998-9938 (in the United States or Canada)
707-829-0515 (international or local)
707-829-0104 (fax)

We have a web page for this book, where we list errata, examples, and any additional information. You can access this page at *http://bit.ly/learn-mcollective*.

To comment or ask technical questions about this book, send email to *bookquestions@oreilly.com*.

For more information about our books, courses, conferences, and news, see our website at *http://www.oreilly.com*.

Find us on Facebook: *http://facebook.com/oreilly*

Follow us on Twitter: *http://twitter.com/oreillymedia*

Watch us on YouTube: *http://www.youtube.com/oreillymedia*

Acknowledgments

I owe significant gratitude to R.I. Pienaar, who created MCollective and continues to provide valuable assistance on support channels. This book would never have been possible without his direct and indirect assistance.

I'd like to thank Richard Clamp and Peter Loubser, who provide the visible support and ongoing development from Puppet Labs.

The Chef portions of this book wouldn't have been possible without the ongoing development of the MCollective Cookbook by Zac Stevens. He and Mischa Taylor of Chef both provided invaluable assistance in their personal time.

I owe a drink and much thanks to the many people who provided input and feedback on the book during the writing process, including but definitely not limited to the technical reviewers, Ryan Dill (StubHub) and Jennifer Davis (Chef).

And finally, I'd like to thank my O'Reilly editors, Courtney Nash and Brian Anderson, who gave me excellent guidance on the book and were a pleasure to work with throughout the project.

## PART I

Getting Started

We will start this part with an overview of what MCollective does, how it works, and how it can be used to orchestrate change. We'll discuss how MCollective differs from control systems that loop through each target, and how true parallel execution can benefit your environment.

Sounds a bit boring, huh? Take a moment and enjoy it, because from that point onward, you're going to be operating live. It's all hands-on from here.

You'll perform a real installation of MCollective servers and clients in your environment. No demo system, no tiny configuration that doesn't match to your needs. You'll build a working MCollective installation and test it out for your exact needs. You'll use the client program to make live but nonoperational calls that are specific and unique to your own servers.

I'll cover network and infrastructure requirements for MCollective and how to confirm that each is configured properly. You'll get in-depth instruction on common installation problems and learn to fix these and related issues on your own.

You can use configuration-management tools to install and configure MCollective. We'll introduce a companion Puppet module that is capable of deploying globally with minimal configuration. If you use Puppet or Chef, you'll install an MCollective agent to control it. Puppet and Chef agents will stop being something that runs periodically and instead become interactive resources you can utilize for immediate change. All this in just Part I of the book!

Introduction

What Is MCollective?

MCollective provides a framework for parallel job execution. It is commonly used to orchestrate change across clusters of servers in near real time. It is not entirely inaccurate to imagine the classic marionette controller with puppets dancing on strings. (Yes it's a pun, but it is more apt than you may realize.)

MCollective is an adjunct tool in your toolbox that cooperates and enhances the capabilities of configuration management tools like Puppet, Chef, and Salt. Whereas these tools analyze and act to ensure complete configuration consistency, MCollective orchestrates specific and often singular actions across systems significantly faster.

Let's talk about the difference between MCollective and using Chef, Puppet, Capistrano, Salt Overstack, or hand-built tools for orchestration. You may have used a parallel execution command like pssh before. You may have built or improved one yourself. And if you have, you're familiar with their limitations, which include any or all of the following:

- Loops through systems in order, processing a few at a time
- Simplistic (or overly complex) authentication mechanisms
- Requires customization for each alternative environment
- Unable to respond to deviations in response
- Too easy to overlook fatal error messages output to the screen
- Doesn't support or extend existing management tools

MCollective differs from these tools in a wide variety of ways:

- Uses a masterless environment that allows parallel execution on thousands of systems
- Allows for custom authentication and authorization mechanisms
- Handles different platforms, architectures, and local environments transparently
- Returns full data sets as result codes, allowing intelligent response
- Directs results to a processor that takes action on responses
- Integrates cleanly with configuration management tools like Puppet and Chef

Let's talk about how MCollective's design makes this possible.

Why Parallel Execution?

All of us have spent time trying to make something happen *at the same time* on a number of systems. How many times have you done something like this?

```
$ for host in bunch of hosts
  do
      scp config-file $host:/some/path
      ssh $host "service apache restart"
  done
```

You tell yourself that this is happening all at once, but you know better. Even with more complex parallel execution processors like `pssh`, `ClusterSSH`, or `Fabric`, the sequential ordering ensures a delay that creates *drift* between hosts.

If you have more than a few hosts, the output from the commands scrolls off the screen. Did you notice that the 15th host command failed? The better parallel SSH processors will keep the output from each host, but you need to examine it for errors. None of them can identify an error in the middle of a multicommand sequence and bring it to your attention.

When it's time to do something on a lot of hosts, you want it to happen fast, and you need to know that it succeeded.

Puppet (or Chef, Salt, etc.) users might want to stand up right now to say, "But I can do this! My configuration agent can ensure that these things happen on a whole bunch of systems all at once!"

You're right, Puppet/Chef/etc. are great tools for making changes on systems and ensuring that those changes happen. But they don't make this happen on *many systems at the same time*. Each agent pulls from the server periodically, allowing the server to process a few at a time. The agents receive their configuration changes spread out over time and then combine many different inputs to produce a consistent configuration. This resolution process usually takes at least 30 seconds and often many minutes.

In very few environments could every configuration management agent get a catalog from the server and execute it at the same moment. Additionally, each agent would take differing times to process their catalogs. MCollective is the perfect complement for configuration management agents, designed specifically to orchestrate actions quickly across many nodes.

How MCollective Works

MCollective was designed from the ground up to achieve true parallel execution with consistent and repeatable results. MCollective avoids the use of a centralized master for command and control, thus avoiding centralized resource problems. It also doesn't reach out to the clients in an ordered loop, thus avoiding drift between each of the systems.

MCollective uses *publish/subscribe middleware* to transport requests between *clients* and *servers*. Controlled nodes run an application server named mcollectived*. This server subscribes to message topics. Clients are applications that publish requests to the message topics. The publish and subscribe operations are done through persistent connections to a middleware *broker*.

The mcollectived server registers with the middleware broker and remains in a listening or IDLE state. Whenever a client sends a request to the middleware, each server receives and evaluates the request immediately and independently. mcollectived validates the request and then hands it off to an agent to process the request. The agent processes the request and sends the reply back. All resources consumed are local to the node without any pull from or push to a centralized resource, like a Puppet master or Chef server.

In this model, you can have a command execute on tens, hundreds, or thousands of nodes at exactly the same time. This publish/subscribe infrastructure delivers a scalable and fast parallel execution environment. The model is illustrated in Figure 1-1.

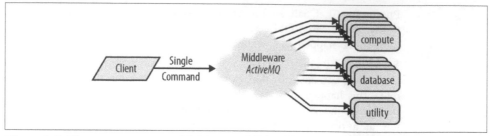

Figure 1-1. The one-to-many publishing model used by MCollective

Now you might be thinking to yourself, "What if I only want the command executed on a subset of nodes?" MCollective provides a rich language for describing which nodes should execute the commands. You can send filters based on hostname, operating system, packages installed, processes running, and many other criteria. Best of all, new criteria custom to your environment will be available when you create your own agent.

Is This Like Multicast IP?

If you are familiar with IP networking and are thinking to yourself that this looks like multicast, then you are correct—it shares a lot of the same benefits. The sending client submits a single message, thus consuming very few resources. Each node that receives the message determines if the message applies to itself and either acts on or discards the message. Like multicast, IP latency is the only factor that influences drift between nodes around the world.

Why Use MCollective

As we have already discussed, MCollective provides an infrastructure designed for orchestrating change on large numbers of systems simultaneously. Here are a few reasons to use it:

- MCollective uses decentralized publish/subscribe middleware to avoid the resource problems associated with centralized master/slave environments.

- MCollective allows you to filter operations based on customizable criteria—not just hostname, operating system, or other common criteria, but anything that can be defined in a custom module.

- MCollective agents implement host-specific routines internally, allowing you to issue the same command to different operating systems without being concerned about the differences between them.

- MCollective agents report back success, failure, and specific return codes or data types for the entire process initiated.
- There are MCollective agents to control, reuse, and interact cleanly with Puppet and Chef. I've heard people discuss agents for CFengine, Ansible, and Salt as well.
- MCollective has replaced `puppet kick` for controlling Puppet agents.

 If you have used `puppet kick` in the past, you are likely aware that Puppet Labs has deprecated `puppet kick` and will be removing support for it in a future release. MCollective replaces `puppet kick` in both the community and Puppet Enterprise product lines and provides significantly more features and functionality.

At the end of Part I, we will introduce how to use both Puppet and Chef to install and configure MCollective. The remainder of the book will include instructions for making each change manually or through the Puppet module and Chef cookbook we document in the book. However, you can leverage every bit of information in this book without using Puppet or Chef. All configuration-management systems (Salt, Cfengine, Ansible, etc.) can be used to install MCollective, and you can build a custom agent to allow MCollective to control them. We will cover how to build these agents in Part III.

Although MCollective plays very well with configuration-management systems, it works above and outside of them. I've used MCollective to manage nodes in more than a hundred co-location facilities around the world without any configuration management available. I've seen MCollective used for multicontinent distributed data collection without any shared management core.

Don't get tied up thinking of the control MCollective provides you as only *puppets dancing on your strings*. Consider a fishing model where the marionette holds the strings cautiously, waiting for the strings to go taut. I've built auto-healing components that listen passively to server inputs and take action to correct a problem without any human involvement.

There are far more ways to use MCollective than I can make marionette and string metaphors for. After reading this book, you'll likely have thought of a way to use it that even the developers didn't imagine. You'll find that MCollective's framework not only supports but encourages creativity.

How to Fail with MCollective

Some sites don't succeed at using MCollective.

Wow. You may be surprised to a statement this strong at the front of this book. However, I have found examining sites that fail with MCollective to be instructive in how to succeed with it. So we're going to evaluate some reasons I have seen MCollective not be widely deployed at sites:

MCollective is installed. How do I make it work? What does it do for me?

> MCollective is not a software package that provides a singular feature set out of the box. MCollective provides a framework for orchestrating change. As such, MCollective doesn't *do anything* until you install agents to answer requests and process actions for you.

> Immediately after Chapter 2, you'll move directly to install a baseline set of plugins that provide valuable and useful features. By the end of Part I, you'll have a feature-rich set of tools for your evaluation of MCollective's power.

MCollective kept timing out in our network.

> In a standard configuration, MCollective will work in a variety of small and large networks, but any given environment may require tuning. MCollective and ActiveMQ contain hundreds of tuning options capable of supporting almost any global environment.

> In Chapter 10, we review in depth the configuration options and discuss the changes necessary in large-scale or specialized environments.

I went to the mailing list or IRC channel and nobody answered my questions.

> MCollective has active support by both Puppet Labs staff and friendly users. However, all are busy people, and none are mind readers. A question without a clear meaning may get overlooked. The best way to get help is to:

> - Phrase your question clearly. Instead of what you see (i.e., "MCollective doesn't work."), tell the list what you did and what errors you received. Specific queries like, "The agents on one node won't respond. The logs from that server say…" are likely to get helpful responses.
> - Show the testing you have done. Provide the relevant configuration and log files when posting to the mailing list, or use a service like Gist (*https://gist.github.com/*) (preferred) or Pastebin (*http://pastebin.com/*) when posting to the #mcollective IRC channel.

Posting to the help channels with specific information like this allows people to quickly determine if they can help you and whether they have seen the problem before. Even a busy person might be able to point you in the right direction.

In summary, MCollective provides a flexible framework for orchestrating change. The changes are implemented by agents designed for that specific request on each server. If an agent isn't doing what you expect, read through this book and see if your question is already answered. Reach out to the support resources provided in the book with specific questions about what you are trying to accomplish. Other people may have solved problems just like yours.

Developing new functionality with MCollective is a creative endeavor. If no agent available today meets your needs, this book provides you with the technical bits necessary to create your own agent plugins. When you are done reading this book, you'll have all of the tools at your disposal. You'll only fail if you don't reach out and use them.

Time to Get Started

As we proceed, this book will show you how MCollective can help you do more and do it faster and yet more precisely than ever before. You'll learn how to extend MCollective to meet your specific needs:

- You'll install MCollective and get it working seamlessly to control files, packages, services, and the Puppet daemon.
- You'll learn the knobs available to tune in the middleware, allowing you to extend your MCollective environment across the campus or around the globe.
- You'll tour through the security plugins available to cryptographically validate every request in your MCollective environment.
- You'll discover an active community of MCollective developers who develop agents, clients, and other MCollective plugins on GitHub.
- You'll build your own custom agent and client. You'll test the agent using raw RPC calls, then build a native Ruby script to invoke MCollective features.

By the time you finish this book, you will understand not just how powerful MCollective is, but you'll know exactly how MCollective works. You'll have the knowledge and understanding to debug problems within any part of the infrastructure. You'll know what to tune as your collective grows. You'll have a resource to return to as your knowledge and experience expands.

Let's get moving! Your servers are marionettes waiting to dance for you—it's time for you to take hold of the strings.

## CHAPTER 2

Installation

In this part of the book, we will walk you through building a fully functional MCollective environment on several of your hosts. You will deploy a simple configuration for your initial tests. We will use this baseline configuration as we expand your knowledge in each of the following chapters.

We will not review every configuration parameter or utilize every feature in this initial installation. The initial installation will provide a basic setup suitable for learning. In Part II, we'll step back and review this configuration in detail, along with optional changes that can be used to fine-tune your installation.

This baseline configuration will use:

- ActiveMQ as the *messaging broker middleware*
- The Pre-Shared Key (PSK) plugin to validate data sent between the clients and the servers
- A simple *Admin User Has Total Control* authorization scheme

You'll find this baseline configuration useful as a foundation to build upon as your MCollective installation grows.

Requirements

Before you install MCollective, you will need to check that you have all of the required elements, as listed in the next two sections.

Puppet Labs Repositories

If you are using RedHat, Fedora, CentOS, Debian, or Ubuntu Linux and are willing to use the Puppet Labs repositories, you can skip this section, as all of these components are available in your operating system packages or supplied in the Puppet Labs Products or Dependencies repositories.

Operating System

The operating system requirements are as follows:

Working time synchronization

Many problems are due to systems having a different idea of what time it is. It is essential that all systems in the collective have a consistent view of the current time through use of Network Time Protocol (NTP). Active Directory/W32Time, the Unix Time Protocol used by `rdate`, and the original Daytime protocol are not accurate enough to provide sufficiently high-resolution time synchronization.

Ruby 1.8.7, 1.9.3, 2.0

MCollective does not work with Ruby versions below 1.8.7. If your operating system does not provide you with a modern version of Ruby, refer to Appendix B for assistance.

Ruby STOMP Gem 1.2.10, 1.3.2, or higher

STOMP is the Simple Text Oriented Messaging Protocol used by MCollective.

5 MB of disk space

256 MB of RAM

A git client, usually available from your operating system package repository

The git client is only necessary when installing MCollective or plugins from source. It is possible to finish this book without using git.

Are These Versions Higher Than Puppet Labs Documentation?

The versions specified here are chosen to avoid known bugs and common problems as reported in the MCollective email, IRC, and ticketing support channels. You can use the lower versions from the Puppet Labs documentation, but you may encounter well-known issues you'd avoid by using these versions.

Middleware Broker

And these are the middleware broker requirements:

- 500 MB of memory minimum
- One of the following messaging middleware options:
  - ActiveMQ 5.8 or higher (preferred) with the STOMP connector (*http://activemq.apache.org/stomp.html*)
  - RabbitMQ 3.2 or higher with the STOMP connector (*http://www.rabbitmq.com/stomp.html*)
- Disk space dependent on middleware service installed (45 MB for ActiveMQ and 10 MB for RabbitMQ)

The middleware broker will not require any disk space beyond the installation packages but will need processor and network capacity for handling at least two concurrent connections for each server node. Most modern systems can handle hundreds of MCollective server connections. Instructions for tuning the broker to handle thousands of concurrent connections is provided in "Large-Scale Broker Configurations" on page 118.

Where to Install

In the remainder of this book, we discuss MCollective as if you are installing it in your production environment. I would imagine that you are smarter than that, but just in case, here are some great ways to build a suitable environment to test and learn MCollective:

- An already established test lab you maintain
- A group of VMware or Openstack host instances
- Vagrant machines running on your personal computer (you can find good Vagrant images at *http://puppet-vagrant-boxes.puppetlabs.com/*)

The choice of virtualization platform is entirely up to you. As you read earlier, MCollective's needs are minimal. Until your broker is supporting hundreds of connected servers, its needs are likewise very minimal. A t1.micro free Amazon Web Services (AWS) instance is suitable for any role in a small MCollective environment. I've built a complete test installation on my Macbook using a total of 4 GB of RAM to support a half-dozen Vagrant nodes.

In all cases, I recommend using either CentOS 6.5 or Ubuntu 13.10 x86 for learning purposes. These platforms are fully supported by every stock MCollective plugin, allowing you to breeze through the learning exercises without distractions. After you have a working MCollective setup, you'll be able to find help in Appendix A for other operating systems.

A nice thing about MCollective is that the names of your nodes aren't important. The only name that will be hardcoded in your configuration files is the name of your middleware broker. This means that you can build your test environment and then easily transition to production hosts while changing only a single value. As you are likely thinking right now, you can simplify even further by using a DNS alias or CNAME and then avoid any configuration file changes.

Dirty Little Secret

I have a dirty little secret to share with you. I've run every single command in this book against a live production environment. Simply put, there's no command example in this book that will cause a production outage. If your environment is safe for testing out ideas in, or if you're just running cowboy, there are no commands shown in this book that will cause an outage.

Naturally, if you run `mco destroy the world`, well you knew what you were doing when you blew your foot right off. You'll have a lot of powerful features in hand by the end of this book. You'll know what each command does, and how to filter your targets effectively. If you're operating cowgirl[1] in a live environment, you'll want to be careful what you ask MCollective to do. But every command shown in this book should be safe to run in production.

Build yourself a group of nodes, physical or virtual, to learn on. Use CentOS 6.5 or Ubuntu 13.10 if possible while learning. Pick one of the nodes to be your middleware broker, and let's get started.

Passwords and Keys

We are going to simplify the initial installation of MCollective to make it easy for you to understand and work with it initially. For this installation, we will need three unique strings used for authentication. You won't type these strings at a prompt— they'll be stored in a configuration file. So we shall cryptographically generate long and complex random passwords.

Run the following command three times and save the values:

```
$ openssl rand -base64 32
```

---

1 Cowboys and cowgirls both shoot from the hip.

Copy the three random strings into your Sticky app, text editor, or write them down on a piece of paper. We're going to use them in the next few sections when configuring your service.

The first string will be the Client Password used by clients to connect to ActiveMQ with permissions to issue commands to the server hosts.

The second string will be the Server Password used by servers to connect to ActiveMQ with permissions to subscribe to the command channels.

The third string will be a Pre-Shared Key used as a salt in the cryptographic hash used to validate communications between server and client, ensuring that nobody can alter the request payload in transit.

Ensure That the Client and Server Passwords Are Different

Many online guides for setting up MCollective suggest using the same username and password for clients and servers. This leads to a problem where the compromise of any server allows control messages to be sent from the compromised server to any host in the collective. We'll explain this problem in "Detailed Configuration Review" on page 101.

You want the username and password installed on every server to be able to subscribe to topics, but not to be able to send requests to them. If you use the same username and password for both, someone who can read any one server's configuration file will be able to issue requests to every host in the collective. Keep these usernames and passwords distinct and separate.

In Chapter 13, we will discuss alternative security plugins. The SSL/TLS security plugins can encrypt the transport and provide complete cryptographic authentication. However, the simplicity of the pre-shared key model is useful to help get you up and running quickly and provides a reasonable level of security for a small installation.

Puppet Labs Repository

Puppet Labs provides APT and YUM repositories containing packages for open source products and their dependencies. These community repositories are intended to supplement the OS vendor repositories for the more popular Linux distributions. These repos contain the Puppet Labs products used in this book, including MCollective, Puppet, and Facter, and packages for the dependencies of these products, including Ruby 1.8.7 for RHEL 5.x systems.

Supported Platforms

Puppet Labs maintains Product and Dependency repositories for the operating systems listed in the following sections. Other operating systems can use MCollective by following the instructions in Appendix B.

Enterprise Linux 6

To install the repositories on Enterprise Linux 6, run the following command:

```
$ sudo yum install http://yum.puppetlabs.com/puppetlabs-release-el-6.noarch.rpm
```

Enterprise Linux versions include RedHat, CentOS, Scientific, Oracle, and all downstream Linux distributions using the same number.

Enterprise Linux 5

This repository includes a build of Ruby 1.8.7 for RHEL-based 5.x systems, which is essential for MCollective:

```
$ sudo yum install http://yum.puppetlabs.com/puppetlabs-release-el-5.noarch.rpm
```

Fedora

At the time this book was written, Fedora 19–20 are supported and available as shown here:

```
$ sudo yum install
  http://yum.puppetlabs.com/puppetlabs-release-fedora-20.noarch.rpm
```

Debian and Ubuntu

For Debian and Ubuntu systems, you have to download the *.deb* file appropriate for your release. It is best to browse to *http://apt.puppetlabs.com/* and look at the files available there to decide the appropriate one to install.

If you are running the unstable release of Debian (Sid) at the time this book was written, you should install the repository as follows:

```
$ wget http://apt.puppetlabs.com/puppetlabs-release-sid.deb
$ sudo dpkg -i puppetlabs-release-sid.deb
$ sudo apt-get update
```

Likewise, if you are running the latest Ubuntu (Trusty Tahr), you should use the following:

```
$ wget http://apt.puppetlabs.com/puppetlabs-release-trusty.deb
$ sudo dpkg -i puppetlabs-release-trusty.deb
$ sudo apt-get update
```

Other platforms

Most platforms (e.g., Solaris and FreeBSD) have package repositories that contain binary packages for MCollective. Consult Appendix A for specific instructions to get MCollective packages installed on other operating systems.

Configuring ActiveMQ

The one thing that every MCollective environment must have is publish/subscribe middleware. In this section, we will install ActiveMQ, the middleware recommended by Puppet Labs for being best performing, most scalable, and well tested. After you have a working installation, instructions for changing the middleware to RabbitMQ are provided in "Using RabbitMQ" on page 237.

Install the Software

The first step is to install the middleware used for communication between clients and servers. You can install this on an existing Puppet or Chef server. Unless you have hundreds of nodes, it won't require a dedicated system. Its resource needs are very minimal.

For RedHat, CentOS, and Fedora-based systems, run the following:

```
$ sudo yum install activemq
$ sudo chkconfig activemq on
```

For Debian or Ubuntu, run:

```
$ sudo apt-get install activemq
$ sudo update-rc.d activemq multiuser
```

And for FreeBSD, run:

```
$ sudo pkg add activemq
$ echo "activemq_enable=YES" | sudo tee -a /etc/rc.conf
```

Tune the Configuration File

Next, we will tune the ActiveMQ configuration file, which should be installed in the appropriate *etc/* directory for your platform (on most Linux systems, this will be */etc/activemq/activemq.xml*). Edit the default file installed by the ActiveMQ package according to the following suggestions. At the time this book was written, even the default configuration provided by the Puppet Labs-provided package needs some tweaking.

We'll cover the configuration file in depth in Part II. During this installation, we will only cover the minimum changes necessary to get ActiveMQ working for MCollective.

Enable purging in the broker

Look for the `broker` statement (usually located five lines into most default configurations I have seen). You'll need to add `schedulePeriodForDestinationPurge` to this:

```
<broker
  xmlns="http://activemq.apache.org/schema/core"
  brokerName="hostname"
  dataDirectory="leave this untouched"
  schedulePeriodForDestinationPurge="60000"
>
```

`schedulePeriodForDestinationPurge` is necessary to clean up stale queues. This will be explained comprehensively in "Detailed Configuration Review" on page 101.

Disable producerFlowControl

Here we will use `policyEntry` statements to disable flow control on both topics and queues, and to enable garbage collection on stale queues:

```
<destinationPolicy>
    <policyMap>
      <policyEntries>
        <!-- MCollective expects producer flow control to be turned off. -->
        <policyEntry topic=">"
          producerFlowControl="false"
          memoryLimit="1mb"
        />
        <!-- MCollective generates a reply queue for most commands.
              Garbage-collect these after five minutes to conserve memory.
        -->
        <policyEntry queue=">"
          producerFlowControl="false"
          memoryLimit="10mb"
          gcInactiveDestinations="true"
          inactiveTimoutBeforeGC="300000"
        />
      </policyEntries>
```

In topic and queue names, the > character is a wildcard that will match any character until the end of the string. Since it is the first character used, all topic and queue names will match these rules.

Define logins for clients and servers in simpleAuthenticationPlugin

You will find the `plugins` section in the ActiveMQ configuration provided by Puppet Labs, but you may have to add it to most vendor or stock Apache configurations. If the configuration file has a `plugins` section, then replace it completely with the example that follows. Otherwise, place this just below the `destinationPolicy` section.

In this section, we will define the usernames and passwords used by the MCollective servers and clients:

```
<plugins>
  <simpleAuthenticationPlugin>
    <users>
      <authenticationUser
        username="client"
        password="Client Password"
        groups="servers,clients,everyone"
      />
      <authenticationUser
        username="server"
        password="Server Password"
        groups="servers,everyone"
      />
    </users>
  </simpleAuthenticationPlugin>
```

These lines are pretty easy to understand. You are entering the username and password to be used for clients and servers to authenticate. The groups parameter assigns this user to the following groups used for authorization.

Note that `plugins` does not terminate here. We have broken the `plugins` block in two halves for ease of reading. The `plugins` XML block closes at the end of the authorization section.

Define permissions for clients and servers in authorizationPlugins

In the remainder of the `plugins` block, we define rights and permissions for the users we created in the previous section. Be very careful to get this text exactly correct, as periods, wildcards, and > characters in particular are significant:

```
<authorizationPlugin>
  <map>
    <authorizationMap>
      <authorizationEntries>
        <authorizationEntry queue="mcollective.>"
          write="clients" read="clients" admin="clients"
        />
        <authorizationEntry topic="mcollective.>"
          write="clients" read="clients" admin="clients"
```

```
        />
        <authorizationEntry queue="mcollective.nodes"
          read="servers" admin="servers"
        />
        <authorizationEntry queue="mcollective.reply.>"
          write="servers" admin="servers"
        />
        <authorizationEntry topic="mcollective.*.agent"
          read="servers" admin="servers"
        />
        <authorizationEntry topic="mcollective.registration.agent"
          write="servers" read="servers" admin="servers"
        />
        <authorizationEntry topic="ActiveMQ.Advisory.>"
          read="everyone" write="everyone" admin="everyone"
        />
      </authorizationEntries>
    </authorizationMap>
  </map>
  </authorizationPlugin>
</plugins>
```

We will review this configuration in great detail in Chapter 10. At this time, it is simply essential that it is entered exactly as it appears here.

Transports

Only one transport should be enabled. Comment out or remove all other transports and leave only the STOMP transport enabled:

```
<transportConnectors>
  <transportConnector name="stomp+nio" uri="stomp+nio://[::0]:61613"/>
</transportConnectors>
```

Disable the web console

ActiveMQ comes with a web console for management. This is unnecessary for MCollective and could have security implications if left open for abuse. Comment this out:

```
<!-- disabled for security implications
<import resource="jetty.xml"/>
-->
```

Start the Service

Now that we've updated the configuration file, it is time to start the service:

```
$ service activemq start
Starting ActiveMQ Broker...
```

After starting the service, check to see that ActiveMQ is listening on TCP port 61613:

```
$ netstat -an | grep 61613
```

If you don't see a LISTEN socket available for incoming connections, check the logfile (Java errors can be verbose, so page through the output carefully):

```
$ tail -200f /var/log/activemq/activemq.log
```

Firewall Change

You should ensure that inbound TCP sessions to port 61613 can be created from every MCollective server and client.

Most Linux systems use `iptables` firewalls. On a Linux system, you could use the following steps to add a rule before the global deny. If all of your servers will fit within a few subnet masks, it is advisable to limit this rule to only allow those subnets, as shown here:

```
$ sudo iptables --list --line-numbers
Chain INPUT (policy ACCEPT)
num  target     prot opt source      destination
1    ACCEPT     all  --  anywhere    anywhere        state RELATED,ESTABLISHED
...etc

$ sudo iptables --list --line-numbers
Chain INPUT (policy ACCEPT)
num  target     prot opt  source      destination
1    ACCEPT     all        anywhere    anywhere        state RELATED,ESTABLISHED
2    ACCEPT     ipv6-icmp  anywhere    anywhere
...etc
```

Look through the output and find an appropriate line number for the new rule. Then use the following syntax to insert the rule into this location in the list:

```
$ sudo iptables -I INPUT 20 -m state --state NEW -p tcp \
    --source 192.168.200.0/24 --dport 61613 -j ACCEPT

$ sudo ip6tables -I INPUT 20 -m state --state NEW -p tcp \
    --source 2001:DB8:6A:C0::/24 --dport 61613 -j ACCEPT
```

Don't forget to save that rule to your initial rules file. For RedHat-derived systems, this can be as easy as this:

```
$ sudo service iptables save
iptables: Saving firewall rules to /etc/sysconfig/iptables:[  OK  ]
$ sudo service ip6tables save
ip6tables: Saving firewall rules to /etc/sysconfig/ip6table:[  OK  ]
```

 I've shown the syntax here for both IPv4 and IPv6 using non-routed networks. Customize to suit your local networks. You can ignore the steps for one protocol or the other if you don't have nodes using both protocols. You can find more details about how to best handle dual-stack nodes in "IPv6 Dual-Stack Environments" on page 100.

Check Appendix A for platform-specific instructions.

Installing Servers

The `mcollectived` application server runs on nodes that will process requests from clients. You should pick several target nodes that you desire to make requests of and install the server as described in the following section.

Install the Software

For RedHat, CentOS, and Fedora-based systems, run the following:

```
$ sudo yum install mcollective
$ sudo chkconfig mcollective on
```

For Debian or Ubuntu, run:

```
$ sudo apt-get install ruby-stomp mcollective
$ sudo update-rc.d mcollective multiuser
```

And for FreeBSD, run:

```
$ sudo pkg add mcollective
$ echo "mcollectived_enable=YES" | sudo tee -a /etc/rc.conf
```

Server Configuration File

The following is the MCollective server configuration file, which should be installed on every host you want to control. Edit the default */etc/mcollective/server.cfg* file installed by the package to look like this:

```
# /etc/mcollective/server.cfg
daemonize = 1
direct_addressing = 1

# ActiveMQ connector settings:
connector = activemq
plugin.activemq.pool.size = 1
plugin.activemq.pool.1.host = activemq.example.net
plugin.activemq.pool.1.port = 61613
plugin.activemq.pool.1.user = server
plugin.activemq.pool.1.password = Server Password
plugin.activemq.heartbeat_interval = 30

# How often to send registration messages
registerinterval = 600

# Security provider
securityprovider = psk
plugin.psk = Pre-Shared Key
```

```
# Override platform defaults?
libdir = /usr/libexec/mcollective
#logger_type = file
#loglevel = info
#logfile = /var/log/mcollective.log
#keeplogs = 5
#max_log_size = 2097152
#logfacility = daemon
```

Note that you have to replace two of the passwords in this file and also the *libdir* directory.

Note that *libdir* will vary between operating systems. For this stage of the learning process, either test on a single operating system or adjust it by hand as necessary for each different OS. In Chapter 7, we'll introduce you to a Puppet module and a Chef cookbook that will handle this cleanly for you.

Start the Service

To start the service, run the following command:

```
$ service mcollective start
Starting mcollective:                              [  OK  ]
```

At this time, you should see the server bound to the ActiveMQ server on the port listed in both the *server.cfg* and *activemq.xml* files:

```
$ netstat -an | grep 61613
tcp   0   0 192.168.200.10:58006      192.168.200.5:61613        ESTABLISHED
```

If you are using IPv6, the response may look like this:

```
$ netstat -an -A inet6 | grep 61613
tcp   0   0 2001:DB8:6A:C0::200:10:45743 2001:DB8:6A:C0::200:5:61613  ESTABLISHED
```

You may find that you are using IPv6 when you didn't expect it. This isn't generally a problem in most sites, so don't rush to turn it off. How to control which protocol to use is covered in "IPv6 Dual-Stack Environments" on page 100.

Creating a Client

You only need to install the client software on systems from which you will be sending requests. This may be your management hosts, a bastion host, or could be your laptop or desktop systems in the office.

Install the Software

For RedHat, CentOS, and Fedora-based systems, run the following:

```
$ sudo yum install mcollective-client
```

For Debian or Ubuntu, run:

```
$ sudo apt-get install mcollective-client
```

And for FreeBSD, run:

```
$ sudo pkg add mcollective-client
```

Client Configuration File

The following is the client configuration file, which should be installed only on hosts from which you will submit requests. Edit the */etc/mcollective/client.cfg* file installed with the package to look like this:

```
# /etc/mcollective/client.cfg
direct_addressing = 1

# Connector
connector = activemq
plugin.activemq.pool.size = 1
plugin.activemq.pool.1.host = activemq.example.net
plugin.activemq.pool.1.port = 61613
plugin.activemq.pool.1.user = client
plugin.activemq.pool.1.password = Client Password
plugin.activemq.heartbeat_interval = 30

# Security provider
securityprovider = psk
plugin.psk = Pre-Shared Key

# Use auto-discovery
default_discovery_method = mc
direct_addressing_threshold = 10
# ...or pre-configure the list of nodes
#default_discovery_method = flatfile
#default_discovery_options = /etc/mcollective/nodes.txt

# Miscellaneous settings
color = 1
rpclimitmethod = first

# Performance settings
direct_addressing_threshold = 10
ttl = 60

# Override platform defaults?
libdir = /usr/libexec/mcollective
```

```
#logger_type = console
#logfacility = daemon
#loglevel = warn
#logfile = /var/log/mcollective.log
#keeplogs = 5
#max_log_size = 2097152
```

 Note that you have to replace two of the passwords in this file and also the *libdir* directory if the operating systems differ.

Security Considerations

With the pre-shared key security model, anyone who can read the *client.cfg* file can find the password used to publish requests. I recommend that you limit the people who can read the client file to the people who you trust to execute commands on every system:

```
$ sudo chmod 640 /etc/mcollective/client.cfg
$ sudo chown root:wheel /etc/mcollective/client.cfg
```

 The Puppet module provided in this book does this step for you. You only need to execute the commands just shown during our initial learning installation. Later on, if you are using the provided Puppet module, this will be handled for you.

We'll cover more flexible security designs in Chapter 13.

Installing from Source

If you have installed the packages from the Puppet Labs repository, you can skip directly down to "Testing Your Installation" on page 28.

If there are no suitable packages for your operating system, you can install MCollective from source. The installer will place the files in the standard Ruby locations for your platform, or to directories which you give it as options.

You will need to set up init scripts for your operating system on your own. We'll show you where the examples are that you can build from.

Do not attempt to install from RubyGems. The version in Ruby-Gems was not created by Puppet Labs and is quite a bit older than, and incompatible with, recent versions of MCollective. It also does not install the connector or security plugins.[2]

Using the Installer

Download a source tarball from *https://github.com/puppetlabs/marionette-collective/tags/*.

Use the installer to place the files in your standard system locations:

```
$ tar xzf marionette-collective-2.5.3.tar.gz
$ cd marionette-collective-2.5.3
$ sudo ./install.rb
                        mc-call-agent:
                                mco:
                        mcollectived:
                            log.rb: mcc.............
            agent_definition.rb: mmc.....
        standard_definition.rb: mmc....
    ...snip test results...

Files:   113
Classes: 137
Modules: 151
Methods: 788
Elapsed: 23.397s
mkdir -p -m 755 /etc/mcollective
install -c -p -m 0644 etc/facts.yaml.dist /etc/mcollective/facts.yaml
mkdir -p -m 755 /etc/mcollective
install -c -p -m 0644 etc/server.cfg.dist /etc/mcollective/server.cfg
mkdir -p -m 755 /etc/mcollective
install -c -p -m 0644 etc/client.cfg.dist /etc/mcollective/client.cfg
mkdir -p -m 755 /etc/mcollective
...snip many more files...
```

You could also install to a different path and use the RUBYLIB environment variable to add it to Ruby's load path:

```
$ cd marionette-collective-2.5.3
$ sudo /path/to/ruby ./install.rb  \
        --configdir=/opt/mcollective/etc      \
        --bindir=/opt/mcollective/bin         \
        --sbindir=/opt/mcollective/sbin       \
        --plugindir=/opt/mcollective/plugins  \
        --sitelibdir=/opt/mcollective/lib
```

---

2 This may be fixed; check Improvement MCO-320 (*https://tickets.puppetlabs.com/browse/MCO-320*).

```
$ export PATH=${PATH}:/opt/mcollective/bin
$ export RUBYLIB=${RUBYLIB}:/opt/mcollective/lib
```

Creating an Init Script

If you didn't install MCollective from a package, you'll need to create an init script to start MCollective at system boot time. There are a few startup scripts in the MCollective source tree to use as starting points:

- *ext/debian/mcollective.init*
- *ext/redhat/mcollective.init*
- *ext/solaris/mcollective.init*

Start with these examples to tailor an appropriate startup script for the MCollective server daemon.

Creating a Package

You may want to create a package for your platform to avoid installing from source on every node. To create a package for your operating system, invoke the installer with an option to build a chroot tree for you:

```
$ cd marionette-collective-2.5.3
$ ./installer.rb --destdir=/package/root/mcollective

No newer files.

Files:    0
Classes:  0
Modules:  0
Methods:  0
Elapsed:  0.009s
mkdir -p -m 755 /package/root/mcollective/etc/mcollective
install -c -p -m 0644 etc/facts.yaml.dist
/package/root/mcollective/etc/mcollective/facts.yaml
mkdir -p -m 755 /package/root/mcollective/etc/mcollective
install -c -p -m 0644 etc/server.cfg.dist
/package/root/mcollective/etc/mcollective/server.cfg
mkdir -p -m 755 /package/root/mcollective/etc/mcollective
install -c -p -m 0644 etc/client.cfg.dist
/package/root/mcollective/etc/mcollective/client.cfg
...snip many more files...
```

Once you have done this, copy the init script you created into the package root, adjust the configuration files if necessary, and then build the package according to your operating system standards.

Testing Your Installation

After you have set up a middleware host, at least one server and one client, you can run a test to confirm that your configuration settings are correct. At this point, the installation used for this chapter looks like the diagram shown in Figure 2-1.

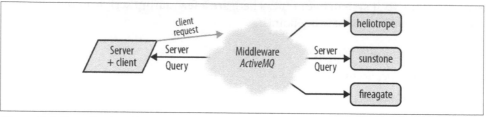

Figure 2-1. Installation diagram

Note that host `geode` has both the server and client software installed. It will receive requests through the middleware the same as every other server.

The *ping* test is a low-level query that confirms that the server node is communicating through the middleware:

```
$ mco ping
sunstone                          time=88.09 ms
geode                             time=126.22 ms
fireagate                         time=126.81 ms
heliotrope                        time=127.32 ms

---- ping statistics ----
4 replies max: 127.32 min: 88.09 avg: 117.11
```

If you get back a list of each server connected to your middleware and its response time, then congratulations! You have successfully created a working MCollective framework.

Troubleshooting

If you didn't get the responses we expected, here are some things to check.

Passwords

The number one problem you'll see is that you didn't use the correct passwords in each location. Ensure that the three passwords we created are used correctly, and replace them if you need to do so for testing purposes:

Client Password

Should be assigned to the user `client` in the */etc/activemq/activemq.xml* file and used for *plugin.activemq.pool.1.password* in */etc/mcollective/client.cfg*

Server Password

> Should be assigned to the user `server` in the */etc/activemq/activemq.xml* file and used for *plugin.activemq.pool.1.password* in */etc/mcollective/server.cfg*

Pre-Shared Key

> Should be used as the value for *plugin.psk* in both */etc/mcollective/server.cfg* and */etc/mcollective/client.cfg*

Networking

The second most likely problem is a firewall blocking access between the server and the middleware, or the client and the middleware. Test the server connectivity by going to the middleware system and confirm that you see connections to port 61613 from each of the servers:

```
$ netstat -a |grep 61613
tcp   0   0 :::61613                      :::*                       LISTEN
tcp   0   0 192.168.200.5.61613           192.168.200.10:58028       ESTABLISHED
tcp   0   0 192.168.200.5.61613           192.168.200.11:22123       ESTABLISHED
tcp   0   0 192.168.200.5.61613           192.168.200.12:42488       ESTABLISHED
tcp   0   0 2001:DB8:6A:C0::200:5:61613 2001:DB8:6A:C0::200:5:32711  ESTABLISHED
tcp   0   0 2001:DB8:6A:C0::200:5:61613 2001:DB8:6A:C0::200:13:45743 ESTABLISHED
```

If you don't see connections like these, then there is a firewall that prevents the servers from reaching the middleware broker.

Connector Names

One potential point of confusion is that ActiveMQ defines the `transportConnector` very differently than MCollective's `connector` setting. These settings will not match.

In the MCollective configuration files for the server and client, it should indicate `activemq`, like so:

```
connector = activemq
plugin.activemq.heartbeat_interval = 30
plugin.activemq.pool.size = 1
plugin.activemq.pool.1.host = activemq.example.net
```

This tells MCollective that it is communicating with ActiveMQ. MCollective always uses the STOMP protocol when connecting with ActiveMQ, but this is not listed here.

In the ActiveMQ configuration, you don't mention MCollective but instead tell the `transportConnector` to provide STOMP protocol transport using the New IO (NIO) Java library. (We'll cover what this means in "Detailed Configuration Review" on page 101.)

```
<transportConnectors>
  <transportConnector name="stomp+nio" uri="stomp+nio://[::0]:61613"/>
</transportConnectors>
```

 When doing searches on the Internet, you may find references to a
stomp connector. This connector was deprecated in MCollective
2.2.3 and removed in 2.3 (*http://bit.ly/1wW72Du*). Always use the
native activemq and rabbitmq connectors.

## CHAPTER 3

Command-Line Client

In this chapter, I'm going to introduce some key terms and concepts you'll hear continuously throughout the book. Each section will introduce and explain the concept, and (if applicable) the plugin that implements its usage.

The most common way to interact with mcollective is the mco command-line client, which can be used interactively or in scripts. It's also relatively easy to write other clients in Ruby, which can be used as backends for GUI apps or as glue in a reactive infrastructure. We'll cover how to build your own clients in Part III. In this chapter, we're going to focus on the command-line client.

As I introduce each concept, I'll show you command lines that use that feature. As we will only use the ping and find commands, these are safe to run in your own MCollective setup. Feel free to run each of them and see what results you receive.

Configuration File

The global configuration file for an MCollective client will be stored in the installation directory, usually */etc/mcollective/client.cfg*.

Users can create their own configuration files. The default file name is *.mcollective* in the user's home directory. Alternative config files can be specified with -c config file on the command line. Each configuration file must be whole and complete. If you specify a configuration file, then the global configuration file is ignored.

In the first part of this book, user-specific configuration files are not necessary. All changes can be made to the global configuration file. It will be necessary to create user-specific files when using SSL keys for authentication, as described in Part II.

Connector

For requests from the client to reach your servers, the client utilizes two plugins:

- A connector plugin to establish a link with the middleware and publish to topics
- A security plugin to sign (and optionally encrypt) the data payload

These two connectors must be the same throughout your environment. For the baseline setup described in Chapter 2, we used:

connector = activemq

> The alternative would have been to use RabbitMQ or to build a custom middleware connector.

securityprovider = psk

> Alternative security plugins will be covered in Part II.

For our initial build, the plugin configuration will be the same for every client.

Facts

The most comprehensive way to identify related groups of systems is by *facts*, which are key/value pairs with information about your server. The most common way to get facts is by using the facter program from Puppet Labs. You run this to see the facts that facter knows about your system:

```
$ sudo yum install facter      # RedHat, CentOS, Fedora Based Systems
$ sudo apt-get install facter  # Debian, Ubuntu
$ sudo pkg add facter          # FreeBSD

$ facter
architecture => x86_64
augeasversion => 1.0.0
bios_release_date => 01/01/2007
bios_vendor => Seabios
bios_version => 0.5.1
blockdevice_sr0_model => QEMU DVD-ROM
...snip many more lines...
```

If you don't use facter, you can generate fact data from any source you like.

We use facts extensively in the following examples. It's a good idea to populate the *facts.yaml* file with some facts to use as you proceed through the exercises. It doesn't matter at this point what the facts are, so you can name them to amuse yourself during your learning process. Before the end of this chapter, you'll come to understand their value.

First, edit the *server.cfg* file (often at */etc/mcollective/server.cfg*) to contain the following:

```
# Facts
factsource = yaml
plugin.yaml = /etc/mcollective/facts.yaml
```

The target for the `plugin.yaml` parameter could include multiple filenames separated by a colon in Unix systems or a semicolon for Windows servers.

The most flexible way to get facts for MCollective is to let Puppet or Chef supply them for you, which we will show you in Chapter 7. For now, a quick way to store many useful facts is to have `cron` invoke `facter` and store the results:

```
/etc/cron.d/facts.sh:
    */30 * * * *   facter -y > /etc/mcollective/facts.yaml
```

Alternatively, you can simply create this file and enter some random facts for learning purposes. The file needs to be in YAML dictionary format (*http://bit.ly/WBwsfa*). Here's a quick example:

```
---
architecture: x86_64
operatingsystem: CentOS
operatingsystemrelease: 6.5
yamltest: true
```

After you create the *facts.yaml* file, you need to restart `mcollectived` for the facts to be loaded and available:

```
$ sudo service mcollective restart
Shutting down mcollective:                       [  OK  ]
Starting mcollective:                            [  OK  ]
```

Once you have made the changes, you can use the `inventory` request and read through the output to see if the facts are available on the node:

```
$ mco inventory nodename
read down through the output...
    Facts:
        architecture => x86_64
        augeasversion => 1.0.0
        bios_release_date => 01/01/2007
        bios_vendor => Seabios
...etc...
```

I rather like using awk to skip all of the other inventory output (naturally, this is not guaranteed against future changes in the output of inventory):

```
$ mco inventory nodename | awk '/Facts:/','/^$/'
```

You can also query for how many nodes share the same value for facts. For example, every node in the following command output has the operatingsystem fact but only four nodes have the hostname fact:

```
$ mco facts operatingsystem
Report for fact: operatingsystem

        CentOS                          found 2 times
        FreeBSD                         found 1 times
        Ubuntu                          found 1 times
        Windows                         found 1 times


Finished processing 5 / 5 hosts in 61.45 ms

$ mco facts hostname
Report for fact: hostname

        fireagate                       found 1 times
        geode                           found 1 times
        heliotrope                      found 1 times
        sunstone                        found 1 times


Finished processing 5 / 5 hosts in 68.38 ms

$ mco facts chef_environment
Report for fact: chef_environment

        dev                             found 3 times
        prod                            found 2 times


Finished processing 5 / 5 hosts in 60.51 ms
```

There is a plugin named mcollective-facter-facts on the Puppet Labs GitHub. This agent can be slow to run, as it invokes facter for each evaluation. In theory, this would be more accurate than reading a file where the output was flushed to disk. In practice, queries time out randomly and inconsistently. Nearly every time someone reports problems with nodes disappearing or not responding, this fact source was the culprit.

I recommend staying with the YAML source to avoid this difficulty. MCollective consistently responds quickly and accurately when reading the facts from a YAML file.

Inventory

One of the basic commands provided in the MCollective client is the `inventory` command. This command allows you to see how a given server is configured, what collectives it is part of, and various running statistics.

For our purposes, the most important part of this output is what agents and plugins are installed on the host. It will also tell you what Puppet classes it knows about (if Puppet is running on the host) and what facts are known about the host (if you set up facts in the previous section). You should run this command against one of your servers and examine the output. We won't do anything with this just now, but we will be coming back to this throughout the next two chapters:

```
$ mco inventory heliotrope
Inventory for heliotrope:

    Server Statistics:
                      Version: 2.5.3
                   Start Time: Mon Jul 26 03:11:12 -0700 2014
                  Config File: /etc/mcollective/server.cfg
                  Collectives: mcollective
              Main Collective: mcollective
                   Process ID: 1334
               Total Messages: 16
       Messages Passed Filters: 13
             Messages Filtered: 3
             Expired Messages: 0
                  Replies Sent: 12
          Total Processor Time: 38.56 seconds
                  System Time: 128.22 seconds

    Agents:
       discovery       rpcutil

    Data Plugins:
       agent           fstat

    Configuration Management Classes:
       No classes applied

    Facts:
       No facts known
```

Inventory Reports

You can pull bulk reports from the inventory service as well. Create a small Ruby script to output the values and pass it to the `script` argument of the inventory command.

The following example file, named *inventory.mc*, provides a list of hosts in the format: Hostname Architecture Operating System OS Release Ver:

```
$ cat inventory.mc
inventory do
  format "%20s %8s %10s %-20s"
  fields {[ identity, facts["architecture"],
    facts["operatingsystem"], facts["operatingsystemrelease"]
  ]}
end

$ mco inventory --script inventory.mc
           geode    x86_64     CentOS 6.4
        sunstone     amd64     Ubuntu 13.10
      heliotrope    x86_64     CentOS 6.5
       tanzanite    x86_64     Windows 7 Ultimate SP1
       fireagate     amd64     FreeBSD 9.2-RELEASE
```

Discovery

One of the most basic operations performed by the MCollective client is to discover which servers are available in the collective. It will use this information when deciding how to issue commands. Let's take a look at a basic example of this:

```
$ mco find --with-identity /a/ --verbose
Discovering hosts using the mc method for 2 second(s) .... 2

tanzanite
fireagate

Discovered 2 nodes in 2.00 seconds using the mc discovery plugin
```

How did the client determine which servers matched the filter? The answer is that it used the mc discovery plugin configured in the *client.cfg* file to ask the servers. Let's use the built-in help to see what this plugin does:

```
$ mco plugin doc mc

MCollective Broadcast based discovery
DISCOVERY METHOD CAPABILITIES:
      Filter based on configuration management classes
      Filter based on system facts
      Filter based on mcollective identity
      Filter based on mcollective agents
      Compound filters combining classes and facts
```

The mc discovery plugin sends out a broadcast query to all servers with the filter you specify. If more than 10 servers respond, then it will send out the request as a broadcast. If fewer than 10 servers respond, it will send direct messages to each server.

You can change the threshold for when to use broadcast versus direct addressing queries by altering the `direct_addressing_thresh old` parameter in the client configuration file (see Figure 3-1).

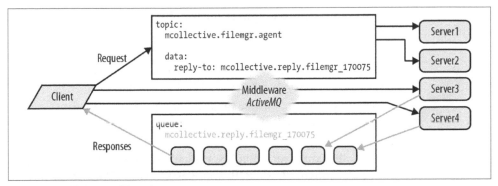

Figure 3-1. Direct addressing

One way to avoid the broadcast discovery used by mc is to use a different discovery plugin. The other discovery plugins provided by default are the `flatfile` and `stdin` discovery plugins. These are more limited discovery mechanisms that use a list of hostnames from a file or standard input. Any of the following invocations achieve exactly the same thing:

- Use the `--nodes filename`.
- Use `--disc-method flatfile --discovery-option filename`.
- Use `--disc-method stdin` and send a list of identities on standard input.

With any of these invocations, no broadcast query will be used. The request will be sent directly to a queue specific to each node:

```
$ mco plugin doc flatfile

Flatfile based discovery for node identities
DISCOVERY METHOD CAPABILITIES:
      Filter based on mcollective identity

$ cat /path/to/hostlist
fireagate
heliotrope

$ mco rpc rpcutil ping --disc-method flatfile --disc-option /path/to/hostlist
Discovering hosts using the flatfile method .... 2

  * [ ============================================================> ] 2 / 2
```

```
heliotrope
    Timestamp: 1385012042
fireagate
    Timestamp: 1385012044

Finished processing 2 / 2 hosts in 146.13 ms
```

Responses to the request are compared against the list of servers identified in discovery, so as to know if any nodes failed to respond.

 `mco rpc` is a method to send a request to the agent without using the client application. You'll learn how to do this in Part III.

The only way to use the flatfile discovery method with `ping` is to use the RPC invocation.[1]

There are a number of other discovery plugins available for MCollective, including ones for PuppetDB, Chef, MongoDB, RiakDB, and Elastic Search. We'll cover how to build your own discovery plugin in Part III.

You might assume that using customized discovery plugins is a good way to limit your commands, but it really isn't. MCollective depends on a consistent discovery view. To limit which servers you affect with a command, let's talk about filtering.

Filters

In general, you will find it wasteful and time-consuming to build a custom list of targets for each MCollective command. You will find it much easier to use the default broadcast discovery method and use filters instead. Filters are used by the Discovery plugin to limit which servers are sent a request. Filters can be applied to any MCollective command.

The syntax for filters are documented in the online help:

```
$ mco help

Host Filters
  -W, --with FILTER              Combined classes and facts filter
  -S, --select FILTER            Compound filter combining facts and classes
  -F, --wf, --with-fact fact=val Match hosts with a certain fact
  -C, --wc, --with-class CLASS   Match hosts with a certain config class
  -A, --wa, --with-agent AGENT   Match hosts with a certain agent
  -I, --wi, --with-identity IDENT Match hosts with a certain configured identity
```

---

1 Improvement request MCO-224 (*https://tickets.puppetlabs.com/browse/MCO-224*) documents this issue.

There are long and short versions of every filter option. We're going to use the long versions throughout the documentation because they are easier to read on the page and easier to remember.

 In the following examples, you will see facts, classes, and agents—concepts I haven't introduced yet. Don't worry about this for now. At this point, you should see how flexible and powerful the filtering language is. In the following sections, we'll walk you through how to enable these features.

Here are some examples of using filters. Each one outputs a list of MCollective servers that match the criteria. These are good to run before executing a command, to ensure that your request will be processed by the nodes you expect to match. In our first example, we'll find all hosts with an *i* in their name:

```
$ mco find --with-identity /i/
heliotrope
fireagate
```

List all web servers named web followed by a number:

```
$ mco find --with-identity /^web\d/
```

List all nodes that have the Puppet class webserver applied to them:

```
$ mco find --with-class webserver
```

Show all nodes that run the CentOS operating system:

```
$ mco find --with-fact operatingsystem=CentOS
```

Show all nodes that have the package agent installed on them:

```
$ mco find --with-agent package
```

 Requires Discovery Plugin Support

If you look back at the previous section, you'll notice that the flat file discovery plugin only supports the identity filter. This is why we use and recommend the mc discovery plugin, to ensure that all of these powerful filters are available to you.

Combination Filters

There are two types of combination filters. The first type combines Puppet classes and facter facts. Here is an example where we ping only CentOS hosts with a Puppet class nameserver:

```
$ mco ping --with "/nameserver/ operatingsystem=CentOS"
```

The second type is called a `select` filter and is the most powerful filter available.

The `select` filter allows you to create searches against Puppet facts and classes with complex Boolean logic. This is the only filter where you can use the operands and and or. You can likewise negate terms using not or ! in the logic.

For example, ping only Ubuntu nodes that have the `webserver` class applied to them:

```
$ mco ping --select "operatingsystem=Ubuntu and /nameserver/"
```

Ping every CentOS node that isn't in the dev environment:

```
$ mco ping --select "operatingsystem=CentOS and !environment=dev"
```

Ping every virtualized webserver:

```
$ mco ping --select "( /httpd/ or /nginx/ ) and is_virtual=true"
```

The final example showed how to match virtualized nodes with either the `httpd` or `nginx` Puppet class applied to them which also have the fact `is_virtual`. This search is only possible using the `select` filter type.

Not All Filters Are Available with Every discovery Plugin

If you are using the `flatfile` or `stdin` `discovery` method, only the `identity` filter can be used. Consult the documentation for each `discovery` method to determine which filters are available.

Using a `select` filter will cause the `mc` `discovery` plugin to be used, even if a different plugin is provided on the command line.

Limits

Beyond what filters can do, you may also want to limit how many servers receive the request or how many process it at the same time. We're going to cover how to do this.

To control how many servers receive your request, use the option `--one` to get a random server or `--limit` to specify either a fixed number of servers or a percentage of the servers matching a filter.

For example, 15 servers of any type:

```
$ mco find --limit 15
```

Only one CentOS server:

```
$ mco facts architecture --one --with-fact operatingsystem=CentOS
```

Five servers that have the `webserver` Puppet class applied to them:

```
$ mco facts osfamily --limit 5 --with-class webserver
```

One-third of the servers that have the `webserver` Puppet class applied to them:

```
$ mco facts is_virtual --limit 33% --with-class webserver
```

By default, every server that matches the filter will be sent the request at the same time. While it is impressive to see every server in your network jump to perform your request at exactly the same instant, there are times that you may want to limit this. For example, you probably don't want every node in a load balancer pool to upgrade themselves at the same moment. Here are some options to control how many servers receive the request in a batch, and how far apart between each batch.

Query `sudo` package version in batches of 10 servers spaced 20 seconds apart:

```
$ mco package status sudo --batch 10 --batch-sleep 20
```

Query the Puppet version of all German servers, processing five every 30 seconds:

```
$ mco package status puppet --batch 5 --batch-sleep 30 --with-fact country=de
```

Ping every server with a *w* in its name without delay—no batching:

```
$ mco ping --with-identity /w/
```

 Ping is a very low-level request that doesn't honor either `--batch` or `--limit`.

Output

Beyond controlling which servers receive the request and how quickly, you can also control the output you receive in response. Here are some useful examples to change the way you receive your responses.

This provides structured data instead of friendly text in response:

```
$ mco plugin --json command options...
```

This avoids display of the status bar:

```
$ mco plugin --no-progress command options...
```

This tells you how long discovery takes, and gives you full RPC statistics at the bottom:

```
$ mco plugin --verbose command options...

Discovering hosts using the mc method for 2 second(s) .... 3

...normal output...

---- command plugin results ----
```

```
        Nodes:  3 / 3
   Pass / Fail:  3 / 0
    Start Time:  Mon Feb 10 23:26:06 -0800 2014
Discovery Time:  2003.32ms
    Agent Time:  178.30ms
    Total Time:  2181.62ms
```

This sends the commands but ignores the response queue entirely:

```
$ mco plugin --no-results command options...
```

One request option that I particularly like is to display only failed or only successful responses to a query.

This should show you only the servers who failed to execute the request:

```
$ mco plugin --display failed command options...
```

Only the servers who successfully executed the request:

```
$ mco plugin --display ok command options...
```

All of the responses from any servers who received the request:

```
$ mco plugin --display all command options...
```

> At the time this book was written, few of the applications I tested honored the display input. I received the same results from each of them no matter what value I provided. Hopefully this option will become better supported.

Classes

Classes are the named blocks of code used by Puppet to apply policy to a node. For example, you may apply a webserver class to an MCollective server that runs Apache. We can use filters to limit requests to servers that have certain Puppet classes applied to them.

> If you aren't using Puppet or Chef, this section won't be useful to you.
>
> If you are using Puppet or Chef, the language gets tricky in this section. The MCollective server runs on nodes in your collective. A Puppet or Chef server compiles catalogs on request for agents, which run on nodes with MCollective servers—just to confuse you.

Puppet

The Puppet agent writes out the classes from the node's Puppet catalog to *classes.txt* in the `$statedir` (which is usually */var/lib/puppet/state*). MCollective knows where this is by default.

Puppet allows you to override the location where the classes are stored. If so, you'll need to update the MCollective configuration to match using the `classfile` directive in *server.cfg*:

```
# puppet.conf
[agent]
  classfile = /only/tigger/knows/classes.txt

# server.cfg
classesfile = /only/tigger/knows/classes.txt
```

If you have a heterogenous environment, you may find that Puppet's default location differs on every platform. I have found it best to leave Puppet and MCollective with the same default locations, rather than trying to control it by tweaking both configurations.

 On Red Hat, CentOS, and Fedora systems, the Puppet Labs packages install a default *puppet.conf* that contains an incorrect/not-default location for the `classfile`. This breaks MCollective's ability to read classes on these hosts. You have to either hardcode the `classfile` in *mcollective/server.cfg* or remove the `classfile` override from the EL default *puppet.conf*. The latter fix is easiest.

You can check here to see if this bug is resolved yet: PUP-1610 (*https://tickets.puppetlabs.com/browse/PUP-1610*).

Chef

The Chef cookbook documented in Chapter 7 will place all roles and recipes in a file named */var/tmp/chefnode.txt*. It will configure MCollective to use it by placing the following configuration line in *server.cfg*:

```
classesfile = /var/tmp/chefnode.txt
```

You can reference the roles and recipes in your filters like so:

```
$ mco find --with-class role.webserver --with-class /apache/
```

Bash Completion

MCollective provides a plugin for bash to enable command-line completion. Unfortunately, this plugin isn't installed by default on any platform I found a package for. Here's a way to install and enable this.

If you have the source available you can install it from there:

```
$ cd marionette-collective-2.5.3
$ sudo cp ext/bash/mco_completion.sh /etc/bash_completion.d/
```

If you installed from packages, you can simply download it directly from GitHub:

```
$ wget https://raw.githubusercontent.com/puppetlabs/marionette-collective/
  master/ext/bash/mco_completion.sh
$ sudo cp mco_completion.sh /etc/bash_completion.d/
```

Once bash completion is installed and you start a new shell session, you can hit Tab to get information on possible completions for your mco command line. For example:

```
$ mco service [TAB]
-A          --discovery-timeout --help   -t        -v          --wc   --with-agent
-c          --dt                --I       -T        --verbose --wf   --with-class
-C          -F                  -q        --target  -W          --wi   --with-fact
--config -h                     --quiet  --timeout --wa         --with --with-identity
```

## CHAPTER 4

Web Clients

Puppet Enterprise

There are two web UIs available for managing MCollective. Puppet Labs provides a web UI for controlling MCollective in their Puppet Enterprise (*http://puppetlabs.com/puppet/puppet-enterprise*) product line. Videos demonstrating the Puppet Enterprise products are available at Puppet Labs webinars (*http://bit.ly/1nw8N5d*).

mcomaster

There is a free web UI named mcomaster (*http://mcomaster.org/*) that is available on GitHub at *https://github.com/ajf8/mcomaster*:

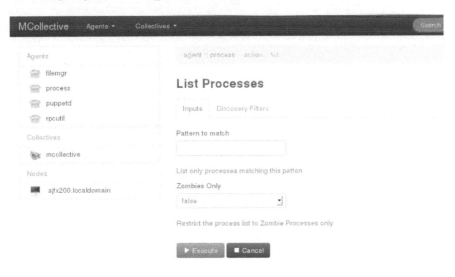

mcomaster is a useful way to explore the query options available from the MCollective plugins you have installed.

 Do not try to install and use mcomaster until MCollective is working properly in your environment. mcomaster requires Ruby 1.9 or 2.0 and will not work with any version of Ruby 1.8.

I've gone through the setup and installation of mcomaster a few times now, and in my experience, most administrators use it a few times and then drift away. The WebUI is slower to use than the command line.

Setting up mcomaster is nontrivial and beyond the scope of this book. If I have enough free time, I may add an mcollective::mcomaster class to my MCollective module for Puppet (*https://github.com/jorhett/puppet-mcollective*).

CHAPTER 5

Agent and Client Plugins

The software installed on the nodes you control through MCollective is a daemon called mcollectived. We will install several agents in this chapter to provide powerful new features. mcollectived is called a server because it functions as an application server. Its abilities are expanded by installing agent plugins to extend and enhance what we can control on the node.

Each agent has a matching client or application that knows how to issue requests specific to that agent. We'll install and use the client applications to communicate with the agent.

Connector Plugins

On each node in your environment, we have installed the mcollectived service. For this daemon to operate correctly, it requires two plugins:

- A connector plugin to establish a link with the middleware and subscribe to topics
- A security plugin to encrypt and decrypt the communications

These two connectors must be the same throughout your environment. In most situations, the configuration for these plugins will be the same for every server.

For the baseline setup described in Chapter 2, we used:

```
connector = activemq
```

The alternative would have been to use RabbitMQ or to build a custom middleware connector.

```
securityprovider = psk
```

We will discuss alternative security plugins like SSL in Chapter 13.

Installing Agents from Packages

Puppet Labs provides a number of MCollective agents that know how to do common systems-management tasks (e.g., query, start, and stop processes, and query, install, and remove packages). We'll start with just the plugins they provide for now.

If you are using the Puppet Labs repositories as described in "Puppet Labs Repository" on page 15, you can simply install the baseline set of agents as follows:

```
# for RedHat, CentOS, and Fedora-based nodes
$ sudo yum install mcollective-filemgr-agent
$ sudo yum install mcollective-nettest-agent
$ sudo yum install mcollective-package-agent
$ sudo yum install mcollective-service-agent

# for Debian and Ubuntu hosts
$ sudo apt-get install mcollective-filemgr-agent
$ sudo apt-get install mcollective-nettest-agent
$ sudo apt-get install mcollective-package-agent
$ sudo apt-get install mcollective-service-agent
```

You'll need to do this on every server in your environment. On the client nodes, you'll need to install the corresponding client package, for example:

```
$ sudo yum install mcollective-filemgr-client
```

For any other operating systems, you should install from the operating system repository or from source, as described in the next section.

Installing Agents from Source

Installing mcollective plugins from source is actually quite easy and is exactly the same on every operating system I've tested the process on. You'll need to have git installed and working on your host to perform these steps:

```
$ git clone git://github.com/puppetlabs/mcollective-filemgr-agent.git
Cloning into 'mcollective-filemgr-agent'...
remote: Reusing existing pack: 49, done.
remote: Total 49 (delta 0), reused 0 (delta 0)
Unpacking objects: 100% (49/49), done.
Checking connectivity... done
$ cd mcollective-filemgr-agent
$ mco plugin package .
Building packages for mcollective-filemgr plugin.
Completed building all packages for mcollective-filemgr plugin.
```

If MCollective does not know how to build packages for your operating system yet, then you'll need to copy the files into the MCollective *plugins* directory.

Copy to Plugins Directory

MCollective plugins are expected to mimic the structure of the *libdir/mcollective* directory. This means that the plugin will have an *agent* directory for the agent plugin and an *application* directory for the client. You can ignore any Rakefiles or *spec* directories in the plugin.

All MCollective plugins must be copied into the *libdir*, as specified in the client and server config files. *libdir* should be the standard Ruby *lib* directory containing an MCollective directory, under which lies an *agent* directory for the agent plugins and an *application* directory for the client.

In short: agent plugin files are named *libdir/mcollective/agent/NAME.(rb|ddl|erb)*. There is usually a client application in *libdir/mcollective/agent/NAME.rb*. There may be *util* or other directories, which should be copied verbatim.

For example, here are the agent files installed for the package plugin:

For RedHat, CentOS, and Fedora-based systems:

```
$ cp agent/package.rb /usr/libexec/mcollective/mcollective/agent/
$ cp agent/package.dll /usr/libexec/mcollective/mcollective/agent/
$ cp application/package.rb /usr/libexec/mcollective/mcollective/application/
```

For Debian and Ubuntu systems, use:

```
$ cp agent/package.rb /usr/share/mcollective/plugins/mcollective/agent/
$ cp agent/package.dll /usr/share/mcollective/plugins/mcollective/agent/
$ cp application/package.rb /usr/share/mcollective/plugins/mcollective/application/
```

And for other platforms, use:

```
$ cp agent/package.rb /opt/mcollective/plugins/mcollective/agent/
$ cp agent/package.dll /opt/mcollective/plugins/mcollective/agent/
$ cp application/package.rb /opt/mcollective/plugins/mcollective/application/
```

You'll probably want to use configuration management to deploy these files to all of your servers.

The *mcollective* directory goes inside *libdir*. In the Red Hat case, this means the complete path contains the string *mcollective/mcollective*; be careful not to accidentally skip the second *mcollective*.

More details are available at *http://bit.ly/WBy7RV*.

Notify mcollectived

After you have installed new agents on a server node, you tell mcollectived to reload the agents. The simplest method is to restart mcollectived for the agents to be loaded and active:

```
$ sudo service mcollective restart
Shutting down mcollective:                    [  OK  ]
Starting mcollective:                         [  OK  ]
```

You can also send the daemon a *USR1* signal to effect the reload. On many platforms, you can do this with pkill. The -x option can be used to ensure you don't kill any other program with a partial name match:

```
$ sudo pkill -USR1 -x mcollectived || echo "pkill failed: $?"
```

Once you have made the changes, you can use the inventory request and read through the output to see if the new agents are available on the node:

```
$ mco inventory nodename
read down through the output...
Agents:
      discovery      rpcutil
      filemgr        nettest
      package        service
```

I rather like using awk to remove all other output (naturally, it's not guaranteed against future changes in the output):

```
$ mco inventory nodename | awk '/Agents:/','/^$/'
```

You can also query to get a list of every server that has the agent installed:

```
$ mco find --with-agent filemgr
geode
heliotrope
sunstone
```

To interact with these agents, we need to have installed the client plugins on any system from which we will be sending requests to these agents, as discussed in "Using Client Plugins" on page 51.

 I have seen inconsistent response when using the USR1 signal to reload the agent. It seems to work most times for making newly added agents available, but is less consistent when reloading an upgraded agent. If you don't see what you expect, it is best to perform a full restart of mcollectived.

Disabling Agents

What if you want to disable an agent on a machine? For example, if there was a problem with the agent but you didn't want to go through uninstalling it yet.

There are two ways to disable an agent. The first option is within the server configuration file:

```
plugin.plugin_name.activate_agent = false
```

The other way is to create a configuration file for that particular agent:

```
$ echo "activate_agent = false"
  | sudo tee -a /etc/mcollective/plugins.d/plugin_name.cfg
```

 When using the Puppet Enterprise, product changes to the main server config file are not supported. You must create plugin configuration files in */etc/puppetlabs/mcollective/plugin.d/*.

Any time this parameter is changed, you'll need to signal mcollectived to reload as documented in "Notify mcollectived" on page 50.

Using Client Plugins

Client plugins provide an application to issue commands to their matching agents. They are only useful when you install the corresponding agent on the servers.

If you are using the Puppet Labs repositories (as described in "Puppet Labs Repository" on page 15), you can install a baseline set of safe and well-tested clients like this:

```
# RedHat, CentOS, Fedora Based Systems
$ sudo yum install mcollective-filemgr-client
$ sudo yum install mcollective-nettest-client
$ sudo yum install mcollective-package-client
$ sudo yum install mcollective-service-client

# Debian or Ubuntu
$ sudo apt-get install mcollective-filemgr-client
$ sudo apt-get install mcollective-nettest-client
$ sudo apt-get install mcollective-package-client
$ sudo apt-get install mcollective-service-client
```

After you install the client plugins, you can get a list of applications available on a node with the doc command:

```
$ mco plugin doc
Please specify a plugin. Available plugins are:
```

```
Agents:
   filemgr                   File Manager
   nettest                   Agent to do network tests from a mcollective host
   package                   Install and uninstall software packages
...etc
```

The applications add custom subcommands (called *faces*) to the `mco` client, allowing easy access to the commands provided by each client plugin. You can get documentation for how to use the plugin from the `help` command:

```
$ mco help package

Install, uninstall, update, purge and perform other actions to packages

Usage: mco package [OPTIONS] [FILTERS] <ACTION> <PACKAGE>
Usage: mco package <PACKAGE> <install|uninstall|purge|update|status>

The ACTION can be one of the following:

    install    - install PACKAGE
    uninstall  - uninstall PACKAGE
    purge      - uninstall PACKAGE and purge related config files
    update     - update PACKAGE
    status     - determine whether PACKAGE is installed and report its version
```

```
$ mco package update mcollective -I heliotrope
 * [ ===================================================> ] 1 / 1

Summary of Ensure:
   2.5.3-1.el6 = 1

Finished processing 1 / 1 hosts in 5923.31 ms
```

You'll find the `help` command useful for determining command syntax, but extensive details about inputs and outputs can be found only in the plugin's documentation:

```
$ mco plugin doc agent/package
package
=======

Install and uninstall software packages

      Author: R.I.Pienaar
     Version: 4.3.1
     License: ASL 2.0
     Timeout: 180
   Home Page: https://github.com/puppetlabs/mcollective-package-agent

   Requires MCollective 2.2.1 or newer

ACTIONS:
========
    apt_checkupdates, apt_update, checkupdates, install, purge, status, uninstall,
```

```
      update, yum_checkupdates, yum_clean

   apt_checkupdates action:
   ------------------------
      Check for APT updates

      INPUT:
          This action does not have any inputs

      OUTPUT:
          exitcode:
              Description: The exitcode from the apt command
              Display As: Exit Code
   ...etc
```

Finding Community Plugins

You may have needs that are custom and unique to your environment. MCollective is extensible, and you'll find many user-provided agents available on the Puppet Forge. You will also find it easy to build your own agents and clients. In those situations, you can orchestrate actions that the MCollective maintainers never dreamed about. I'll show you how to do this in Part III.

Before you set out to build your own plugin, you should look around to ensure that someone hasn't built it already. There are many benefits to using something that is easy to extend. One of them is that it builds a large community of people who extend the software to meet their own needs. The other is that members of the community can share the plugins with one another. So before you go off to build a module yourself, you should check to make sure someone hasn't already made an agent for this.

The first location to look for plugin agents and clients should always be the Puppet Labs Yum or APT repositories (this repo and how to use it is documented in "Puppet Labs Repository" on page 15):

```
$ yum search --enablerepo=puppetlabs* mcollective # RedHat
$ apt-cache search mcollective                     # Debian
```

Puppet Labs maintains a wiki page with links to many of the plugins (*http://bit.ly/WBzrUP*).

At the time this book was written, the only place where I saw significant community MCollective plugin development was on GitHub. GitHub contains hundreds of MCollective plugins that others have already developed. Running a GitHub search for "mcollective" (*https://github.com/search?q=mcollective*) will return most of the plugins available for download.

Unfortunately, many of the modules available on GitHub are made for older versions of MCollective. It can be difficult to sift through everything to find the gems. As the requirements for plugins have changed significantly in the last two years, I would recommend avoiding any plugin that hasn't been updated in 2013 or later.

It is always best if you can build packages of the plugins with the `mco plugin pack age` command. Install the `-agent` packages on servers and the `-client` packages on clients. You'll need to follow the steps outlined in "Notify mcollectived" on page 50 so that the server will pick up the new agents.

If you can't build a package with the plugin, the process for installing plugins from source is documented in "Installing from Source" on page 25.

Recommended Plugins

I am not responsible or affiliated with any of these plugins, but I have found each of them useful at one site or another in the last year:

Plugin name	Description
Puppet Labs Plugins (*https://github.com/puppetlabs/mcollective-plugins*)	Agents for mongodb-registration, NRPE, and many others
mcollective-test (*https://github.com/ripienaar/mcollective-test*)	A set of helpers to assist in writing unit and integration tests for MCollective agents and applications
iptables agent (*https://github.com/puppetlabs/mcollective-iptables-agent*)	Puppet Labs agent for controlling iptables
Shell Agent (*https://github.com/cegeka/mcollective-shell-agent*)	Agent for running arbitrary shell commands
PuppetDB Discovery (*https://github.com/ploubser/mcollective-puppetdb-discovery*)	Discovery plugin that uses PuppetDB as the source
Nadeau's Plugins (*https://github.com/nadeau/mcollective-plugins*)	Agents for `procfs`, `lvm`, `lxc`, `drbd`
OMRY's Agents (*https://github.com/omry/mcollective-plugins*)	Agents for `grep`, `monit`, `status files`, `up time`, `reboot`...
Zcollective (*https://github.com/scalefactory/zcollective*)	Configure Zabbix using data discovered using MCollective
Logstash Audit (*https://github.com/puppetlabs/mcollective-logstash-audit*)	An audit plugin that produces logs suitable for Logstash

There are many more plugins available on GitHub every day. Go take a look at *https://github.com/search?q=mcollective*.

## CHAPTER 6

Maintenance

Now that you have MCollective working, and have an idea of how powerful MCollective can be, let's go over some of the steps involved in maintaining and debugging MCollective.

Time Sync

Many of the weirder problems end up being due to the clients and servers having a different idea of what time it is. Before you take any other debugging steps, ensure that your systems have a consistent view of the time:

```
client$ date +%s
1396310400
server$ date +%s
1396310402
```

Allowing for the difference in time taken for you to run the commands on these two systems, they should be within a few seconds. In modern NTP time-sync, 1/100 of a second is a considerable gap, so most systems should be easily within the same second.

The reason this is important is due to how messages are constructed. Every MCollective message sent out contains the current timestamp and a `ttl` to indicate how long the message is valid:

```
{
  :msgtime    => 1396310400,
  :ttl        => 60,
  :filter     => {
                    "fact"   => [{:fact=>"operatingsystem", :value=>"Debian"}],
                    "agent"  => ["package"]
                 },
  :senderid   => "desktop.example.net",
```

```
:msgtarget   => "/topic/mcollective.discovery.command",
:agent:      => 'discovery',
:collective' => 'mcollective',
:body        => body,
:hash        => "88dd360f13614b7db83616ba49deb130",
:requestid   => "70141ca8a465954706a51ef6a7d4914e"
}
```

In the situation described by this packet, the request is valid from *1396310400* until *1396310460*. If your server receives a request from a client too far in the past, then the request will be ignored because the TTL has already expired. Even weirder problems can occur with clients in the future, from the server's perspective. It is absolutely essential that all of the systems in the collective have a consistent view of the time.

 We aren't talking about timezones here. Computers track time in UTC time and display it to you in the timezone-offset you have configured in your preferences. To computers, all time is stored and compared in UTC time, as represented here. The commands just shown give the UTC epoch time, or seconds since January 1, 1970 UTC.

If you know how to translate that number back to Pacific standard time, then you'll know the exact minute I wrote this particular chapter.

Best practice is to have Puppet, Chef, or any other configuration management tool ensure that NTP is configured properly on every node.

Keeping Sessions Alive

If you have a firewall or flow-tracking switch (e.g., Juniper) between your servers and your middleware, you may need to tweak the settings to ensure the connections remain open.

MCollective's STOMP sessions are idle unless a client is actively issuing requests. MCollective does set the keep-alive flag on the TCP session, but many operating systems send the first keep-alive packet long after most firewalls drop the session from their active table. The server will not be aware that the session has been cut. The middleware will not learn until it tries to forward a message from a client.

STOMP heartbeats were introduced with STOMP 1.1 and have generally solved this problem. The configuration provided in Chapter 2 utilizes these heartbeats, and should keep the connection alive.

Prior to STOMP heartbeats, to keep the sessions alive, one had to configure the server to send updated registration information on a period shorter than the time the firewall will time out the session. In most cases, every 10 minutes was more than sufficient:

```
# server.cfg
registerinterval = 600  # seconds
```

The default registration agent is `AgentList`, which sends a list of only the installed server plugins. You can create your own registration agents to send other information, as we'll document in Chapter 21.

Activating Changes

After any server or agent configuration change, you'll need to restart `mcollectived` before the changes will be visible:

```
$ sudo service mcollective restart
Shutting down mcollective:                               [  OK  ]
Starting mcollective:                                    [  OK  ]
```

You can send the `mcollectived` daemon a to make it reload agent plugins. On most platforms you can do this with `pkill`. The `-x` option can be used to ensure you don't kill any other program with a partial name match. The following command will cause MCollective to reload the agents, but also report back any failures from the `pkill` command:

```
$ sudo pkill -USR1 -x mcollectived || echo "pkill failed: $?"
```

Note that this won't report back any failures from MCollective. For that purpose, you'd have to read the log files:

```
$ tail -20 /var/log/mcollective.log
```

Server Statistics

In addition to the list of agents available on a server, MCollective also reports back a fair number of statistics from the `inventory` request:

```
$ mco inventory heliotrope
Inventory for heliotrope:

    Server Statistics:
                      Version: 2.5.3
                   Start Time: Wed Jul 28 23:27:32 -0700 2014
                  Config File: /etc/mcollective/server.cfg
                  Collectives: mcollective
             Main Collective: mcollective
                   Process ID: 29427
               Total Messages: 5
       Messages Passed Filters: 5
             Messages Filtered: 0
```

```
          Expired Messages: 0
             Replies Sent: 4
     Total Processor Time: 2.66 seconds
             System Time: 3.65 seconds


   Agents:
      discovery      filemgr       nettest
      package        puppet        rpcutil
      service
```

...several hundred other lines of output

As the output of `inventory` is very verbose, I rather like using `awk` to stop after the first blank line:

```
$ mco inventory heliotrope | awk '/Server/','/^$/'
```

Logging

The following are defaults for logging used if not overridden in the *server.cfg* file:

```
logger_type = file
loglevel = info
logfile = /var/log/mcollective.log
keeplogs = 5
max_log_size = 2097152
logfacility = user
```

In this default configuration, `mcollectived` writes its own logs to disk and does its own log rotation. It keeps five logs on disk, and rotates when each log reaches 2 MB.

This may work for many underutilized hardware systems but may be nonoptimal in many situations where storage is expensive or the systems are virtualized. Personally, I prefer to utilize the existing logging and analysis infrastructure and recommend the following settings:

```
logger_type = syslog
loglevel = debug
logfacility = daemon
```

These settings are documented in detail at *http://docs.puppetlabs.com/mcollective/ configure/server.html#logging* and *http://docs.puppetlabs.com/mcollective/configure/ client.html#logging*.

Monitoring Servers

There are two ways to check whether MCollective servers are alive: actively and passively.

An active check would be to issue a call to an agent available on every node and validate the results. This could be something as simple as `mco ping`, which is a low-level connectivity test that doesn't require authentication or authorization. Or you could test to a specific plugin (e.g., an NRPE test). We provide a script to do this in Chapter 19.

A passive check would be to listen to the registration agent topic and look for servers that haven't checked in recently. We discuss how to build a registration agent in Chapter 21. An example of how to check this with Nagios can be found at Puppet Labs wiki AgentRegistrationMonitor (*http://bit.ly/1wWHpCB*).

## CHAPTER 7

Configuration Management

By now you must be thinking to yourself, "Wow, this is a lot of configuration data." Yes, you are absolutely right.

It is best to use Puppet, Chef, or another configuration-management system to deploy and maintain MCollective. As you proceed through this book, you will be constantly tweaking the MCollective configuration and adding new plugins. Most changes will need to be synchronized across servers, yet many servers will also have customized settings. In previous sections, we have gone over how to set up MCollective by hand, but across many systems it becomes a lot of work. It's best to manage your MCollective installation with configuration management.

As the installation documentation on the Puppet Labs website says (*http://bit.ly/ 1wWHENY*):

> [MCollective] is the textbook example for why you need config management:
>
> - It has multiple components that run on many different machines.
> - It has pieces of global configuration that must be set harmoniously, everywhere.
> - Most of its settings are identical for machines in a given role (e.g. every server), but some of its settings have per-system differences. This is easy to manage with a template, and incredibly frustrating to manage by hand.
> - Its configuration *will* change over time, and the changes affect many many systems at once.
>
>   New/updated agents must be deployed to all servers; when a new admin user is introduced, every server must be made aware of their permissions.
>
> In summary, its configuration requirements are strict, and configuration drift will cause it to stop working. Use Puppet.

For what it is worth, you could just as easily use Chef, Salt, Cfengine, Ansible, or another configuration-management tool to install and configure MCollective. We focus on Puppet since MCollective and Puppet are both maintained by Puppet Labs, and their integration is something you can get support for.

Documentation for Chef can be found in "Chef" on page 75.

If you are already invested in a different configuration management tool, there is no need to worry. MCollective does not depend on Puppet. You can adapt the configuration recipes from this book to your chosen tool or look to see if someone has already provided a plugin for you.

Puppet

I have created a Puppet module for installing and configuring MCollective. This module implements every feature discussed in the book with a minimum of external dependencies. Every chapter following this one will contain configuration examples which utilize this module.

You might notice that there is a `puppetlabs-mcollective` module available on the Puppet Forge. We are not using this module for teaching MCollective for several reasons:

- If you don't override some defaults values, the setup will use well-known usernames and passwords. A mistype would make your setup vulnerable to attack.

- It doesn't separate client and server permissions, which creates a security problem if any server is compromised or untrustable.

- It doesn't separate client permissions and broker link permissions.

- The Puppet Labs module has numerous external dependencies that could be distracting to set up when trying to follow the book.

The module provided in this book allows a simple setup to work immediately and then the ability to add more as you read each chapter in the book.

Installing the Puppet Module

So there are two different ways to install the Puppet module to manage MCollective.

Using r10k

If you already use r10k, you can get a configuration and Puppetfile from *http://github.com/jorhett/learning-mcollective* to install the modules for you. This will also pull down an example Hiera configuration and data files. As this is not really an MCollective concern, documentation for the r10k setup can be found in "Using r10k to install Puppet Modules" on page 234.

Straight from GitHub

If you don't use r10k, you can pull the module down from GitHub, like so:

```
$ git clone git://github.com/jorhett/puppet-mcollective.git
Cloning into 'puppet-mcollective'...
remote: Counting objects: 65, done.
remote: Compressing objects: 100% (56/56), done.
remote: Total 65 (delta 11), reused 59 (delta 5)
Receiving objects: 100% (65/65), 34.83 KiB, done.
Resolving deltas: 100% (11/11), done.
```

If you have your own Puppet module forge internally, the following optional step will build a module package appropriate for uploading to the forge:

```
$ cd puppet-mcollective
$ puppet module build
Notice: Building /home/jorhett/src/puppet-mcollective for release
Module built:
/home/jorhett/src/puppet-mcollective/pkg/jorhett-mcollective-0.1.0.tar.gz
```

Or you can move the module directly into your modulepath:

```
$ mkdir -p /etc/puppet/environments/learning_mcollective/modules
$ mv puppet-mcollective
  /etc/puppet/environments/learning_mcollective/modules/mcollective
```

You'll need to get the Puppet Labs stdlib module if you don't have it already:

```
$ puppet module install puppetlabs-stdlib
  --modulepath=/etc/puppet/environments/learning_mcollective/modules
Notice: Preparing to install into
/etc/puppet/environments/learning_mcollective/modules ...
Notice: Downloading from https://forgeapi.puppetlabs.com ...
Notice: Installing -- do not interrupt ...
/etc/puppet/environments/learning_mcollective/modules
└── puppetlabs-stdlib (v4.2.1)
```

We created a new environment specific to testing MCollective here. The example assumes you are using directory environments as documented at Puppet Docs: Directory Environments (*http://bit.ly/1wWJpuv*) or the older config file–based environments. As both config file environments and "no environment" are scheduled for deprecation, it is best to do all new deployments in the manner documented at *http://bit.ly/1wWJpuv*.

Feel free to place these modules in another environment name if you already have an appropriate testing environment. The environment name is not special.

In the next section, you'll define the site configuration in the manifests and/or Hiera data.

Configuring MCollective Using Puppet

The following Puppet manifest will perform a basic MCollective setup and initialization for you. If you don't yet use Puppet, consider how easy it is to replace the entire Chapter 2 section of the book with these small recipes.

This module contains all of the manifests and templates shown in this book, plus examples of ActionPolicy configurations.

This module could be extended to cover more middleware configurations if it relied on other Forge modules for managing ActiveMQ and RabbitMQ configurations. For the purposes of simple, one-shot setup, I wanted to focus on a simplified configuration that serviced only MCollective clients and servers. If you prefer to manage the middleware configuration yourself, simply don't use the `mcollective::middleware` class in this book.

For a simple example, the following declarative policy could be used to configure your nodes:

```
manifests/site.pp:
# This sets the defaults for all subclasses
node default {
  class { '::mcollective':
    hosts           => ['activemq.example.net'],
    client_password => 'Client Password ',
    server_password => 'Server Password',
    psk_key         => 'Pre-Shared Key',
  }
  # Every node installs the server
  include mcollective::server
}
# This node is the ActiveMQ broker
```

```
node 'activemq.example.net' inherits default {
  include mcollective::middleware
}
# This node is my admin host where I'll submit requests
node 'admin.example.net' inherits default {
  include mcollective::client
}
```

For most nodes on your network, you would use only the mcollective and mcollec
tive::server classes. You should put the mcollective::client class on any hosts
from which you wish to submit requests.

Hiera Configuration Data

You can supply parameters to each of the classes just described, or you can simply
define all of the settings in Hiera. What follows is the most minimal set of parameters
you'll need to supply.

First, you enable class assignment from Hiera in the site manifest:

```
# manifests/site.pp
hiera_include('classes')
```

Then you set up the Hiera data hierarchy to look for data in files based on the hostname first, with a fallback to a common file:

```
# /etc/puppet/hiera.yaml
---
:backends:
    - yaml
:yaml:
    :datadir: '/etc/puppet/environments/learning_mcollective/hieradata'
:hierarchy:
    - hostname/%{::hostname}
    - common
```

Put all shared parameters in the common file. In this case we define that every node
will load the server:

```
# hieradata/common.yaml
classes:
  - mcollective::server

mcollective::hosts:
  - 'activemq.example.net'
mcollective::client_password: 'Client Password '
mcollective::server_password: 'Server Password'
mcollective::psk_key         : 'Pre-Shared Key'
```

Finally, we create two files that contain classes specific to their hostname:

```
# hieradata/hostname/activemq.yaml
classes:
```

```
    - mcollective::middleware

# hieradata/hostname/admin.yaml
classes:
  - mcollective::client
```

Hiera

Hiera is a key/value lookup tool for configuration data, built to let you define Puppet configuration data without repeating yourself.

If you are not familiar with using Hiera, the best reference can be found at Hiera Overview (*http://bit.ly/1wWKnHl*). In particular, read carefully "Usage with Puppet" (*http://bit.ly/1wWKrGT*) for how Puppet modules automatically include Hiera data.

The MCollective Puppet module has dozens of parameters available to customize the settings to your specific needs. This module can be used to create high-security configurations or build a large distributed network of brokers. What follows is a much more complex example that does the following:

1. Directs clients to their local broker (depending on the Hiera hierarchy)
2. Sets up site→site links between the brokers
3. Uses SSL encryption for all connections
4. Sets up file logging at debug loglevel
5. Loads up package, service, and Puppet agents at both sites
6. Installs the client programs only on machines at site1

The following Hiera files break up the configuration between the London and Philadelphia offices. Each office has its own ActiveMQ server. All of the admins are in London, so the client packages are loaded there. All other parameters are the same for the MCollective framework:

```
# /etc/puppet/hiera.yaml
---
:backends:
    - yaml
:yaml:
    :datadir: '/etc/puppet/environments/learning_mcollective/hieradata'
:hierarchy:
    - hostname/%{::hostname}
    - domain/%{::domain}
    - common

# hieradata/hostname/activemq.yaml
classes:
```

```
  - mcollective::middleware

# hieradata/domain/philadelphia.example.net.yaml
mcollective::hosts:
  - 'activemq.philadelphia.example.net'

# hieradata/domain/london.example.net.yaml
mcollective::hosts:
  - 'activemq.london.example.net'

classes:
  - mcollective::client
mcollective::client::package_ensure: 'latest'
mcollective::plugin::clients:
  package:
    version: 'latest'
  service:
    version: 'latest'
  puppet:
    version: 'latest'

# hieradata/common.yaml
classes:
  - mcollective::server

mcollective::hosts:
  - 'activemq.london.example.net'
  - 'activemq.philadelphia.example.net'
mcollective::collectives:
  - 'mcollective'
  - 'london'
  - 'philadelphia'
mcollective::client_password: 'Client Password '
mcollective::server_password: 'Server Password'
mcollective::broker_password: 'Broker Password'
mcollective::psk_key          : 'Pre-Shared Key'

mcollective::connector          : 'activemq'
mcollective::connector_ssl      : true
mcollective::connector_ssl_type: 'anonymous'

# Server configuration
mcollective::server::logger_type: 'file'
mcollective::server::log_level  : 'debug'

# Client configuration
mcollective::client::package_ensure: 'absent'
mcollective::client::unix_group    : 'wheel'

# Middleware configuration
mcollective::middleware::keystore_password  : 'Keystore Password'
mcollective::middleware::truststore_password: 'Truststore Password'
```

```
# Plugins to install
mcollective::plugin::agents:
  package: {}
  service: {}
  puppet :
    version: 'latest'
```

Don't worry about understanding this complex example just yet—this is skipping way ahead into chapters much later in the book! We'll be spending the remainder of this book walking you through different things you can achieve with MCollective, and each and every section will contain Puppet/Hiera parameters you can apply to enable those features.

Sharing Facts with Puppet

As discussed in "Filters" on page 38, one of the most flexible ways to match related groups of systems is by facts. The easiest way to get `facter` facts for MCollective is to let Puppet supply them for you. This is much better than the simple cron method we showed you earlier, as it allows you to add both custom Puppet facts and variables to the list.

To get this more flexible usage, add the following to your Puppet manifests:

```
node myhost.example.net {
  include mcollective::server
  include mcollective::facts
}
```

Or add the following if you're using Hiera:

```
# hieradata/common.yaml
classes:
  - mcollective::server
  - mcollective::facts
```

 Did you enable fact creation using the cron script we documented in "Facts" on page 32?

If so, you'll want to remove the */etc/cron.d/facts.sh* cron script. Otherwise, Puppet and cron will keep overwriting each other's results. Puppet has more facts available and more flexibility in adding new facts from Puppet variables, so this is the better of the two choices.

Installing Agents with Puppet

Here are some example manifests for adding agents to your systems, assuming the agent packages are available in a package repository. For the first one, we show you how to define an explicit version, but this is not necessary:

```
node nodename {
  mcollective::plugin::agent { 'filemgr':
    version => '1.0.1-1',
  }
}
```

If you use Hiera, this can be done even easier. The module we provided looks for agent and client names to be defined in YAML and installs them using the parameter hash supplied. The following Hiera data is identical to the Puppet policy we defined previously:

```
mcollective::plugin::agents:
  filemgr:
    - version: 1.0.1-1
```

It must be broken out exactly as it is here. The data type for `mcollective::plu gin::agents` is a list of agents to install. Each agent should have a dictionary of attributes. In this sense, the Hiera data is identical to the declarative invocation shown earlier.

You can also define an array of dependencies for an agent. Here's an example where we want to install the MCollective agent for Puppet, but only if the Puppet package is installed. We look up the name of the package from a variable in the `puppet::client` class to ensure we get the appropriate package name for each operating system:

```
node nodename {
  mcollective::plugin::agent { 'puppet':
    version      => latest,
    dependencies => [ Package[ $puppet::client::package_name ] ],
  }
}
```

Naturally, you can express the exact same idea in Hiera data:

```
mcollective::plugin::agents:
  puppet:
    version: latest
    dependencies:
      - Package[ %{puppet::client::package_name} ]
```

On hosts where you execute the client commands, you should install the client plugins. Here's a simple example where we install client plugins using the default values:

```
node nodename {
  mcollective::plugin::client { 'filemgr': }
  mcollective::plugin::client { 'nettest': }
```

```
  mcollective::plugin::client { 'package': }
  mcollective::plugin::client { 'service': }
  mcollective::plugin::client { 'puppet':  }
}
```

When using Hiera to load agents or clients, specify default values with an empty dictionary. Here is a complete Hiera example showing both agents and client plugins, some with versions and dependencies and some without:

```
mcollective::plugin::agents:
  filemgr:
    - version: 1.0.1-1
  nettest: {}
  package: {}
  service: {}
  puppet:
    version    : latest
    dependencies:
      - Package[ %{puppet::client::package_name} ]

mcollective::plugin::clients:
  filemgr: {}
  nettest: {}
  package: {}
  service: {}
  puppet:
    version: latest
```

I'm sure you've noticed by now that Hiera uses plural names (agents and clients) but the declarative policy invocation uses a single name (agent or client). This should be intuitive to remember, since the single name loads a single plugin, whereas the Hiera plural name accepts a list of plugins.

Validating the Installation

Run the puppet client to reconfigure one of your nodes:

```
$ puppet agent --test --environment learning_mcollective
```

Now, verify that Puppet has configured the servers and clients as you expect. Test that your nodes are reachable the same way we did in "Testing Your Installation" on page 28:

```
$ mco ping
sunstone                       time=88.09 ms
geode                          time=126.22 ms
fireagate                      time=126.81 ms
heliotrope                     time=127.32 ms

---- ping statistics ----
4 replies max: 127.32 min: 88.09 avg: 117.11
```

If you get back a list of each server connected to your middleware and its response time, then congratulations! You have successfully deployed MCollective using Puppet. If it doesn't work, check out "Troubleshooting" on page 28 and validate the settings used in this chapter.

Debugging

Here we'll go through some common errors you might encounter with MCollective and Puppet interaction.

Unable to match server with class

If you are unable to match a host using the `--with-class` filter option, the first thing to do is get an inventory of the node with `mco inventory hostname`. If you find that the inventory does not list any classes for a host, then the *classes.txt* file that `mcollectived` is trying to read is not being written to by Puppet.

The *classes.txt* file is written out by the Puppet agent during each run. In the `[agent]` section of *puppet.conf* is a variable `classfile`. This defaults to *$statedir/classes.txt* and *$statedir* defaults to *$vardir/state*. MCollective defaults to the same location as Puppet does on every platform.

However, this variable can be overridden in both *puppet.conf* and *mcollective/server.cfg*. If you do not see Puppet classes in the output of an inventory request for a puppetized node, you should check the following two values and ensure that they match up:

```
$ sudo puppet apply --configprint classfile
/var/lib/puppet/state/classes.txt
$ grep classesfile /etc/mcollective/server.cfg
$ mco rpc rpcutil get_config_item item=classesfile -I heliotrope
heliotrope
    Property: classesfile
        Value: /var/lib/puppet/state/classes.txt
```

If the `classfile` from Puppet matches this, then MCollective doesn't need an override in *server.cfg*. If any different value is found, you may want to set them explicitly to match in both files:

```
# /etc/puppet/puppet.conf
[agent]
  classfile = $statedir/classes.txt

# /etc/mcollective/server.cfg
classesfile = /var/lib/puppet/state/classes.txt
```

Unable to match server with fact

If you are unable to match a host using the `--with-fact` filter option, the first thing to do is get an inventory of the node with `mco inventory hostname`. If you find that the inventory does not list any facts for a server, then the *facts.yaml* file that `mcollectived` is trying to read is not being written to by `facter` or Puppet.

For MCollective to know about facts, a parameter named `plugin.yaml` must be defined in mcollective's *server.cfg*. This parameter names a file that contains the server's facts in YAML format, usually */etc/mcollective/facts.yaml*:

```
# /etc/mcollective/server.cfg
factsource = yaml
plugin.yaml = /etc/mcollective/facts.yaml
```

The target for the `plugin.yaml` parameter could include multiple filenames separated by a colon in Unix systems, or a semicolon for Windows servers. If the facts do not show up after restarting `mcollectived`, then the most likely problem is the formatting of the YAML within the file.

The most basic way to collect system facts was described in "Facts" on page 32. A more elegant and flexible solution, which can use Puppet-generated facts or values, was introduced earlier in this chapter in "Sharing Facts with Puppet" on page 68. It doesn't matter how you generate your system facts, as long as they are written in YAML format to the listed file.

Confirm that one of the following is configured to write out facts to this file:

- A cron job that generates YAML (as described in "Facts" on page 32)
- A puppet module that writes out `facter` facts and other variables (as described in "Sharing Facts with Puppet" on page 68)
- Some other script or process you have that can generate YAML key/value pairs

You can install facts plugins other than YAML from the Puppet Labs Forge, GitHub, or other repositories, as discussed in "Finding Community Plugins" on page 53. You can also build your own, as documented in Chapter 20.

 There is a plugin named `mcollective-facter-facts` on the Puppet Labs GitHub. This agent can be slow to run, as it invokes `Facter` for each evaluation. This has been observed to cause problems with nodes going offline randomly. The plugin used here to load facts from a YAML-format text file works much better.

Unable to match server by hostname

If you are unable to match a host using the `--with-identity` or `-I` filter option, your first action should be to confirm that `mcollectived` is running on the server. This is the most likely reason for a failed response by name.

The next step is to check and see what the configured identity in the server configuration might be:

```
$ grep identity /etc/mcollective/server.cfg
#identity=
```

In this situation, the identity is not hardcoded in the server configuration, so we'll have to use a different fact to identify the node.

The default identity for the node is the output of the `hostname` command. If you are using Puppet, we can query Puppet for its `certname`, which we can use as a filter to query the node and gather its identity.

On the node with the MCollective server, run this command:

```
$ sudo puppet apply --configprint certname
heliotrope.example.net
```

On a node with the MCollective client installed, run this command:

```
$ mco rpc rpcutil get_config_item item=identity --wf \
    clientcert=heliotrope.example.net

heliotrope
    Property: identity
       Value: heliotrope
```

 No, that's not a misprint. The configuration variable `certname` is provided by Puppet as `facter` fact `clientcert`. No idea why the inconsistency—it's just how Puppet is.

Likewise, you can use any other fact or class to locate the node. For example, there are only two CentOS hosts in my testlab:

```
$ mco rpc rpcutil get_config_item item=identity --wf operatingsystem=CentOS

Discovering hosts using the mc method for 2 second(s) .... 2
 * [ ============================================> ] 2 / 2

geode
    Property: identity
       Value: geode

heliotrope
```

```
    Property: identity
       Value: heliotrope

Summary of Value:
        geode = 1
    heliotrope = 1

Finished processing 2 / 2 hosts in 18.38 ms
```

If you want an MCollective node to think of itself with a different name, then set identity in *server.cfg*:

```
identity = iambatman
```

If you are using configuration management *like any sane person*, you can set the variable from the configuration management's knowledge of the node. For example, here's a Puppet template fragment to ensure the MCollective node identifies itself by the Puppet certificate name, rather than the output of hostname:

```
identity = <%= scope.lookup('::clientcert') -%>
```

The most common source of node name confusion is based around the use of node names or FQDNs in the hostname of a system. For example, you can set a node's hostname to either a simple name, or you can include the domain:

```
$ grep HOSTNAME /etc/sysconfig/network   # RedHat location
HOSTNAME=heliotrope
$ hostname
heliotrope
$ hostname -f
heliotrope.example.net
```

With this setup, the MCollective identity was *heliotrope*, while the Puppet certname was *heliotrope.example.net*. You can resolve that mismatch by changing */etc/sysconfig/ network* on RedHat-derived systems or */etc/hostname* on Debian-derived systems or */etc/rc.conf* on *BSD systems. Or you can leave it alone, so long as you understand the difference.

The lack of matching between Puppet and MCollective does not create any explicit problems. My test setup uses short node names (e.g., "heliotrope") for MCollective, while Puppet always uses the FQDN of the host.

Absolutely nothing breaks out of the box by having different identities in Puppet and MCollective; it only affects how you might write your custom plugins. In my opinion, if you have many hosts with unique hostnames, you can save a lot of typing by leaving the domain name off of the hostname. Other people have different opinions drawn from their experiences. YMMV (your mileage may vary).

Chef

You can find a Chef cookbook for MCollective at *http://community.opscode.com/cook books/mcollective* or *https://github.com/zts/cookbook-mcollective*. You should download the cookbook and its dependencies to your local cookbooks repo. For example, this was the process I followed:

```
~$ cd chef_repo/cookbooks
cookbooks$ knife cookbook site download mcollective
Downloading mcollective from the cookbooks site at version 0.14.3
   to /home/jorhett/chef-repo/mcollective-0.14.3.tar.gz
Cookbook saved: /home/jorhett/chef-repo/mcollective-0.14.3.tar.gz
cookbooks$ knife cookbook site download chef_handler
Downloading chef_handler from the cookbooks site at version 1.1.6
   to /home/jorhett/chef-repo/cookbooks/chef_handler-1.1.6.tar.gz
Cookbook saved: /home/jorhett/chef-repo/cookbooks/chef_handler-1.1.6.tar.gz
cookbooks$ knife cookbook site download apt
Downloading apt from the cookbooks site at version 2.4.0
   to /home/jorhett/chef-repo/cookbooks/apt-2.4.0.tar.gz
Cookbook saved: /home/jorhett/chef-repo/cookbooks/apt-2.4.0.tar.gz
cookbooks$ knife cookbook site download yum
Downloading yum from the cookbooks site at version 3.2.2
   to /home/jorhett/chef-repo/cookbooks/yum-3.2.2.tar.gz
Cookbook saved: /home/jorhett/chef-repo/cookbooks/yum-3.2.2.tar.gz
cookbooks$ tar xzf mcollective-0.14.3.tar.gz
cookbooks$ tar xzf chef_handler-1.1.6.tar.gz
cookbooks$ tar xzf apt-2.4.0.tar.gz
cookbooks$ tar xzf yum-3.2.2.tar.gz
```

Then upload the cookbooks to your server's cookbooks repo. For example, this was the process I followed:

```
cookbooks$ knife cookbook upload mcollective chef_handler apt yum
Uploading mcollective   [0.14.3]
Uploading chef_handler  [1.1.6]
Uploading apt           [2.4.0]
Uploading yum           [3.2.2]
Uploaded 4 cookbooks.
```

Configuring MCollective using Chef

Add recipe[mcollective::server'] to the *run_list* for every node and recipe [mcollective::client] to the nodes from which you'll issue requests.

Some Chef attributes you need to tune to match the setup used in this book are:

Configuration variable	Value
['mcollective']['package']['version']	2.6.0 or higher
node['mcollective']['identity']	node['hostname']

Configuration variable	Value
node['mcollective']['group']	wheel
node['mcollective']['connector']	activemq
node['mcollective']['stomp']['hostname']	activemq.*example.net*
node['mcollective']['stomp']['port']	61613
node['mcollective']['stomp']['username']	server
node['mcollective']['stomp']['password']	*Server Password* from "Passwords and Keys" on page 14
node['mcollective']['stomp']['client_username']	client
node['mcollective']['stomp']['client_password']	*Client Password* from "Passwords and Keys" on page 14
node['mcollective']['securityprovider']	psk
node['mcollective']['psk']	*Pre-Shared Key* from "Passwords and Keys" on page 14
node['mcollective']['factsource']	yaml
node['mcollective']['enable_puppetlabs_repo']	true

For example, here is how it looked when I set up a single node to be an MCollective client:

```
~$ knife node edit sunstone.example.net
{
  "name": "sunstone.example.net",
  "chef_environment": "_default",
  "normal": {
    "mcollective": {
      "connector": "activemq",
      "securityprovider": "psk",
      "psk": "Pre-Shared Key",
      "stomp": {
        "hostname": "activemq.example.net",
        "port": "61613",
        "username": "server",
        "password": "Server Password"
        "client_username": "client",
        "client_password": "Client Password"
      }
    },
    "tags": [
    ]
  },
  "run_list": [
    "recipe[mcollective::client]",
    "recipe[mcollective::server]"
  ]
}
```

By default, this Chef cookbook will install MCollective packages from the Puppet Labs APT or YUM repositories. If you have your own package repositories, you can disable this behavior by setting node['mcollective']['enable_puppetlabs_repo'] to false.

You can find all possible variables to tune in *attributes/default.rb* (*http://bit.ly/ 1wWO53B*).

Sharing Ohai Data with Chef

As discussed in "Filters" on page 38, one of the most flexible ways to filter requests for related groups of systems is by facts. The easiest way to generate useful facts for MCollective is to get them from the Chef *Ohai* data. This is significantly more flexible than the simple cron method we showed you previously.

This Chef cookbook writes out a *facts.yaml* file containing facts from a set of Ohai keys. This means that Ohai data is available as facts for use in filters without any changes on your part.

An alternative value for factsource is *ohai*. This method is similar to the facter source for facts in that mcollectived executes the command periodically and caches the response.

In practice, this has the same problem as the facter source—many queries time out randomly and inconsistently. I recommend staying with the YAML source to avoid this difficulty.

You can control which Ohai keys are available as facts by adjusting the following attribute:

```
node['mcollective']['fact_whitelist'] = [
                        'fqdn', 'hostname', 'domain',
                        'ipaddress', 'macaddress', 'os',
                        'os_version', 'platform', 'platform_version',
                        'ohai_time', 'uptime', 'uptime_seconds',
                        'chef_packages', 'keys', 'instmaint',
                        'virtualization', 'cpu', 'memory'
                        ]
```

Did you enable fact creation using the cron script we documented in "Facts" on page 32?

If so, you'll want to remove the */etc/cron.d/facts.sh* cron script. Otherwise, Chef and cron will keep overwriting each other's results. The Ohai data has more facts available and more flexibility in adding new facts from Chef recipes, so this is the better of the two choices.

Sharing Chef Roles and Recipes as Classes

This Chef cookbook writes out the roles and recipes used on the node to MCollective's *classfile*. So you can filter your requests against a Chef role or recipe that is applied to a node.

Installing Agents with Chef

To install and configure MCollective plugins using the Chef cookbook, follow these steps:

1. Install the agent plugin and DDL in the *agent/* subdirectory of node['mcollec tive']['site_plugins'].

2. Install the client plugin in the *application/* subdirectory of node['mcollective'] ['site_plugins'].

3. Install any supporting libraries in the *util/* subdirectory of node['mcollective'] ['site_plugins'].

4. Place any plugin configuration files in the node['mcollective']['plu gin_conf'] directory.

Make a change to the *server configuration* so that the server daemon will be restarted when the recipe runs.

> The default location to install agents, applications, DDLs, and such is site_plugins at */etc/mcollective/site_plugins/mcollective/*.
>
> The default location for plugin configuration files is plugin_conf at */etc/mcollective/plugin.d/*.

TLS Security Limitations

Later on in this book, you'll learn how to enable TLS security options. The author of the MCollective Chef cookbook intends to add support for these options, but they were not available at the time this book was written. Check the cookbook's main page (*https://github.com/zts/cookbook-mcollective*) for an update on this.

This will be covered in the next update to the electronic editions of *Learning MCollective*.

Validating the Installation

At this point, you should verify that Chef has configured the servers and clients as you expect. Test that your nodes are reachable the same way we did in "Testing Your Installation" on page 28:

```
$ mco ping
sunstone                                 time=88.09 ms
geode                                    time=126.22 ms
fireagate                                time=126.81 ms
heliotrope                               time=127.32 ms

---- ping statistics ----
4 replies max: 127.32 min: 88.09 avg: 117.11
```

If you get back a list of each server connected to your middleware and its response time, then congratulations! You have successfully deployed MCollective using Chef. If it doesn't work, check out "Troubleshooting" on page 28 and validate the settings used in this chapter.

 The Chef cookbook for MCollective creates configuration files that look very different from the examples documented in this book. In particular, it places the connector settings in the plugin configuration directory, as documented in Chapter 15. This is a different approach that achieves the same goal. The order of the parameters is not important.

Debugging

Here we'll go through some common errors you might encounter with MCollective and Chef interaction.

Unable to match server with class

If you are unable to match a host using the --with-class filter option, the first thing to do is get an inventory of the node with mco inventory *hostname*. If you find that the inventory does not list any classes for a host, then it is most likely that mcollec tived is not configured to read the file created by the cookbook.

The MCollective cookbook writes out all roles and recipes to the file specified by node['mcollective']['classesfile'] (default */var/tmp/chefnode.txt*) during each run. The MCollective configuration in */etc/mcollective/server.cfg* needs to reference that location as the source of data for classes.

This variable can be overridden in both the Chef node attributes and */etc/mcollective/server.cfg*. If you do not see the Chef roles and recipes in the output of an inventory request for a Chef node, you should check the following two values and ensure that they match up:

```
$ knife node show heliotrope.example.net --attribute mcollective.identity
heliotrope.example.net:
    mcollective.identity: heliotrope.example.net
$ grep classesfile /etc/mcollective/server.cfg
$ mco rpc rpcutil get_config_item item=classesfile -I heliotrope
```

```
heliotrope
   Property: classesfile
      Value: /var/tmp/chefnode.txt
```

If the `classesfile` from Chef matches this, then MCollective doesn't need an override in *server.cfg*. If any different value is found, you should set them explicitly to match in both files:

```
$ knife node edit heliotrope.example.net (all literal, everything except $ bold)
  "normal": {
    "mcollective": {
      "classesfile": "/var/tmp/chefnode.txt",
    }
  }

$ sudo $EDITOR /etc/mcollective/server.cfg
classesfile = /var/tmp/chefnode.txt
```

Unable to match server with fact

If you are unable to match a host using the `--with-fact` filter option, the first thing to do is get an inventory of the node with `mco inventory` *hostname*. If you find that the inventory does not list any facts for a server, then the *facts.yaml* file that `mcollectived` is trying to read is not being written to by Chef.

For MCollective to know about facts, there needs to be a parameter named `plugin.yaml` defined in mcollective's *server.cfg*. The value of this parameter should be a filename that lists the server's facts in YAML format, usually */etc/mcollective/facts.yaml*:

```
# /etc/mcollective/server.cfg
factsource = yaml
plugin.yaml = /etc/mcollective/facts.yaml
```

The target for the `plugin.yaml` parameter could include multiple filenames separated by a colon in Unix systems or a semicolon for Windows servers. If the facts do not show up after restarting `mcollectived`, then the most likely problem is the formatting of the YAML within the file.

With Chef, the MCollective cookbook writes out Ohai keys and values in YAML format to the listed file.

Confirm that one of the following is configured to write out facts to this file:

- The Chef cookbook writes out Ohai keys and their values as described in "Sharing Ohai Data with Chef" on page 77.
- Some other script or process generates YAML key/value pairs.

You can install facts plugins other than YAML from the Chef Site Cookbooks, Git-Hub, or other repositories, as discussed in "Finding Community Plugins" on page 53. You can also build your own, as documented in Chapter 20.

## CHAPTER 8

Controlling Puppet Agent

In the previous chapter, we showed how to use Puppet to install and configure MCollective. In this chapter, we're going to show you how MCollective can:

- Use the Puppet classes applied to the node in filters
- Use facts known by Puppet in filters
- Query, start, stop, and restart the Puppet agent
- Run the Puppet agent with special command line options
- Query and make changes to the node using Puppet resources

If you are using Puppet, you will be quite happy with the level of control MCollective gives you. MCollective allows new ways of using Puppet that simply aren't possible from agent, cron-run, or even command-line usage of Puppet.

Install the Puppet Agent

The first thing we need to do is install the MCollective Puppet agent. Installation of this is identical to the agents we installed in Chapter 5. Since we know you have Puppet installed, we'll dispense with the command-line installation and show you to do it with Puppet:

```
node nodename {
  mcollective::plugin::agent  { 'puppet': }  # for servers
  mcollective::plugin::client { 'puppet': }  # for clients
}
```

If you use Hiera, you can install the agent with a simple listing of the Puppet agent in the `mcollective::plugin::agents` array. In this example, we're going to show you an example where we set the Puppet agent dependencies to ensure that the Puppet client is installed on the host:

```
mcollective::plugin::agents:
  puppet:
    version: latest
    dependencies:
      - Package[%{puppet::client::package_name}]
      - Service[%{puppet::client::service_name}]

mcollective::plugin::clients:
  puppet:
    version: latest
```

 This is obviously a bit redundant (because Puppet is enforcing this policy, so we already know that it is installed), but this makes for a good example because the MCollective agent for Puppet can't function without Puppet installed.

Checking Puppet Status

Once you have installed the MCollective Puppet agent and restarted mcollectived (which the Puppet module does for you), you should install the MCollective Puppet client on one of your admin nodes. The first thing you should do is confirm which systems have the MCollective Puppet agent installed:

```
$ mco find --with-agent puppet
geode
heliotrope
sunstone

$ mco puppet count
Total Puppet nodes: 3

          Nodes currently enabled: 3
         Nodes currently disabled: 0

Nodes currently doing puppet runs: 0
          Nodes currently stopped: 3

        Nodes with daemons started: 1
     Nodes without daemons started: 2
        Daemons started but idling: 1

$ mco puppet summary
Summary statistics for 3 nodes:

              Total resources: ▄_____█_____  min: 0.0    max: 17.0
          Out Of Sync resources: _____  min: 0.0    max: 0.0
```

```
       Failed resources: _____      min: 0.0   max: 0.0
      Changed resources: _____      min: 0.0   max: 0.0
Config Retrieval time (seconds): ▊_____        min: 0.0   max: 1.8
   Total run-time (seconds): ▊_____        min: 0.0   max: 2.3
Time since last run (seconds): ▊_____▊   min: 221.0 max: 2.5k
```

You'll notice that these Puppet runs are very fast, with fairly few resources involved. Only a few resources are used for the minimum test environment for the MCollective module provided in this book. A production setup will usually have much longer run times and thousands or tens of thousands of resources involved.

Controlling the Puppet Daemon

During maintenance, you may want to disable the Puppet agent on certain nodes. When you disable the agent, you can supply a message letting others know what you are doing:

```
$ mco puppet disable --with-identity heliotrope message="Disk replacement"

 * [ ============================================> ] 1 / 1

Summary of Enabled:
   disabled = 1

Finished processing 1 / 1 hosts in 85.28 ms
$ mco puppet runonce --with-identity heliotrope

 * [ ============================================> ] 1 / 1

heliotrope                          Request Aborted
   Puppet is disabled: 'Disk replacement'
   Summary: Puppet is disabled: 'Disk replacement'

Finished processing 1 / 1 hosts in 84.22 ms
```

Re-enabling the Puppet agent on the node is just as easy as disabling it:

```
$ mco puppet enable --with-identity heliotrope

 * [ ============================================> ] 1 / 1

Summary of Enabled:
   enabled = 1

Finished processing 1 / 1 hosts in 84.36 ms
```

Use these same commands to enable or disable the Puppet agent on nodes matching any filter criteria, as discussed in "Filters" on page 38.

Invoking Ad Hoc Puppet Runs

The MCollective Puppet agent provides a powerful tool for controlling Puppet runs. If you examine `help` for the Puppet client, you'll find many familiar options for controlling Puppet runs, exactly as you would from the command line with `puppet agent` or `puppet apply`:

```
$ mco help puppet

Application Options
    --force                      Bypass splay options when running
    --server SERVER              Connect to a specific server or port
    --tags, --tag TAG            Restrict the run to specific tags
    --noop                       Do a noop run
    --no-noop                    Do a run with noop disabled
    --environment ENVIRONMENT Place the node in a specific environment for this run
    --splay                      Splay the run by up to splaylimit seconds
    --no-splay                   Do a run with splay disabled
    --splaylimit SECONDS         Maximum splay time for this run if splay is set
    --ignoreschedules            Disable schedule processing
    --rerun SECONDS              When performing runall do so repeatedly
                                      with a minimum run time of SECONDS
```

The simplest invocation is naturally to run Puppet immediately on one system:

```
$ mco puppet runonce --with-identity heliotrope

 * [ ============================================================> ] 1 / 1

Finished processing 1 / 1 hosts in 193.99 ms

$ mco puppet status --with-identity heliotrope

 * [ ============================================================> ] 1 / 1

    heliotrope: Currently idling; last completed run 02 seconds ago

Summary of Applying:
   false = 1

Summary of Daemon Running:
   running = 1

Summary of Enabled:
   enabled = 1

Summary of Idling:
   true = 1

Summary of Status:
   idling = 1
```

```
Finished processing 1 / 1 hosts in 86.43 ms
```

What if you needed to run Puppet instantly on every CentOS host to fix the *sudoers* file? Notice in the output here that one of these hosts had Puppet agent running, and the other did not. However, both ran Puppet when we asked them to:

```
$ mco puppet runonce --tags=sudo --with-fact operatingsystem=CentOS

 * [ ============================================================> ] 2 / 2

Finished processing 2 / 2 hosts in 988.26 ms

$ mco puppet status --wf operatingsystem=CentOS

 * [ ============================================================> ] 2 / 2

     geode: Currently stopped; last completed run 1 minutes 52 seconds ago
heliotrope: Currently idling; last completed run 2 minutes 21 seconds ago

Summary of Applying:
   false = 2

Summary of Daemon Running:
   stopped = 1
   running = 1

Summary of Enabled:
   enabled = 2

Summary of Idling:
    true = 1
   false = 1

Summary of Status:
   stopped = 1
    idling = 1

Finished processing 2 / 2 hosts in 42.17 ms
```

 At this time, it is only possible to pass options like `tags` and `noop` if the Puppet daemon is not active on the host. In order to run Puppet with custom command-line options, the Puppet daemon needs to be invoked from cron periodically or only run using MCollective. If you leave the service running, you can still use `runonce` or `runall`, but you cannot pass runtime options.[1]

---

1 This is being tracked in Feature Request MCO-134 (*https://tickets.puppetlabs.com/browse/MCO-134*).

How about prompting Puppet to update immediately on every host in your environment? If you are using only local manifests, you can trigger a run affecting thousands of hosts. In most server-based environments, the Puppet servers won't be able to handle every client checking in for a fresh catalog all at the same time. Likewise, you may want to limit the number of hosts evaluating their policies at the same time to prevent too many of them being out of service simultaneously.

Here is any example where we *slow roll* Puppet on all servers, processing only two at a time:

```
$ mco puppet runall 2
2014-02-10 23:14:00: Running all nodes with a concurrency of 2
2014-02-10 23:14:00: Discovering enabled Puppet nodes to manage
2014-02-10 23:14:03: Found 39 enabled nodes
2014-02-10 23:14:06: geode schedule status: Signalled the running Puppet Daemon
2014-02-10 23:14:06: sunstone schedule status: Signalled the running
                     Puppet Daemon
2014-02-10 23:14:06: 37 out of 39 hosts left to run in this iteration
2014-02-10 23:14:09: Currently 2 nodes applying the catalog; waiting for
                     less than 2
2014-02-10 23:14:17: heliotrope schedule status: Signalled the running
                     Puppet Daemon
2014-02-10 23:14:18: 36 out of 39 hosts left to run in this iteration
...etc
```

Run Puppet on all web servers, up to five at at time:

```
$ mco puppet runall 5 --with-identity /^web\d/
```

Note that runall is like batch except that instead of waiting for a sleep time, it waits for one of the Puppet daemons to complete its run before it starts another. If you didn't mind some potential overlap, you could use the batch options instead:

```
$ mco puppet --batch 10 --batch-sleep 60 --tags ntp
```

Manipulating Puppet Resource Types

The MCollective Puppet agent is so powerful that you can make arbitrary changes based on Puppet's Resource Abstraction Layer (RAL). For example, if you wanted to ensure the httpd service was stopped on a given host, you could do the following:

```
$ mco puppet resource service httpd ensure=stopped --with-identity geode

 * [ ==================================================> ] 1 / 1

geode
   Changed: true
    Result: ensure changed 'running' to 'stopped'

Summary of Changed:
   Changed = 1
```

```
Finished processing 1 / 1 hosts in 630.99 ms
```

You can obviously limit this in all the ways specified in "Filters" on page 38. For example, you probably only want to do this on hosts where Apache is not being managed by Puppet:

```
$ mco puppet resource service httpd ensure=stopped --wc !apache
```

You could also fix the root alias on hosts:

```
$ mco puppet resource mailalias root recipient=me@example.net
```

This Way Lies Danger

This section documents some extremely powerful controls. Enabling the Puppet RAL allows direct, instantaneous, and arbitrary access to any resource type Puppet knows how to affect. Read carefully through the next section for how to protect yourself.

Restricting Which Resources Can Be Controlled

By default, no resources can be controlled from MCollective. The feature is enabled in the MCollective agent, but it has an empty whitelist. Consider this feature a really powerful shotgun. The whitelist protects you and everyone who depends upon that foot you are aiming at. *Be careful.*

These are the default configuration options:

```
plugin.puppet.resource_allow_managed_resources = true
plugin.puppet.resource_type_whitelist = none
```

If you want to allow resource control, you would need to edit the *mcollective/server.cfg* file with either a whitelist (Example 8-1) or a blacklist (Example 8-2) of resources that can be controlled.

Example 8-1. Whitelist allows only specified resources

```
plugin.puppet.resource_type_whitelist = package,service
```

Example 8-2. Blacklist allows everything except specified resources

```
plugin.puppet.resource_type_blacklist = exec
```

MCollective does not allow you to mix white and black lists.

Block MCollective from Puppet Resources

By default, no resource defined in the Puppet catalog can be controlled from MCollective, so as to prevent mcollective from making a change against the Puppet policy. Sending alternative options for a resource in the Puppet catalog is most likely to simply be overwritten the next time Puppet runs without the same options. In a worst case, well... sorry about the foot.

To allow MCollective to alter resources under Puppet's control, enable the following setting:

```
plugin.puppet.resource_allow_managed_resources = true
```

## CHAPTER 9

Waking the Chef

In Chapter 7, we showed how to use Chef to install and configure MCollective. In this chapter, we're going to show how MCollective can:

- Use the Chef recipes and roles applied to the node in filters
- Use Ohai data as facts for MCollective filters
- Query, start, stop, and restart the Chef client
- Wake the Chef client to evaluate the node immediately

To control the Chef daemon, you'll need to upload the chef-client cookbook and its dependencies. I did it like this:

```
~$ cd chef_repo/cookbooks
cookbooks$ knife cookbook site download chef-client
Downloading chef-client from the cookbooks site at version 3.6.0
  to /home/jorhett/chef-repo/cookbooks/chef-client-3.6.0.tar.gz
Cookbook saved: /home/jorhett/chef-repo/cookbooks/chef-client-3.6.0.tar.gz
cookbooks$ knife cookbook site download cron
Downloading cron from the cookbooks site at version 1.4.0
  to /home/jorhett/chef-repo/cookbooks/cron-1.4.0.tar.gz
Cookbook saved: /home/jorhett/chef-repo/cookbooks/cron-1.4.0.tar.gz
cookbooks$ knife cookbook site download logrotate
Downloading logrotate from the cookbooks site at version 1.6.0
  to /home/jorhett/chef-repo/cookbooks/logrotate-1.6.0.tar.gz
Cookbook saved: /home/jorhett/chef-repo/cookbooks/logrotate-1.6.0.tar.gz
cookbooks$ tar xzf chef-client-3.6.0.tar.gz
cookbooks$ tar xzf cron-1.4.0.tar.gz
cookbooks$ tar xzf logrotate-1.6.0.tar.gz
cookbooks$ knife cookbook upload chef-client cron logrotate
Uploading chef-client    [3.6.0]
Uploading cron           [1.4.0]
```

```
Uploading logrotate      [1.6.0]
Uploaded 3 cookbooks.
```

Then you need to add the chef-client recipe to the node's run_list:

```
~$ knife node edit sunstone.example.net
{
  "run_list": [
    "recipe[chef-client]",
    "recipe[mcollective::client]",
    "recipe[mcollective::server]"
  ]
}
```

Install the Chef Agent

The MCollective agent for Chef and a Chef handler to provide Chef information to
MCollective are both installed by default. You can disable the MCollective agent or
Chef handler by setting either of the following attributes to false:

Chef attributes	Value
node['mcollective'][install_chef_handler?]	true (default) or false
node['mcollective'][install_chef_agent?]	true (default) or false

The MCollective agent for Chef must be installed on both client and server nodes in
order for requests to "Wake the Chef" to work.

Checking Chef Status

Once you have installed the MCollective Chef agent and restarted mcollectived
(which the Chef cookbook does automatically), you will be able to query and "Wake
the Chef" client. The first thing you should do is confirm which systems have Chef
installed:

```
$ mco filemgr --file /etc/chef/client.rb status
geode
heliotrope
sunstone
```

Now we should confirm that all Chef nodes respond to requests for the MCollective
Chef agent:

```
$ mco find --with-agent chef
geode
heliotrope
sunstone
```

Now we shall use the client application to send requests to the Chef agent:

```
$ mco chef status
Discovering hosts using the mc method for 2 second(s) .... 3
 * [ ================================================> ] 3 / 3

Summary of Status:

          OK = 2
     Stopped = 1
     Missing = 0

Finished processing 3 / 3 hosts in 45.15 ms
```

Invoking Ad Hoc Chef Client Runs

The following two commands will do exactly as you expect:

```
$ mco chef stop -I hostname
$ mco chef start -I hostname
```

 Chef client does not have the concept of enable or disable provided by the Puppet agent.

In Chef parlance, you don't tell the agent to runonce but instead to wake:

```
$ mco chef wake -I hostname
```

This command will wake the Chef client to initiate a run immediately. The output of this request includes only the nodes on which the Chef client failed to respond.

## PART II

Complex Installations

Now that you have a working MCollective environment, we're going to slow the pace down a bit and go on a nuts-and-bolts tour inside MCollective's ecosystem.

We'll review the architecture, backbone, transport, and security components involved in making MCollective transactions seamless. You'll go through each tunable parameter, why we recommend the values we do, and what you can achieve by changing it.

You'll learn how to create a *network of brokers* for multisite or redundancy requirements. You'll learn how to create and use *collectives* to handle thousands of MCollective agents spread around the world.

You'll learn to enable cryptography-based security plugins for MCollective that utilize various cryptographic methods to authenticate clients, from distributed salts and hashes to centrally signed and validated public/private key infrastructure. You'll write per-client and per-command granular authorization rules, and you'll use detailed audit logs to confirm the results.

After finishing this section, you'll be able to fine-tune MCollective for any environment: small but globally diverse, immense in scale but localized, from tightly secured and audited to permissive and enabling. MCollective can support all of these modes, and you'll know how to utilize all of them.

## CHAPTER 10

Middleware Configuration

In this chapter, we will go deeper into the configuration of the middleware and explain each option and parameter in more detail. If you are just learning MCollective, it is not essential that you understand everything in this chapter. If MCollective is working properly in your environment and meets your needs, you can set this chapter aside and read it later.

Here are some reasons to carefully read this chapter:

- You are having difficulty with connectivity to your middleware broker.
- You are tuning ActiveMQ to handle more hosts.
- You wish to implement a network of brokers at remote sites.
- You are looking for master/slave redundancy.

For any change to the middleware, most especially for changes intended to handle growth issues, it will be essential for you to understand the middleware configuration in detail. That is what this chapter will provide for you.

Messaging Brokers

MCollective uses publish/subscribe middleware to provide a messaging service between clients, servers, and listeners. By design, MCollective uses connector plugins to communicate with the middleware broker, thus allowing flexibility in the choice of middleware and the type of communication. As of this writing, the core installation contains the following middleware plugins (note, however, that it is possible to create your own middleware connector based on a different technology):

- ActiveMQ 5.8 or higher (preferred) (*http://activemq.apache.org/*)

- RabbitMQ 2.8 or higher (*http://www.rabbitmq.com/*)

Each of these middleware technologies is widely used and actively supported by developer communities. Each of these is suitable for small deployments, large clusters, and wide-scale hierarchical deployments. They are both used in thousands of environments every day.

Apache Apollo is a next-generation messaging server intended to replace ActiveMQ. It works with MCollective using the ActiveMQ connector. It does not yet support clustering at the time this book was written.

By leveraging popular and actively maintained open source message brokers, MCollective is freed from having to create and support a proprietary communications infrastructure.

Let's review in depth the middleware configuration file *activemq.xml* from "Configuring ActiveMQ" on page 17.

Network Security

These are some of the security considerations you should take into account when configuring your middleware broker.

Transport Connectors

You should disable any transport connector that you are not using. For example, if you have enabled TLS encryption for ActiveMQ middleware, you should comment out the unencrypted connector:

```
<transportConnectors>
  <!-- # disable the unencrypted connector as we are using TLS
  <transportConnector name="stomp+nio" uri="stomp+nio://0.0.0.0:61613"/>
  -->
  <!-- this would be IPv4 only
  <transportConnector name="stomp+ssl" uri="stomp+ssl://0.0.0.0:61614"/>
  -->
  <!-- this accepts IPv4 and IPv6 both -->
  <transportConnector name="stomp+ssl" uri="stomp+ssl://[::0]:61614"/>
</transportConnectors>
```

If you have multiple IP addresses on the host, you may replace 0.0.0.0 or ::0 with the specific IP you'd like ActiveMQ to answer on. Remember that every server and client must be able to reach this address. Repeat if necessary for each IP separately:

```
<transportConnector name="stomp+nio" uri="stomp+nio://192.168.2.5:61613"/>
<transportConnector name="stomp+nio"
 uri="stomp+nio://[2001:DB8:6A:C0::200:5]:61613"/>
```

Firewall Configurations

MCollective depends on the ability of both servers and clients to initiate inbound sessions to the appropriate TCP port on the middleware broker. The following table lists which ports are used for which middleware brokers and/or their administrative interfaces:

Middleware	Usage	TCP Port	Action
ActiveMQ	RMI Port	1098	Limit to management hosts
ActiveMQ	JMX Console	1099	Limit to management hosts
ActiveMQ	Web Console and Jolokia	8161	Limit to management hosts
ActiveMQ	STOMP unencrypted	61613	Allow
ActiveMQ	STOMP+SSL	61614	Allow
ActiveMQ	OpenWire unencrypted	61616	Limit to brokers
ActiveMQ	OpenWire+SSL	61617	Limit to brokers
RabbitMQ	STOMP unencrypted	61613	Allow
RabbitMQ	STOMP+SSL	61614	Allow

Most Linux systems use `iptables` firewalls. On a Linux system, you could use the following steps to add a rule before the global deny. If all of your servers will fit within a few subnets, it is advisable to limit this rule to only allow those subnets to connect:

```
$ sudo iptables --list --line-numbers
Chain INPUT (policy ACCEPT)
num  target     prot opt  source      destination
1    ACCEPT     all  --   anywhere    anywhere        state RELATED,ESTABLISHED
2    ACCEPT     icmp --   anywhere    anywhere
... Look through the output and find an appropriate line number for this rule
$ sudo ip6tables --list --line-numbers
Chain INPUT (policy ACCEPT)
num  target     prot opt  source      destination
1    ACCEPT     all       anywhere    anywhere        state RELATED,ESTABLISHED
2    ACCEPT     ipv6-icmp anywhere    anywhere
...etc
```

Look through the output and find an appropriate line number for the new rule. Then use the following syntax to insert the rule into this location in the list:

```
$ sudo iptables -I INPUT 20 -m state --state NEW -p tcp \\
    --source 192.168.200.0/24 --dport 61613 -j ACCEPT

$ sudo ip6tables -I INPUT 20 -m state --state NEW -p tcp \\
    --source 2001:DB8:6A:C0::/24 --dport 61613 -j ACCEPT
```

Don't forget to save that rule to your initial rules file. For RedHat-derived systems, this can be as easy as the following:

```
$ sudo service iptables save
iptables: Saving firewall rules to /etc/sysconfig/iptables:[  OK  ]
$ sudo service ip6tables save
ip6tables: Saving firewall rules to /etc/sysconfig/ip6table:[  OK  ]
```

Check Appendix A for platform-specific instructions for other operating systems.

IPv6 Dual-Stack Environments

If you have both IPv4 and IPv6 deployed on your network, you may find that some hosts are using IPv4 and others are using IPv6. You'll also notice that all of these hosts can communicate with each other just fine. As long as the host can connect to the middleware broker, it really doesn't matter which protocol they used to get there.

However, there are situations where you may need to control which protocol is used —for example, if you want to ensure IPv6 is used in all places. Or perhaps you have a remote site where the provider doesn't provide IPv6 transit yet. How does one control which protocol is used?

The answer is that this choice is determined by your operating system. If a remote host has both IPv4 and IPv6 addresses, then the operating system will decide which one to attempt to connect to first. If the first protocol fails, MCollective will attempt a fallback query on the other address.

At the time I tested, every OS I checked will go first to the IPv6 address and then fall back to the IPv4 address if the first attempt fails. As MCollective server connections are very long lived, a short delay for initial connection will not matter.

There are no parameters in MCollective to define the protocol used for the connection.

Is there nothing you can define in the configuration to influence the protocol used for the middleware connection? Nope, not by the connection parameters. The only way to control the protocol used is to use an IP address appropriate for that protocol.

If a remote host has both IPv4 and IPv6 addresses, then the operating system will decide which one to attempt to connect to first.

To ensure that a client uses a certain protocol to connect to your middleware broker, set the broker's name in the configuration file to a name that resolves to one type of address. For example:

```
$ host activemq.example.net
activemq.example.net has address 192.168.200.5
activemq.example.net has IPv6 address 2001:DB8:6A:C0::200:5
$ host activemq-v6.example.net
activemq-v6.example.net has IPv6 address 2001:DB8:6A:C0::200:5
$ host activemq-v4.example.net
activemq-v4.example.net has address 192.168.200.5
```

For hosts that I want to connect only over IPv6, I could use this Hiera config:

```
mcollective::hosts:
  - 'activemq-v6.example.net'
```

Or here is an IPv4-only connection:

```
mcollective::hosts:
  - 'activemq-v4.example.net'
```

And believe it or not, the following will cause the server to connect over *both* protocols:

```
mcollective::hosts:
  - 'activemq-v6.example.net'
  - 'activemq-v4.example.net'
```

ActiveMQ Config Structure

The ActiveMQ configuration file is quite long, and it can be easy to lose your place within the file. So before we start, let's review the structure of the file:

- There is a single broker element that handles all MCollective configuration.
- Flow control and garbage collection are defined by `policyEntry` elements.
- Users are defined in `authenticationUser` elements.
- Access rules are defined in `authorizationEntry` elements.
- System resource limits are defined in `systemUsage` elements.
- Network connectors for clients are defined in `transportConnector` elements.
- Network connectors for other brokers are defined in `networkConnector` elements.
- The SSL `keyStore` and `trustStore` are defined in the `sslContext` element.

You can find example *activemq.xml* configuration files for ActiveMQ 5.8 and 5.9 at *https://github.com/jorhett/learning-mcollective/tree/master/examples/*. These examples match the book contents and the output created by the ActiveMQ template in the Puppet module.

Detailed Configuration Review

The following definitions were missing from the *activemq.xml* configuration skeleton in the previous section. We'll go through each one and document which values should be set, and which values you may want to change.

Broker Definition

The `broker` element defines the ActiveMQ Java application that all servers and clients communicate with. This is the container that encloses all other elements we will be discussing:

```
<broker xmlns="http://activemq.apache.org/schema/core" useJmx="true"
    brokerName="hostname"
    dataDirectory="leave this untouched"
    networkConnectorStartAsync="true"
    schedulePeriodForDestinationPurge="60000"
>
```

`brokerName` can be any name and for a single instance the value *localhost* is just fine. In a network of brokers, each broker will need to have a unique name. We'll cover this in "ActiveMQ Clusters" on page 113.

`networkConnectorStartAsync` tells ActiveMQ to bring up all network connectors in parallel. This parameter only matters if you have a network of brokers, but it's a good default to have.

`schedulePeriodForDestinationPurge` of 60,000 milliseconds tells ActiveMQ to scan for stale queues every minute. This works on queues that have the `policyEntry gcI nactiveDestinations` enabled. These queues will be garbage collected when idle and empty. Documentation of this feature can be found at *http://activemq.apache.org/delete-inactive-destinations.html*.

Topic and Queue Tuning

MCollective works best if producer flow control (*http://activemq.apache.org/producer-flow-control.html*) is disabled. Producer flow control slows down producers when the memory or disk capacity has been exceeded. This usually only occurs when you have many applications delivering large volumes of data to a slow processor that works through a queue on its own timeline.

MCollective requests are small, fast, and transient. The timeout for most queries is 10 seconds. Neither agents nor clients generally submit large amounts of data, and the client expects to receive replies as quickly as possible. It is best to allow MCollective clients and servers to submit without the overhead of flow control:

```
<policyEntries>
  <!-- MCollective works best with producer flow control disabled. -->
  <policyEntry topic=">"
    producerFlowControl="false" memorylimit="1mb"
  >
    <pendingSubscriberPolicy>
      <vmCursor/>
    </pendingSubscriberPolicy>
  </policyEntry>
```

The > character is a wildcard that will match any character. Because it is the first character used, all topics and all queues will match these rules.

The vmCursor value for pending subscriber messages instructs MCollective to keep all topic contents in memory for fast and efficient delivery. This is documented at *http://activemq.apache.org/message-cursors.html*.

In the following configuration, we garbage collect idle queues after five minutes of inactivity (if no new requests enter a queue in five minutes, we clean up the queue and recover the memory):

```
<!-- MCollective generates a reply queue for most commands.
     Garbage-collect these after five minutes to conserve memory. -->
<policyEntry queue=">"
  producerFlowControl="false" memorylimit="1mb"
  gcInactiveDestinations="true"
  inactiveTimeoutBeforeGC="300000"
>
  <pendingQueuePolicy>
    <vmQueueCursor/>
  </pendingQueuePolicy>
</policyEntry>
</policyEntries>
```

Each request creates a new reply queue to collect responses. After the request timeout (the default is 10 seconds), the client stops listening to the reply queue. Without garbage collection, the number of reply queues would grow until ActiveMQ ran out of memory. These rules clean up the abandoned reply queues.

The policyEntry for queues has two extra parameters:

- gcInactiveDestinations instructs the broker to run garbage collection on queues that match the policy (all queues with this example).

- inactiveTimeoutBeforeGC indicates that queues should be removed when they have been idle for five minutes.

If you have many reply queues and they are collected quickly, you could try adjusting inactiveTimeoutBeforeGC back down to its default of one minute (60000).

As with topics, the vmQueueCursor value for pending queue messages instructs MCollective to keep all queue entries in memory for fast and efficient delivery. This is documented at *http://activemq.apache.org/message-cursors.html*.

Authentication and Authorization

The critical parts for middleware authentication are the nodes queue and the agent topics. These deliver messages to the servers that should act on the requests.

To consider the marionette metaphor, these are your strings. Messages to a node's queue will be delivered to exactly one node. Messages published to an agent topic will be received and processed by every mcollectived daemon that has the named agent installed.

Users and groups

This section defines the users and assigns them to groups:

```
<users>
  <authenticationUser username="broker"
    password="Broker Password"
    groups="brokers,everyone"
  />
  <authenticationUser username="client"
    password="Client Password"
    groups="servers,clients,everyone"
  />
  <authenticationUser username="server"
      password="Server Password"
    groups="servers,everyone"
  />
</users>
```

All of the authorization rules defined in the authorizationPlugin section use groups, not usernames. You can create additional usernames and passwords if you like, but remember that these don't control which commands can be run on a server —this only controls who can send requests to each topic or queue. In general, it is best to leave the middleware authentication to these three groups and implement fine-grained control using the authorization rules documented in "Authorization" on page 163.

> You might have noticed that our initial configuration had only two users. We have included a broker user we will introduce later in "ActiveMQ Clusters" on page 113.

Topics and queues the clients send to

The first thing you'll notice is that we define a brokers group and give it the ability to write to every queue and topic (this is used only by brokers to relay data in a cluster configuration; we'll cover this in "ActiveMQ Clusters" on page 113):

```
<authorizationEntry queue=">" write="brokers" read="brokers" admin="brokers" />
<authorizationEntry topic=">" write="brokers" read="brokers" admin="brokers" />
```

Next, we give global read and write on the MCollective topics and queues to clients. The > character in this case is equivalent to a trailing wildcard, allowing access to all topics or queues underneath MCollective:

```
<authorizationEntry topic="mcollective.>"
  write="clients" read="clients" admin="clients"
/>
<authorizationEntry queue="mcollective.>"
  write="clients" read="clients" admin="clients"
/>
```

The admin permission allows the client to create the topic or queue if it doesn't exist already.

 In this example, our collective is named mcollective, which is the default. In Chapter 12, we will discuss using multiple collectives. At that time, you'll need to duplicate the last two lines with each collective's name.

Topics and queues the servers read from

Here we allow the server nodes to read from or create the MCollective agent topics:

```
<authorizationEntry topic="mcollective.*.agent" read="servers" admin="servers" />
```

The agent topics are where the clients place requests intended for multiple nodes that have a given agent. For example, a mco puppet runonce command would be sent out on the mcollective.puppet.agent topic:

```
<authorizationEntry queue="mcollective.nodes" read="servers" admin="servers" />
```

Here we allow the server nodes to read from or create the MCollective node queue. This is where the clients place commands intended for a single MCollective server.

The topics and queues don't use an explicit write permission because the wildcard client rules above them allow clients to write to any of these queues. The servers should not write to these queues.

Topics and queues the servers write to

Next, we allow the server nodes to create or submit data to one of the agent topics—the *registration* agent (this information is submitted during the server connection and periodically thereafter; we'll discuss registration in more depth in Chapter 21):

```
<authorizationEntry topic="mcollective.registration.agent"
  write="servers" read="servers" admin="servers"
/>
```

Then we authorize servers to submit their replies to the queues created to collect them:

```
<authorizationEntry queue="mcollective.reply.>"
  write="servers" admin="clients"
/>
```

For example, if you send a command to the `filemgr` agent and the unique number *170075* was assigned to the request, a reply queue named *filemgr_170075* would be created. Each server that matches the filter (servers 3–4 in Figure 10-1) would send a response on the queue `mcollective.reply.filemgr_170075`. The client would read each reply from the queue, as Figure 10-1 shows.

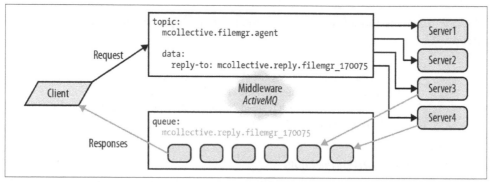

Figure 10-1. Publish to a topic, receive responses on a unique queue

 The writeable queues used by the servers to communicate information can be read by the clients or by specially designed listeners. We'll discuss how listeners collect feedback from the agents in Chapter 22.

Transport Connectors

A `transportConnector` element defines a mechanism for servers and clients to connect with the middleware broker over an IP network.

All MCollective messages are formatted as Streaming Text Oriented Messaging Protocol (STOMP) packets. The following configuration creates a `STOMP` protocol connector utilizing ActiveMQ's New I/O (NIO) library:

```
<transportConnectors>
  <transportConnector name="stomp+nio" uri="stomp+nio://[::0]:61613" />
</transportConnectors>
```

The NIO interface has significantly better performance. The `stomp` connector without NIO is only suitable for a small number of connections.

You could make the IP address specific to just one interface, and you could change the TCP port used if you wanted to. In the following examples, we show specific IPv4 and IPv6 addresses with TCP port 6163:

```
<transportConnector name="stomp+nio" uri="stomp+nio://192.168.200.5:6163" />

<transportConnector name="stomp+nio"
  uri="stomp+nio://[2001:DB8:6A:C0::200:5]:6163" />
```

In "ActiveMQ Clusters" on page 113, you will learn how to use `networkConnector` elements to link to other ActiveMQ brokers.

Chapter 11 will document how to enable TLS encryption to protect the traffic between MCollective nodes and the middleware broker.

Management Interfaces

It is not common to require a management console for ActiveMQ when using it only with MCollective. The needs of MCollective applications are usually small and instantaneous, so tuning for large data streams and long queues simply isn't necessary.

That being said, I've found the tools covered in the following sections to be useful while debugging problems with ActiveMQ implementations.

 Most of my experience with these tools was actually gained while debugging other applications. The MCollective configuration documented in this book moves responses quickly to their destinations.

Web Console

Enabling the Web Console will provide you with a web interface for examining ActiveMQ's queues and topics. This will give you a basic overview of how many messages are going through each topic and queue, to look for queues that may be filling up, and so on.

You access this console by going to your ActiveMQ box on port 8161 (*http://activemq.example.net:8161/admin*). See Figure 10-2.

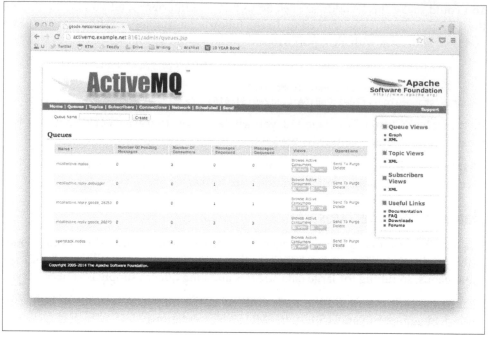

Figure 10-2. Web Console

To enable the Web Console, you simply need to add or enable the Jetty inclusion in the ActiveMQ file:

```
<!-- Allows us to use system properties as variables in this configuration file -->
<bean class="org.springframework.beans.factory.config.PropertyPlaceholderConfigurer">
  <property name="locations">
    <value>file:${activemq.conf}/credentials.properties</value>
  </property>
</bean>

<!--
  Enable web consoles, REST and Ajax APIs and demos
  See ${ACTIVEMQ_HOME}/conf/jetty.xml for more details.
-->
<import resource="jetty.xml"/>
```

If you are using the Puppet module documented in Chapter 7, then you can secure the Web Console by providing a password:

```
# declarative method
node activemq.example.net {
  class { 'mcollective::middleware':
    jetty_password => 'openssl rand -base64 20',
  }
}
```

```
# Hiera method
mcollective::middleware::jetty_password: openssl rand -base64 20
```

 Access to the Web Console is not encrypted by default. To use this safely over the open Internet, edit the *conf/jetty.xml* file and remove the comments around the `SecureConnector` element near the bottom.

You can find more information at *http://activemq.apache.org/web-console.html*.

Jolokia API and HawtIO

If you are using ActiveMQ 5.9 or later, then you can get to all of the same ActiveMQ internals using the Jolokai REST API. Enable the REST API by one of the following:

- Uncomment the inclusion of Jetty at the bottom of the ActiveMQ configuration file.
- Add a `jetty_password` to the class or Hiera parameters for the Puppet module, as described previously.

Access the API on your ActiveMQ box using *http://activemq.example.net:8161/api/jolokia,* or *https://activemq.example.net:8161/api/jolokia* if you have enabled the secure connector.

A popular Jolokia client right now is the hawtio Console (*http://hawt.io/*). This is a pure JavaScript application that you can run inside your Chrome browser, as a local Java server on your desktop, or within another Java app engine.

No matter which way you want to use it, the instructions to install hawtio (*http://hawt.io/getstarted/index.html*) are really easy to follow.

hawtio (*http://hawt.io/*) provides a clean, modern user interface to access the ActiveMQ internals (Figure 10-3).

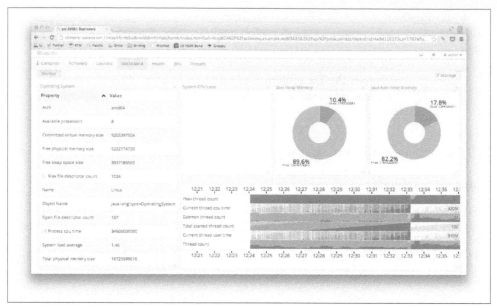

Figure 10-3. The hawtio user interface

JMX MBean Console

The JMX MBeans interface will provide you with a method to query both the JVM
and ActiveMQ statistics directly with a JMX client. To enable JMX MBeans, you need
to enable useJmx attribute on the broker element and then enable managementCon
text:

```
<broker brokerName="hostname" useJmx=true ... >

# ...farther down...
  <managementContext>
    <managementContext
        createConnector="true"
        connectorHost="localhost"
        connectorPort="1099"
        rmiServerPort="1098"
    />
  </managementContext>
```

If you are using the Puppet module documented in Chapter 7, then you can enable
JMX with a simple step:

```
# declarative method
node activemq.example.net {
  class { 'mcollective::middleware':
    use_jmx => true,
  }
}
```

```
# Hiera method
mcollective::middleware::use_jmx : true
```

There is a graphical JConsole application on every system that has Java installed. Simply go to a prompt and run `jconsole` like so (a window like that shown in Figure 10-4 will pop up):

```
$ jconsole service:jmx:rmi:///jndi/rmi://activemq.example.net:1099/jmxrmi
```

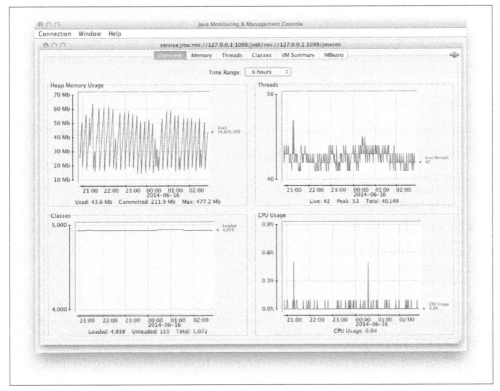

Figure 10-4. JConsole GUI

 The JMX console is unencrypted and unprotected by username and password by default. It is best to protect this behind a firewall. Ensure that both of the port numbers listed are blocked from remote access.

To use this safely over the open Internet, do both of the following:

- Edit the *activemq-wrapper.conf* or *wrapper.conf* file as appropriate for your platform to include: `-Djava.rmi.server.hostname=127.0.0.1`. This will limit the connector to only working with connections from localhost.

- Use SSH Tunneling to reach the interface without allowing plaintext connections, like so:

```
$ ssh activemq -L 1099:localhost:1099 -L 1098:localhost:1098
$ jconsole service:jmx:rmi://localhost:1098/jndi/rmi://localhost:1099/jmxrmi
```

Whether you enable remote connections or not, enabling the JMX console will allow you to use the `activemq-admin` tool on the ActiveMQ server. Leaving this enabled without a password allows you to use `activemq-admin` without crazy syntax. The following are some useful examples of this tool.

Examine the statistics for a single topic or all queues:

```
$ activemq-admin query -QTopic=mcollective.puppet.agent
$ activemq-admin query -QQueue=*
```

Look at the messages in a queue:

```
$ activemq-admin browse --amqurl tcp://localhost:61613 mcollective.reply.*
```

These display useful statistics about the brokers:

```
$ activemq-admin bstat localhost
$ activemq-admin bstat
$ activemq-admin list
```

This command doesn't work for me with ActiveMQ 5.9.1. Using `--jmxlocal` removes the error but does not display any values:

```
$ activemq-admin dstat
$ activemq-admin dstat --jmxlocal
```

This was just a quick overview of the tool. All of these commands have many additional options documented at *http://activemq.apache.org/activemq-command-line-tools-reference.html*.

To enable username and password security, refer to documentation of the JMX connector at *http://activemq.apache.org/jmx.html*.

Statistics plugin

The statistics plugin provides an API you can query for queue and topic statistics. Enable this by adding the following lines to the ActiveMQ configuration file:

```
<plugins>
    <statisticsBrokerPlugin />
...other things...
</plugins>
```

This is already enabled by default in the default ActiveMQ configuration file, the example provided in GitHub, and the templates provided by the Puppet module.

To submit a query, you will have to use an ActiveMQ publisher and listener. The publisher should send a blank message to the `ActiveMQ.Statistics.Broker` and set a `replyTo` header to indicate a queue that the listener is attached to. To get statistics for all topics and queues, send to the destination `ActiveMQ.Statistics`.

Complete details and example Java programs to perform these queries are available at *http://activemq.apache.org/statisticsplugin.html*.

You can learn more about how to do similar programming in Part III. You may find a statistics query utility at the GitHub repository for Learning MCollective (*https://github.com/jorhett/learning-mcollective*).

Conclusion

In this section, we have gone through each tuning parameter in the baseline configuration used for our initial setup.

We have shown the structure of the topics and queues used by MCollective.

We have introduced the `TransportConnector` element and explained why Java's NIO connectors are necessary.

We have introduced you to several management interfaces useful for analyzing ActiveMQ for debugging purposes.

The following sections build on this baseline, showing changes that could be made to increase security or improve reliability in larger environments.

ActiveMQ Clusters

If your collective grows near a thousand nodes, or if you have multiple sites, you may want to:

- Set up a network of brokers to convey messages between sites
- Set up master/slave synchronization to provide redundancy within a site
- Encrypt traffic between sites

You can use all of these options together or in combination. Let's go over how to configure each one.

Network of Brokers

A network of brokers configuration is useful when you want to put ActiveMQ servers in different physical locations (e.g., different data centers) and have them operate as a single consistent messaging space. Here is an example of the lines you'd need to add to both of the ActiveMQ systems to set up the linkage:

```
<plugins>
  <simpleAuthenticationPlugin>
    <users>
      <authenticationUser username="broker"
        password="Broker Password"
        groups="brokers,everyone"
      />
    </users>
  </simpleAuthenticationPlugin>
</plugins>
<transportConnectors>
  <transportConnector name="openwire" uri="tcp://0.0.0.0:61616" />
</transportConnectors>

<networkConnectors>
  <networkConnector
    name="SFO-PVG"
    duplex="true"
    uri="static:(tcp://activemq.london.example.net:61616)"
    userName="broker"
    password="Broker Password"
  />
</networkConnectors>
<transportConnectors>
  <transportConnector name="openwire" uri="tcp://0.0.0.0:61616" />
</transportConnectors>
```

Tuning options for the `networkConnector` can be found at *http://activemq.apache.org/networks-of-brokers.html*.

By putting the `broker` user in the `brokers` group, it will have the ability to write to all topics and queues on the accepting ActiveMQ server. This is necessary for replication to work.

At each location, you configure the client to connect to the nearest middleware broker. All messages will be transmitted between the two locations, thus allowing a single collective to work cleanly across sites. If you are concerned about redundancy, you can configure the client to fall over to the other sites if the local site is down:

```
plugin.activemq.pool.size = number of sites with their own broker
plugin.activemq.pool.1.host = site #1 broker hostname
plugin.activemq.pool.1.setting = settings for this site
plugin.activemq.pool.2.host = site #2 broker hostname
plugin.activemq.pool.2.setting = settings for this site
...etc
```

 The Puppet Labs site indicates that you will need two connections, one for topics and another for queues, at *http://bit.ly/UttA1X*. My tests were unable to confirm this—I used these settings successfully with clients and servers on each side.

The Puppet module provided with this book will configure a network of brokers simply by adding more brokers to the `hosts` Hiera parameter and providing a broker password:

```
mcollective::broker_password: 'openssl rand -base64 32'
mcollective::hosts:
 - site #1 broker hostname
 - site #2 broker hostname
 - site #3 broker hostname
```

All of the other parameters used for connecting to the brokers are assumed to be identical.

You may want to limit clients or servers to use only a local node. Each of the modules can be overridden at its own layer, so you can play with Hiera hierarchy to your heart's content. There are two good ways to do this. The easiest is only to inform the brokers of all nodes:

```
mcollective::hosts:
 - site local broker hostname
mcollective::middleware::hosts:
 - site #1 broker hostname
 - site #2 broker hostname
 - site #3 broker hostname
```

Or you can limit the servers to a local node and let the brokers and clients know about all nodes:

```
mcollective::server::hosts:
 - site local broker hostname
mcollective::hosts:
 - site #1 broker hostname
 - site #2 broker hostname
 - site #3 broker hostname
```

In large environments (about 2,000–3,000 nodes, depending on latency between your brokers), discovery might take longer than the default two seconds. In a production environment with 5,500 nodes, we found that 10 seconds was necessary for discovery to consistently receive responses from all nodes. You will need to modify client apps to extend the discovery timeout (discussed in Part III later) or set an environment variable to avoid having to type this with every CLI command:[1]

```
$ export MCOLLECTIVE_EXTRA_OPTS="--discovery-timeout 10 \
--timeout 5"
```

Master/Slave Redundancy

If you are looking for fast failover response at a single location, you may instead want to use a master/slave cluster setup. For that kind of setup, you want this identical configuration on both brokers:

```
<plugins>
  <simpleAuthenticationPlugin>
    <users>
      <authenticationUser
        username="broker"
        password="Broker Password"
        groups="brokers,everyone"
      />
    </users>
  </simpleAuthenticationPlugin>
</plugins>

<transportConnectors>
  <transportConnector name="openwire" uri="tcp://0.0.0.0:61616" />
</transportConnectors>

<networkConnectors>
  <networkConnector
    uri="masterslave:(tcp://amq1.example.net:61616,tcp://amq2.example.net:61616)"
    userName="broker"
    password="Broker Password"
  />
</networkConnectors>
```

Pay special attention to the `networkConnector uri` here. The first host listed should be the master, and then every hostname listed after it would be slaves. Every ActiveMQ broker should have the list in the same order.

---

1 Puppet Labs Improvement Request MCO-193 (*https://tickets.puppetlabs.com/browse/MCO-193*) requests a configuration file option for this. It may be available by the time this book is printed.

Tuning options for the `networkConnector` can be found at *http://activemq.apache.org/networks-of-brokers.html*.

To enable the servers and clients to fail over to the slave, you will need to make the following changes to both the server and client configuration files:

```
plugin.activemq.pool.size   = count of all ActiveMQ brokers
plugin.activemq.pool.1.host = master broker name
all the settings for the master broker
plugin.activemq.pool.2.host = slave broker #2
all the same settings slave broker 2
plugin.activemq.pool.3.host = slave broker #3
all the same settings slave broker 3
...repeat until done
```

The Puppet module provided with this book supports a master/slave setup with the following Hiera parameter:

```
mcollective::hosts:
  - master broker hostname
  - slave broker #2 hostname
  - slave broker #3 hostname
```

All of the other parameters used for connecting to the brokers are assumed to be identical.

Encrypted Broker Links

You should use SSL/TLS encryption for the links between sites. You should absolutely do this if you are connecting across the public Internet. To do this, you'll need to create both the `keyStore` described in "Anonymous TLS" on page 129 and the `trustStore` from "CA-Verified TLS Servers" on page 132.

Then you would adjust the ActiveMQ configuration between the sites to use the appropriate protocol:

```
<transportConnectors>
  <transportConnector
    name="openwire+ssl"
    uri="ssl://0.0.0.0:61617?needClientAuth=true"
  />
</transportConnectors>
<networkConnectors>
  <networkConnector
    name="SFO-PVG"
    duplex="true"
    uri="static:(ssl://activemq.siteb.example.net:61617)"
    userName="broker"
```

```
      password="Broker Password"
    />
  </networkConnectors>

  <sslContext>
    <sslContext
      keyStore="ssl/keystore.jks"
      keyStorePassword="somethingElseYouWillNeverShare"
      trustStore="ssl/truststore.jks"
      trustStorePassword="anotherThingYouWillNeverShare"
    >
  </sslContext>
```

If you are using the Puppet module provided with this book, you would simply set the following Hiera parameters and Puppet will do all the work for you:

```
mcollective::connector_ssl                    : true
mcollective::middleware::keystore_password    : 'openssl rand -base64 20'
mcollective::middleware::truststore_password: 'openssl rand -base64 20'
```

Conclusion

In this section, we have reviewed two different models for multibroker usage:

- Using a network of brokers to provide connectivity between diverse sites
- Using master-slave redundancy to provide resilience to hardware problems

You can blend both of these options to connect a master/slave pair of brokers to brokers at remote sites.

Large-Scale Broker Configurations

There are two very different types of large-scale broker configurations:

- Many clients using a single broker
- Brokers at many sites around the world

Obviously you can have both configurations in the same organization. We'll try to cover the individual needs of each.

I often see requests for "a high-performance ActiveMQ configuration." There are a few basic recommendations for any configuration, but the truth of the matter is that once an MCollective environment has grown, either by size or by network distance, you'll need to tune in a way specific to your network and your needs.

A Racing Analogy for Tuning

In my personal time, I race motorcycles on closed courses for fun. Let's think about tuning using motorcycle (or car) racing as an analogy.

A street motorcycle/car works on all streets without custom changes because the needs are simple. You only go about half as fast as it can go, and you don't brake to the limits every time you stop. This is like a basic middleware broker: it can easily handle a few hundred nodes without any tuning.

Once you are trying to run at top speed, maintain the highest corner speed, or brake down from the highest speed without losing control, your demands are much higher. So you have to tune your motorcycle/car to perform at that level.

You can get some basic tuning assistance from anyone, but to run with the very best, you must tune your motorcycle to the conditions at each track you go to. Everything from riding style to corner banking to air temperature will play into the tuning equations. The most successful race teams tune their race bike/car to the specific needs of that specific track on that specific day.

Small sites (street drivers) can use MCollective without any special tuning. Big sites with big demands (racers) need to tune MCollective for the special needs of their own racetrack, which will be different than every other racetrack.

This analogy only goes so far—thankfully, you won't need to retune MCollective every day. As your environment grows, you'll need to tune MCollective differently for your specific network (*track*) and for your specific usage (*riding style*). What works on a different network or to support different applications won't necessarily work for you.

In this section, we'll discuss tuning ActiveMQ for high numbers of clients or high volume traffic. There are many tunable parameters for ActiveMQ that aren't relevant to MCollective. We're going to ignore those features and focus on changes that are specific and useful for MCollective.

Understanding MCollective's Needs

The Puppet Labs documentation (*http://bit.ly/UtuwTP*) has very conservative recommendations for middleware sizing:

> Scale—we recommend a maximum of about 800 MCollective servers per ActiveMQ broker, and multiple brokers let you expand past this.

This is a safe rule. The fact of the matter is that *it depends*. I've been involved with sites that have four times that number per broker. I've also been involved with sites that max out brokers well below that number. The answer for your exact needs is something that you may spend some time figuring out and will likely change over time.

First, let's go over what does and doesn't matter for making MCollective feel faster in your network:

✗ Bigger network pipes ✓ Low-latency links

In very few environments will MCollective generate substantial network traffic on the broker, and frankly *you know who you are* because you wrote or are using an agent that transfers large data. Most requests and responses are trivial in size and generate hundreds of minimum-size packets, rather than any substantially sized packets.

MCollective is very sensitive to latency in the network links between brokers. I have found it best practice to implement all networks of brokers as a mesh rather than a star whenever possible. It allows traffic to get to its destination with a single hop, rather than traversing a central routing queue prior to delivery.

✗ Dozens of CPU cores ✓ Gigabytes of RAM

ActiveMQ does not appear to scale vertically. I have never witnessed a performance gain by moving ActiveMQ to a bigger hardware box. In my experience, OpenStack/KVM or VMware ESX virtual hosts provide identical performance to bare metal hosts with equivalent specs. In most circumstances, the ActiveMQ host can be running at very low CPU utilization while ActiveMQ queues are overloaded.

The best way to tune ActiveMQ for higher performance is to make more memory available for it. Many default installations limit the Java application to 512 MB and the ActiveMQ broker to a mere 20 MB of RAM. Because even small-end systems these days have significantly more RAM, I often quadruple or octuple (eight times) this limiter. Java will only use what it needs. I have not witnessed any significant memory leakage in ActiveMQ 5.8 or 5.9.

✗ Less collectives with more machines ✓ Localized collectives avoid transit

A query sent to a collective with 5,000 nodes on it will cause the request to be broadcast to all 5,000 hosts during discovery. Each host must read the filter and decide whether to respond. If you split up your collectives and send most messages to a local subcollective, it will reduce cross-site network traffic significantly. We'll show you how to do this in Chapter 12.

Recommendations for Baseline Tuning

So what does this all mean? Here are the common changes that every site should implement for high-performance middleware:

- Set `org.apache.activemq.UseDedicatedTaskRunner` to `false` in the wrapper configuration file, or use `-Dorg.apache.activemq.UseDedicatedTaskRunner =false` in the command-line arguments.

- Tune *Java Max Memory* to use most of the available memory in the system. A dedicated broker isn't doing much else with that memory, is it? This is `wrapper.java.maxmemory` in *activemq-wrapper.conf* for many platforms, or adjust `-Xmx512m` on the command line.

- Ensure that producer flow control is disabled as discussed in "Detailed Configuration Review" on page 101. If you are seeing queue messages being lost, adjust `systemUsage/systemUsage/memoryUsage` to use 70% of the size of Java Max Memory. For any broker supporting a thousand clients or large reply queues, this should be several gigabytes.

- If you have many distinct networks or widely dispersed sites, create subcollectives for each location or region, as discussed in "Localizing Traffic" on page 145. You can still initiate requests to the entire collective when necessary, but it shouldn't be your default.

Supporting Thousands of Servers

To handle anything near a thousand connections to an ActiveMQ broker, you'll need to tune the TCP stack of the node. I've included some recommendations that I and others have found useful. You may need to find the correct tuneables for non-Linux systems:

```
# More file descriptors == more open TCP connections
ulimit -Hn 8192
ulimit -Sn 8192

# Close and reuse finished TCP sessions faster
/sbin/sysctl -w net.ipv4.tcp_fin_timeout=15
/sbin/sysctl -w net.ipv4.tcp_tw_reuse=1

# Identify failed TCP links faster
/sbin/sysctl -w net.ipv4.tcp_keepalive_time=300
/sbin/sysctl -w net.ipv4.tcp_keepalive_intvl=30
/sbin/sysctl -w net.ipv4.tcp_keepalive_probes=5

# Allow connection backlog of 2000 connections
# Required as STOMP clients reconnect quickly
/sbin/sysctl -w net.core.somaxconn=2000
```

```
/sbin/sysctl -w net.core.netdev_max_backlog=2000

# Increase size of TCP read and write buffers
/sbin/sysctl -w net.core.rmem_default=256960
/sbin/sysctl -w net.core.rmem_max=5242880
/sbin/sysctl -w net.core.wmem_default=256960
/sbin/sysctl -w net.core.wmem_max=5242880

# Disable timestamps
/sbin/sysctl -w net.ipv4.tcp_timestamps=0
```

You would make these changes permanent by storing them in the appropriate files for your platform. On Linux, the ulimit changes should be stored in */etc/security/limits.conf*, and the sysctl changes would be stored in */etc/sysctl.conf*.

Another important thing to change is the discovery timeout. In environments larger than 2,000–3,000 nodes (depending on latency between your brokers), discovery might take longer than the default two seconds. In a production environment with 5,500 nodes, we found that 10 seconds was necessary for discovery to get answers from all nodes consistently.

You will need to modify client apps to extend the discovery timeout (discussed in Part III later) or set an environment variable to avoid having to type this with every CLI command:[2]

```
$ export MCOLLECTIVE_EXTRA_OPTS="--discovery-timeout 10 --timeout 5"
```

As you can see, we did not need to extend the timeout for requests to the same length when all nodes were local to the client. Discovery needed to have twice the timeout as the requests themselves.

Reaching Globally Diverse Servers

The first thing you should consider with globally diverse brokers, especially if the links are high-latency transcontinental links, is to localize as much traffic as possible using distinct *collectives* in each region. If you split up the nodes into local collectives and send most messages to the local collective, it will reduce cross-site network traffic significantly. We'll show you how to do this in Chapter 12.

The second improvement is to set up your broker links in a star configuration if possible, or a modified star configuration if necessary. You want to minimize the *hops* (i.e., the number of brokers that have to process a request) between the client and server. This will improve the latency of the reply and avoid running into timeouts.

---

2 Puppet Labs Improvement Request MCO-193 (*https://tickets.puppetlabs.com/browse/MCO-193*) requests a configuration file option for this. It may be available by the time this book is printed.

Timeouts in large networks are not always avoidable. Multicontinental networks create unavoidable high latency between your brokers. You will need to tune your requests to work around this:

- One tunable is the discovery timeout. In a production environment with seven global sites, we found that five seconds was necessary for discovery to get answers from all nodes.

- The other tunable is the request timeout. In the same environment, we found that the minimum suitable request timeout was the same number.

For command-line applications, you can set environment variables:[3]

```
$ export MCOLLECTIVE_EXTRA_OPTS="--discovery-timeout 5 --timeout 5"
```

For custom client applications, you can tune the timeouts within the application, as documented in Part III.

Upgrading to ActiveMQ 5.9.1

At the time this book went to print, Puppet Labs was providing ActiveMQ 5.8 in its repository. While working with several clients, I found ActiveMQ 5.9 to work significantly better when handling large numbers of SSL/TLS clients.

Originally, ActiveMQ was designed for a small number of connected nodes. As usage of ActiveMQ grew, it was clear that the basic connector couldn't handle large numbers of clients. A new connector was created based on the Java Non-blocking I/O (*http://en.wikipedia.org/wiki/New_I/O*) (NIO) library. This connector was available for non-SSL connections in ActiveMQ 5.8 but did not handle SSL connections well.

In my experience, the standard stomp+ssl connector will start to fail somewhere just over 500 active connections. More TCP connections will be accepted, but the STOMP negotiation will be unsuccessful.

ActiveMQ 5.9 provides a stomp+nio+ssl connector that can handle large numbers of SSL clients. I have created an ActiveMQ 5.9.1 RPM for RedHat/CentOS based on the configuration supplied by Puppet Labs with 5.8 and have made it available at *http://bit.ly/UtwWBU*. I provided this to Puppet Labs in Improvement CPR-32 (*https://tickets.puppetlabs.com/browse/CPR-32*), so it might be available in the repository already. If not, you can download it from my website for evaluation.

Start by making a backup copy of *activemq.xml*, as your configuration will revert to the stock Puppet Labs config after installing this RPM:

---

3 Puppet Labs Improvement Request MCO-193 (*https://tickets.puppetlabs.com/browse/MCO-193*) requests a configuration file option for this.

```
$ sudo cp /etc/activemq/activemq.xml /etc/activemq/activemq.xml_5.8
$ wget -q http://www.netconsonance.com/downloads/activemq-5.9.1-2.el6.noarch.rpm
$ sudo service mcollective stop
Shutting down mcollective:                                    [  OK  ]
$ sudo service activemq stop
Stopping ActiveMQ Broker...
Stopped ActiveMQ Broker.
$ sudo yum install activemq-5.9.1-2.el6.noarch.rpm
Loaded plugins: fastestmirror, security
Loading mirror speeds from cached hostfile
Setting up Install Process
Examining activemq-5.9.1-2.el6.noarch.rpm: activemq-5.9.1-2.el6.noarch
Marking activemq-5.9.1-2.el6.noarch.rpm to be installed
Resolving Dependencies
--> Running transaction check
---> Package activemq.noarch 0:5.9.1-2.el6 will be installed
--> Finished Dependency Resolution

Dependencies Resolved

================================================================================
 Package        Arch         Version        Repository                    Size
================================================================================
Installing:
 activemq       noarch       5.9.1-2.el6    /activemq-5.9.1-2.el6.noarch  41 M

Transaction Summary
================================================================================
Install       1 Package(s)

Total size: 41 M
Installed size: 41 M
Is this ok [y/N]: y
Downloading Packages:
Running rpm_check_debug
Running Transaction Test
Transaction Test Succeeded
Running Transaction
  Updating   : activemq-5.9.1-2.el6.noarch                       1/2
  Cleanup    : activemq-5.8.0-3.el6.noarch                       2/2
  Verifying  : activemq-5.9.1-2.el6.noarch                       1/2
  Verifying  : activemq-5.8.0-3.el6.noarch                       2/2

Installed:
  activemq.noarch 0:5.9.1-2.el6

Complete!
$ sudo service activemq start
Starting ActiveMQ Broker...
$ sudo service mcollective start
Starting mcollective:                                         [  OK  ]
```

To use this version with the Puppet module, you need to inform the module that you want the configuration changes specific to version 5.9. This is accomplished with the following Hiera change:

```
# hieradata/common.yaml
mcollective::middleware::confversion: '5.9'
```

Then run the Puppet agent on your middleware systems like so:

```
$ mco puppet runonce --with-class mcollective::middleware

 * [ ==================================================> ] 1 / 1

Finished processing 1 / 1 hosts in 283.63 ms
```

If you aren't using Puppet to manage the middleware configuration, then start by making a backup copy of */etc/activemq/activemq.xml*, as your configuration will revert to the stock Puppet Labs config. You'll need to reapply by hand many of the changes discussed in "Detailed Configuration Review" on page 101.

Checking for Known Problems

At the time this book was written, several problems exist that you should be aware of. I hope these issues are fixed and obsolete by the time this book reaches your hands, so I've given you the bug numbers and links to check them out:

The ActiveMQ connector does not close TCP sessions when it fails to complete an SSL connection

> An incorrectly configured server will create hundreds of open TCP sessions on the ActiveMQ broker (Bug MCO-196 (*https://tickets.puppetlabs.com/browse/MCO-196*)). You can see this with the following command on your broker:[4]
>
> ```
> netstat -an |grep 6161 |awk '{print $5}' |cut -d: -f1 |sort |uniq -c |sort -n
> ```

ActiveMQ 5.8.0 has only a half-second tolerance for heartbeat failures

> ActiveMQ 5.8 will drop a connection that is more than half a second late. We've found this to be especially problematic with SSL/TLS connections. ActiveMQ 5.9 provides a new transport option (`transport.hbGracePeriodMultiplier` (*https://activemq.apache.org/stomp.html*)), which can be used to make the heartbeat validation less strict. If you are having issues with this, consider upgrading to ActiveMQ 5.9.1 (as documented earlier) and setting this value to *1.5*.

---

4 This shows as *resolved* on the Puppet Labs ticketing system, but I haven't had a chance to test this yet with a sufficiently large site. Please contact me if you can confirm whether this is solved or not.

No more than 500 SSL/TLS connections per broker

Some time after the 500th client has connected to an ActiveMQ 5.8 broker with SSL/TLS, you will start seeing clients that fail to negotiate a session. I have been unable to determine the limitation, but it has not been a lack of CPU or memory on the ActiveMQ broker. It simply ceases to finish the SSL/TLS negotiation after reaching that limit. The ActiveMQ developers indicate that only the NIO transport connectors are designed to handle large numbers of clients.

Update to ActiveMQ 5.9.1, where you can use STOMP+NIO+SSL (*https:// activemq.apache.org/configuring-transports.html*) as your transport. If you are using the Puppet module provided in this book, it will automatically adjust your ActiveMQ configuration to use this connector when `confversion` is set to *5.9*. No client or server configuration changes are necessary.

Conclusion

Tuning ActiveMQ brokers or clusters for scale requires changes at multiple levels. In this chapter, we discussed the following changes:

- Give as much memory as possible to the Java engine, then tune up the size of your broker to match. The broker will only consume memory it needs.

- Tune the system *sysctls* to enlarge the number of open files and to increase the read and write buffers used for network connections.

- Use multiple collectives to isolate traffic for large clusters or geographically diverse sites.

- If you are using TLS authentication with more than a few hundred servers, upgrade to ActiveMQ 5.9.1 to utilize the SSL-enabled NIO connector.

- Use a star or modified star configuration to limit the number of brokers a message has to transit between the server and the client.

- Configuration problems could cause servers or clients to back off and retry connections. Check the number of open connections per IP address on the middleware hosts to identify misconfigured nodes.

- Increase the discovery and request timeouts as necessary for all servers to transmit their responses back to the client.

Growing your network of brokers will require careful tuning to achieve the best performance. None of the tuning done here is limited to MCollective. Most documentation for tuning ActiveMQ connectors will be relevant to the performance of your network of brokers.

Middleware Security

In this chapter, we will discuss two different ways to enhance security of your middleware connection. Both of these options use *Transport Layer Security* (TLS), which is an enhanced version of Secure Sockets Layer (SSL).

Middleware security options control the ability to connect to the broker. Which queues and topics a node can read and write from is controlled by the authorizationEntry configuration documented in "Authentication and Authorization" on page 103.

MCollective has its own authorization system that controls whether or not a given MCollective request is allowed on a server, described in "Authorization" on page 163.

This layer of security only controls whether or not a node can connect to the broker and whether or not the communication is encrypted.

TLS protects traffic by encrypting it with a pre-arranged symmetric key. This key is used to encrypt the traffic flowing between the two sides. Each side of the TLS connection can (optionally) validate the far side's X.509 certificate. This asymmetric cryptography can assure that the far side with whom they are communicating is valid prior to sending any data.

When you connect to your bank's website, the browser does a cryptographic validation that the website is really your bank's site. It does this by ensuring that the bank's public key was signed (in an X.509 certificate) by an authority that the browser recognizes and trusts.

The bank does not usually require your browser to provide a certificate back to it proving who you are, although this is a valid TLS configuration. It relies instead on your username and password, which is protected from eavesdropping by the TLS encryption.

If you wish to implement TLS encryption, it is essential that you understand these configuration choices:

- *Anonymous TLS* provides the easiest way to encrypt transport between the MCollective nodes and the middleware. Similar to web clients connecting to a secure website, the client is not required to have a valid TLS certificate. The secure session is set up, and end-to-end encryption protects the username and password used to connect, as well as all MCollective requests (Figure 11-1).

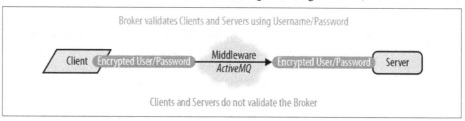

Figure 11-1. TLS encryption without client TLS certificates

- *CA-Verified TLS* provides not only encrypted transport, but also cryptographic authentication between the MCollective nodes and the middleware. This configuration requires that every MCollective node have a pre-signed TLS certificate to access the middleware. This ensures the most extensive security for the middleware (Figure 11-2).

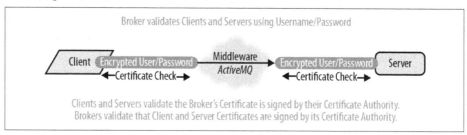

Figure 11-2. TLS encryption with bidirectional TLS certificate verification

There are two parts of enabling CA-Verified TLS: trusted servers and trusted clients, which we'll cover in "CA-Verified TLS Servers" on page 132 and "CA-Verified TLS Clients" on page 139, respectively.

Let's go through how to configure these two options.

Anonymous TLS

Anonymous TLS is the easier-to-configure option to encrypt traffic between MCollective and the middleware. This option uses TLS encryption to protect the connection from snooping of usernames, passwords, and MCollective request data. The clients continue to authenticate to the middleware using the usernames and passwords we configured in "Configuring ActiveMQ" on page 17.

> This is a good security model if you trust your firewall, DNC, and related infrastructure to ensure that nodes always connect to the expected broker, and no unauthorized systems can connect to your broker. You should avoid using this security model when using insecure DNS or Internet transit.

Advantages

The advantages of Anonymous TLS include the following:

- Easy to set up.
- Encrypts the data stream to and from the middleware.
- Prevents sniffing of ActiveMQ logins and passwords.

Disadvantages

The disadvantages of Anonymous TLS include the following:

- Vulnerable to man-in-the-middle attacks when connections can be intercepted.
- If a server password is compromised, an attacker could observe requests sent to servers, and inventory data submitted on the mcollectivr.registration.agent topic.

Puppet Module Setup

If you are using the Puppet module provided with this book, you need only the following Hiera data and all three of the following steps will be done for you. No other changes are required. Once every node has accepted the changes, everything will be working over SSL:

```
mcollective::connector_ssl                  : true
mcollective::connector_ssl_type             : anonymous
mcollective::middleware::keystore_password: openssl rand -base64 32
```

Or if you use declarative Puppet manifests:

```
node something-every-node-inherits {
  class { 'mcollective':
    connector_ssl      => true,
    connector_ssl_type => 'anonymous',
  }
  class { 'mcollective::middleware':
    keystore_password  => 'openssl rand -base64 20',
  }
}
```

Manual Setup

If you don't have Puppet installed, these are the steps for enabling Anonymous TLS manually.

Create a TLS keypair

Create a self-signed keypair for your middleware broker:

```
$ mkdir /etc/activemq/ssl
$ cd /etc/activemq/ssl
$ openssl genrsa -out broker-name_key.pem 2048
............+++
..................................................................+++
e is 65537 (0x10001)
$ openssl req -new -key broker-name_key.pem -out broker-name_cert.pem -days 3650
You are about to be asked to enter information that will be incorporated
into your certificate request.
...snip answers that don't matter...
```

Create a Java keyStore

Next, we want to set up the SSL keyStore used by ActiveMQ for negotiating the encrypted connection:

```
$ cd /etc/activemq/ssl
$ cat broker-name_key.pem broker-name_cert.pem \
    > broker-name_combined.pem
$ openssl pkcs12 -export
  -in broker-name_combined.pem -out broker-name.p12 -name broker-name
Enter Export Password: secret
Verifying - Enter Export Password: secret
$ keytool -importkeystore -storetype JKS -destkeystore keystore.jks \
```

```
    -srcstoretype PKCS12 -srckeystore $broker-name.p12 -alias broker-name
Enter destination keystore password: write down this password
Re-enter new password: use the same as last time
Enter source keystore password: secret
$ sudo chown activemq keystore.jks
$ sudo chmod 0400 keystore.jks
```

The first password can be junk like *secret* because you are removing the file immediately after creating the keyStore. You'll need to save the keyStore password because it will be used in the next section. It is best to use a completely random string like openssl rand -base64 20 and drop the final character, which is always an equals sign (=).

 Alternative ways of creating Java keyStores can be found in the "Setting Up Keystores For ActiveMQ" section (*http://bit.ly/1ruyfha*) of the Puppet Labs MCollective documentation.

Configure the middleware to use the keystore

Now in */etc/activemq/activemq.xml*, let's set up the SSL connector and the keyStore definition:

```
<transportConnectors>
  <transportConnector name="stomp+ssl" uri="stomp+ssl://0.0.0.0:61614"/>
</transportConnectors>
<sslContext>
  <sslContext
    keyStore="ssl/keystore.jks" keyStorePassword="password from creation above"
  />
</sslContext>
```

Configure the client and server by hand

Add the following lines to both the MCollective server and client configuration. The fallback parameter is required to tell MCollective to connect without its own private key information:

```
# mcollective/server.cfg or mcollective/client.cfg
plugin.activemq.pool.1.port = 61614
plugin.activemq.pool.1.ssl = true
plugin.activemq.pool.1.ssl.fallback = true
```

Testing

Once you have completed these steps, validate that the keyStore matches up with your original key:

```
$ keytool -list -keystore /etc/activemq/ssl/keystore.jks
Enter keystore password:

Keystore type: JKS
Keystore provider: SUN

Your keystore contains 1 entry

geode.netconsonance.com, Feb 16, 2014, PrivateKeyEntry,
Certificate fingerprint (MD5): 61:EA:B9:63:BE:C9:AB:D7:C4:D2:2F:F3:D4:66:E2:43

$ cd /var/lib/puppet/ssl/certs
$ sudo openssl x509 -in broker-name.pem -fingerprint -md5 | head -1
MD5 Fingerprint=61:EA:B9:63:BE:C9:AB:D7:C4:D2:2F:F3:D4:66:E2:43
```

After you enable TLS, test in the exact same manner as described in "Testing Your Installation" on page 28. You may also want to examine the packets in Wireshark to confirm that SSL/TLS encryption was used.

CA-Verified TLS Servers

A more complete security improvement is to authenticate connections between MCollective nodes and the middleware using TLS keys and certificates. This option ensures that communications with your middleware is both encrypted and limited to access by pre-authorized client certificates. Access to the middleware will require both:

- The middleware usernames and passwords we configured in "Configuring ActiveMQ" on page 17

- A certificate signed by a Certificate Authority designated in the broker's trust store

 This is a good security model if you want to ensure that every client and server, which connect to the middleware, have been preapproved. It has the added setup cost of creating and signing keys for each server or client which is connecting.

Advantages

The advantages of CA-Verified TLS include the following:

- Validates each incoming connection for a certificate signed by your Certificate Authority

- Encrypts the data stream to and from the middleware broker

- Prevents sniffing of ActiveMQ logins and passwords
- Not vulnerable to man-in-the-middle attacks
- Requires both a server password and the server's private key to be compromised before one could listen in on MCollective topics

Disadvantages

One disadvantage of CA-Verified TLS is that it requires a certificate signed by your Certificate Authority for each server and client.

Setup Paths

There are two different choices for doing TLS authentication. The first and easiest choice is to use the existing key infrastructure of Puppet. This requires very little extra configuration and takes advantage of the existing Puppet Certificate Authority.

The second choice is to create or use your own Certificate Authority and to manually sign each server and client key. This is more labor intensive.

We document both of these choices in the sections that follow.

TLS using Puppet CA

In this section, we will use a Puppet Certificate Authority and the existing Puppet SSL keys and certificates to secure access to the middleware.

Puppet one-step process

If you are using the Puppet module provided with this book, you need only the following Hiera data, and all three of the following steps will be done for you. No other changes are required. Once every node has accepted the changes, all connections will be encrypted using TLS:

```
mcollective::connector_ssl                    : true
mcollective::connector_ssl_type               : trusted
mcollective::middleware::keystore_password  : use a random string, right?
mcollective::middleware::truststore_password: string a random use
```

Or if you use declarative Puppet manifests:

```
node something-every-node-inherits {
  class { 'mcollective':
    connector_ssl      => true,
    connector_ssl_type => 'trusted',
  }
  class { 'mcollective::middleware':
    keystore_password   => 'use a random string, right?',
    truststore_password => 'random use string a',
```

```
        }
    }
```

Create a Java trustStore by hand

The Java `trustStore` will be created based on the Puppet server's public key. We cannot use a public CA, as that would allow anyone signed by the public CA to connect to our system. One of the best sources of this information is the existing key infrastructure provided by Puppet. Here's an example of creating the `truststore` using the Puppet CA:

```
$ sudo mkdir /etc/activemq/ssl
$ cd /etc/activemq/ssl
$ sudo puppet agent --configprint ssldir
/var/lib/puppet/ssl
$ keytool -importcert -alias "puppet.example.net" -file
  /var/lib/puppet/ssl/certs/ca.pem -keystore truststore.jks -storetype JKS
Enter keystore password: write down this pass#1
Owner: CN=Puppet CA: puppet.example.net
Issuer: CN=Puppet CA: puppet.example.net
Serial number: 1
Valid from: Sat Jan 05 14:32:01 PST 2013 until: Fri Jan 05 14:32:01 PST 2018
Certificate fingerprints:
   MD5:  F2:F8:C7:F7:45:92:DF:9A:BB:E0:0E:E9:F0:55:C6:B0
   SHA1: 84:5C:ED:3F:03:C2:19:DC:F9:95:A8:0E:32:65:9D:0E:B5:A4:81:AC
   Signature algorithm name: SHA256withRSA
   Version: 3

...blah Extensions blah ObjectId blah blah Identifier blah...

Trust this certificate? [no]: yes
Certificate was added to keystore
$ sudo chown activemq truststore.jks
$ sudo chmod 0400 truststore.jks
```

You'll need to save this `trustStore` password, because it will be used in the middleware configuration files.

Create a Java keyStore by hand

Next, we want to set up the SSL keys used for negotiating the encrypted connection. The following example uses the existing Puppet keypair to create the Java `keyStore`:

```
$ mkdir /etc/activemq/ssl
$ cd /etc/activemq/ssl
$ sudo puppet agent --configprint ssldir
/var/lib/puppet/ssl
$ export HOSTNAME=$( hostname -f )
$ sudo cat /var/lib/puppet/ssl/certs/$HOSTNAME.pem \
    /var/lib/puppet/ssl/private_keys/$HOSTNAME.pem \
    > $HOSTNAME-combined.pem
```

```
$ openssl pkcs12 -export -in $HOSTNAME-combined.pem -out $HOSTNAME.p12
  -name $HOSTNAME
Enter Export Password: secret
Verifying - Enter Export Password: secret
$ sudo keytool -importkeystore -storetype JKS -destkeystore keystore.jks \
    -srcstoretype PKCS12 -srckeystore $HOSTNAME.p12 -alias $HOSTNAME
Enter destination keystore password: write down this password
Re-enter new password: use the same as last time
Enter source keystore password: secret
$ rm $HOSTNAME.p12 $HOSTNAME-combined.pem
$ sudo chown activemq keystore.jks
$ sudo chmod 0400 keystore.jks
```

The first password can be junk like *secret* because you are removing the file immediately after creating the keyStore. You'll need to save the keyStore password because it will be used in the next section. It is best to use a completely random string like openssl rand -base64 20 and drop the final character, which is always an equals sign (=).

Configure the broker by hand

Here we configure ActiveMQ to use the Java trustStore and keyStore we've created. You'll need to put the passwords you used previously in the appropriate places. Add the following lines to the ActiveMQ configuration file */etc/activemq/activemq.xml*:

```
<transportConnectors>
  <transportConnector
    name="stomp+ssl" uri="stomp+ssl://[::0]:61614?needClientAuth=true"
  />
</transportConnectors>
<sslContext
  keyStore="ssl/keystore.jks"      keyStorePassword="keystore password"
  trustStore="ssl/truststore.jks"  trustStorePassword="truststore password"
/>
</sslContext>
```

Configure the MCollective server by hand

Add the following lines to the MCollective server configuration *server.cfg*:

```
plugin.activemq.pool.1.ssl      = true
plugin.activemq.pool.1.port     = 61614
plugin.activemq.pool.1.ssl.ca   = /var/lib/puppet/ssl/certs/ca.pem
plugin.activemq.pool.1.ssl.cert = /var/lib/puppet/ssl/certs/hostname.pem
plugin.activemq.pool.1.ssl.key  = /var/lib/puppet/ssl/private_keys/hostname.pem
```

TLS using Another CA

If an existing Puppet Certificate Authority is not available or not appropriate, this section provides a process for creating a new CA, or using your existing CA, to secure access to the middleware.

Creating and managing SSL keys is a complex topic beyond the scope of this book. I have found the following commands to work when testing, but Your Mileage May Vary.

Create a new Certificate Authority (optional)

If you do not have an existing Certificate Authority to use, the following steps will create one:

```
$ openssl genrsa -out CA_key.pem 2048
Generating RSA private key, 2048 bit long modulus
............+++
..............................................................................+++
e is 65537 (0x10001)
$ openssl req -x509 -new -nodes -key CA_key.pem -days 10240 -out CA_cert.pem
You are about to be asked to enter information that will be incorporated
into your certificate request.
...snip
```

Hide that key away in a dark place. It is now *literally* the key to access your middleware. If that key is compromised, you will be faced with the very annoying task of replacing it and re-creating *each and every client and node certificate.*

Create a Java trustStore from the Certificate Authority

Next, we create the Java `trustStore` from the public key of our Certificate Authority. We cannot use a public CA, as that would allow anyone signed by the public CA to connect to our system. Here is the process of creating the `trustStore` from the CA's public key:

```
$ keytool -importcert -alias "MyCA" -file CA_cert.pem \
    -keystore truststore.jks -storetype JKS
Enter keystore password: write down this pass#1
Owner: CN=My CA: myca.example.net
Issuer: CN=My CA: myca.example.net
Serial number: 1
Valid from: Sat Jan 05 14:32:01 PST 2013 until: Fri Jan 05 14:32:01 PST 2018
Certificate fingerprints:
  MD5:  F2:F8:C7:F7:45:92:DF:9A:BB:E0:0E:E9:F0:55:C6:B0
  SHA1: 84:5C:ED:3F:03:C2:19:DC:F9:95:A8:0E:32:65:9D:0E:B5:A4:81:AC
  Signature algorithm name: SHA256withRSA
  Version: 3

...blah Extensions blah ObjectId blah blah Identifier blah...

Trust this certificate? [no]: yes
Certificate was added to keystore
```

```
$ sudo chown activemq truststore.jks
$ sudo chmod 0400 truststore.jks
```

You'll need to save this `trustStore` password, because it will be used in the middleware configuration files.

Create a TLS Keypair for every server

Next, create a new key for each host and sign it with your Certificate Authority. Be sure to avoid making the certificate expiration longer than the Certificate Authority's lifetime:

```
$ openssl genrsa -out node1_key.pem 2048
.............+++
...................................................................+++
e is 65537 (0x10001)
$ openssl req -new -key node1_key.pem -out node1.csr
You are about to be asked to enter information that will be incorporated
into your certificate request.
...snip
$ openssl x509 -req -days 5120 -set_serial 01 -CA CA_cert.pem -CAkey CA_key.pem \
    -in node1.csr -out node1_cert.pem
Signature ok
subject=/C=US/ST=California/L=San Jose/O=Example/CN=Node1
Getting CA Private Key
```

Create a Java keyStore

For each middleware broker, you will need to create a Java `keyStore`. Simply combine the PEM files to generate a PKCS12 file, and create the `keyStore` from that:

```
$ cd /etc/activemq/ssl
$ sudo cat /etc/ssl/private/hostname_key.pem /etc/ssl/certs/hostname_cert.pem \
    > combined.pem
$ openssl pkcs12 -export -in combined.pem -out combined.p12 -name $( hostname -f )
Enter Export Password: secret
Verifying - Enter Export Password: secret
$ sudo keytool -importkeystore -storetype JKS -destkeystore keystore.jks \
    -srcstoretype PKCS12 -srckeystore combined.p12 -alias $( hostname -f )
Enter destination keystore password: write down pass#2
Re-enter new password: same as last time
Enter source keystore password: secret
$ rm combined.p12 combined.pem
$ sudo chown activemq truststore.jks
$ sudo chmod 0400 truststore.jks
```

You'll need to save the `keyStore` password, because it will be used in the next section.

Configure the broker to use the stores we made

Here we configure ActiveMQ to use the Java `trustStore` and `keyStore` we've created. You'll need to put the passwords you used in the previous sections in the appropriate places. Add the following lines to the ActiveMQ configuration file */etc/activemq/ activemq.xml*:

```
<transportConnectors>
  <transportConnector
    name="stomp+ssl" uri="stomp+ssl://[::0]:61614?needClientAuth=true"
  />
</transportConnectors>
<sslContext>
  <sslContext
    keyStore="ssl/keystore.jks"     keyStorePassword="password #2"
    trustStore="ssl/truststore.jks" trustStorePassword="password #1"
  />
</sslContext>
```

Configure the MCollective server by hand

Add the following lines to the MCollective server configuration *server.cfg*:

```
plugin.activemq.pool.1.ssl      = true
plugin.activemq.pool.1.port     = 61614
plugin.activemq.pool.1.ssl.ca   = /etc/ssl/certs/CA_cert.pem
plugin.activemq.pool.1.ssl.cert = /etc/ssl/certs/node1_cert.pem
plugin.activemq.pool.1.ssl.key  = /etc/ssl/private/node1_key.pem
```

Validate keyStore and trustStore

No matter which type of CA you chose to use, stop and validate that the keyStore matches up with your original key. In the following examples, we are using the Puppet cert locations, but the same commands work wherever you stored the certificate:

```
$ keytool -list -keystore /etc/activemq/ssl/keystore.jks
Enter keystore password:

Keystore type: JKS
Keystore provider: SUN

Your keystore contains 1 entry

geode.netconsonance.com, Feb 16, 2014, PrivateKeyEntry,
Certificate fingerprint (MD5): 61:EA:B9:63:BE:C9:AB:D7:C4:D2:2F:F3:D4:66:E2:43

$ sudo openssl x509 -in /var/lib/puppet/ssl/certs/activemq.example.net.pem \
   -fingerprint -md5 | head -1
MD5 Fingerprint=61:EA:B9:63:BE:C9:AB:D7:C4:D2:2F:F3:D4:66:E2:43
```

Then validate that the trustStore was imported correctly:

```
$ keytool -list -keystore /etc/activemq/ssl/truststore.jks
Enter keystore password:

Keystore type: JKS
```

```
Keystore provider: SUN

Your keystore contains 1 entry

puppet.example.net, Feb 16, 2014, PrivateKeyEntry,
Certificate fingerprint (MD5): F2:F8:C7:F7:45:92:DF:9A:BB:E0:0E:E9:F0:55:C6:B0

$ sudo openssl x509 -in /var/lib/puppet/ssl/certs/ca.pem \
  -fingerprint -md5 | head -1
MD5 Fingerprint=F2:F8:C7:F7:45:92:DF:9A:BB:E0:0E:E9:F0:55:C6:B0
```

CA-Verified TLS Clients

Each client requires its own certificate in order to connect. A common way would be to make each user have her own certificate. A perhaps less cumbersome way is to create certificates for each team, and ensure that only the team has access to the private key. You can likely think of other ways to break this out. Either way, you will need to create a TLS certificate for each unique entity you wish to validate.

Although this will be cumbersome, you will be able to re-use these certificates for authorization, as described in Chapter 13. The certificate file name minus the *.pem* extension will be the name logged for authentication.

Clients of the Puppet CA

One way to create client certificates is to generate them on a Puppet master with `pup pet cert generate` *username* and then copy them to the desired system. The process as documented at Configure MCollective Clients (*http://bit.ly/1nwamjl*) works well if you have shared network-mounted home directories.

Unfortunately, this requires each user generating a keypair to have root access on a Puppet master. Moving the generated keys back and forth can also be problematic.

Distributing keys in this manner means that someone has another user's private key. If you are all working from the same nodes and you all have root access, then when working as root you can get to another user's private key. But if you want clarity on who issued a command, have users generate their own key and store it on a machine only they have root access to—such as their laptop.

Create a Puppet keypair on the client node

I have found the following process much easier to perform for any logged-in user (it also ensures that the user's private key is not known by anyone else):

```
client$ puppet agent --certname user --server puppetmaster --test
Info: Creating a new SSL key for user
Info: Caching certificate for ca
Info: csr_attributes file loading from /home/user/.puppet/csr_attributes.yaml
Info: Creating a new SSL certificate request for user
Info: Certificate Request fingerprint (SHA256): 83:26:59:C9:A2:A4:93:97:79:...
Info: Caching certificate for ca
Exiting; no certificate found and waitforcert is disabled
```

An admin on the Puppet master need only issue one command:

```
puppetmaster$ sudo puppet cert sign user
Notice: Signed certificate request for user
Notice: Removing file Puppet::SSL::CertificateRequest user at
    '/var/lib/puppet-server/ssl/ca/requests/user.pem'
```

The user can run the following command and have her own key, cert, and CA as necessary for the config:

```
client$ puppet agent --certname user --server puppetmaster --no-daemonize \
--no-client --verbose
Info: Caching certificate for user
Info: Caching certificate for user
Notice: Starting Puppet client version 3.5.1
Error: Could not run: Daemons must have an agent, server, or both
```

That error is the exact response we want to get. The --no-daemonize --no-client options at the end of the second command are necessary to prevent Puppet from trying to run. If you don't supply these options, the Puppet agent will try to run a default catalog on your system. Logged in as a normal user, that may not cause any problems, but it's best to be avoided.

 If you are considering using autosign to avoid having to sign each user's certificate, realize that this removes the *trusted* nature of this configuration. It would provide no more security than the anonymous configuration and yet require so much more effort on your part.

Change the client configuration

For clients to utilize their own keys, they will need to create a personal config file. The default file name looked for by MCollective clients is *.mcollective* in the user's home directory. Alternative configuration files can be specified with -c config on the command line.

Add the following lines to the *~/.mcollective* file for each user:

```
plugin.activemq.pool.1.port     = 61614
plugin.activemq.pool.1.ssl      = true
plugin.activemq.pool.1.ssl.ca   = /home/user/.puppet/ssl/certs/ca.pem
plugin.activemq.pool.1.ssl.cert = /home/user/.puppet/ssl/certs/user.pem
plugin.activemq.pool.1.ssl.key  = /home/user/.puppet/ssl/private_keys/user.pem
```

How about a sneaky little trick? Well, if a user has root access on a Puppetized machine, he will be able to access the middleware using the node's Puppet certificate. It's a perfectly valid certificate signed by the same Puppet CA. This is one more reason that MCollective's authorization is so important.

I don't feel that this is a security problem. If a node is part of the puppet framework, allowing it to connect to the middleware only makes sense. If users have root access, then the server login to the middleware is visible to them anyway. This is one of the many reasons that we ensure that the client passwords and permissions are distinct.

Clients Using Another CA

You'll need to follow the instructions in this section if you don't have or won't be using the Puppet Certificate authority to sign client certificates.

Create a keypair for each client

Each user who wants to connect will need to generate a new keypair and then submit a signing request:

```
$ mkdir -p ~/.mcollective.d
$ cd ~/.mcollective.d
$ mkdir -p certs private_keys public_keys
$ openssl genrsa -out private_keys/user.pem 2048
...........+++
.................................................................+++
e is 65537 (0x10001)
$ openssl req -new -key private_keys/user.pem -out user.csr
You are about to be asked to enter information that will be incorporated
into your certificate request.
...snip
```

Sign the certificate request

The user then submits the resulting CSR file to be signed. An administrator with access to that all-important private key will use the following commands to sign the user's request with the Certificate Authority (be sure to avoid making the certificate expiration longer than the Certificate Authority's lifetime):

```
$ openssl x509 -req -days 5120 -set_serial 01 -CA CA_cert.pem -CAkey CA_key.pem \
    -in user.csr -out user.pem
Signature ok
subject=/C=US/ST=California/L=San Jose/O=Jo Rhett/CN=jorhett
Getting CA Private Key
```

 If you are considering allowing anyone to access and sign keys in order to reduce help requests, realize that this removes the *trusted* nature of this configuration. It would provide no more security than the anonymous configuration and yet require more effort on your part. The ability to sign keys must be limited to people you can trust.

Change the Client Configuration

The resulting PEM file and the certificate *CA_cert.pem* should both be returned to the user. They should be placed in the directories as identified here. Add the following lines to the *~/.mcollective* file for the user, or any other configuration file specified with -c config on the command line:

```
plugin.activemq.pool.1.port     = 61614
plugin.activemq.pool.1.ssl      = true
plugin.activemq.pool.1.ssl.ca   = /home/user/.mcollective.d/certs/CA_cert.pem
plugin.activemq.pool.1.ssl.cert = /home/user/.mcollective.d/certs/user.pem
plugin.activemq.pool.1.ssl.key  = /home/user/.mcollective.d/private_keys/user.pem
```

Conclusion

There are two ways to secure the nodes connections to the ActiveMQ broker:

- Anonymous TLS encryption uses only the server certificate for generating encryption keys. This is the same model used by websites and is easy to implement.

- CA-Verified TLS encryption provides bidirectional authentication where each side confirms that the other side's certificate was signed by the same Certificate Authority. This requires careful signing of unique keys and certificates for every server and client.

Both of these choices will protect the login credentials and the MCollective data from being sniffed on the wire.

## CHAPTER 12

Creating Collectives

A *collective* is a set of ActiveMQ topics and queues used to group request traffic. In small installations, you should use a single collective. The installation we have done in this book uses the default collective name mcollective for all configurations.

You may want to create multiple collectives for the following reasons:

- Collectives can be used to limit traffic in large clusters or between sites.
- Collectives can be used to group nodes together for restricting client access.

Deciding When to Create More

There are a few reasons why you may want to implement multiple collectives in your network:

- You have more than a thousand servers.
- You have multiple locations with high latency between them.
- You have multiple locations and you'd like to reduce the network traffic between them.
- You want to allow local admins control of their own hosts, while allowing a global team to administer all hosts.

Here are a few reasons you wouldn't want to implement multiple collectives:

You want fault tolerance in your middleware setup.

> Collectives do not intrinsically provide fault tolerance. Fault tolerance can be created by using a network of brokers or master/slave setup, which is documented in

"ActiveMQ Clusters" on page 113. Collectives are most effective at limiting traffic when placed on brokers localized to each site.

You want to implement barriers for authorization control.

Although you can restrict clients to specific collectives to limit server access, this isn't a granular authorization mechanism. We suggest using the facilities documented in "Authorization" on page 163.

You have different Puppet domains.

Although Puppet and MCollective play nice together, their domains don't need to overlap. You can use a single MCollective for many Puppet domains or vice versa.

If you didn't find your answer in this list, let's go over how to create collectives.

Collectives != Clustering

One thing to understand up front is that collectives are different from ActiveMQ clusters.

A collective is a set of ActiveMQ topics and queues used to isolate network traffic. An ActiveMQ cluster provides fault tolerance for a set of topics and queues. It's quite possible to run hundreds of collectives on a single ActiveMQ broker, which would provide zero fault tolerance. Likewise, you could use dozens of ActiveMQ brokers to provide extensive fault tolerance and high performance for a single collective.

Most environments use something in between these two extremes, such as:

- A master/slave pair of brokers that support all collectives for single-site redundancy
- A network of brokers with one ActiveMQ broker in each location which hosts all collectives at that site
- A network of brokers with multiple ActiveMQ brokers in each location
- A combination of these three options

We provide some examples of ActiveMQ cluster configuration in "ActiveMQ Clusters" on page 113. For now, it is only important to realize that these are distinct. The collective is a message path configured on top of network of brokers.

 If you are familiar with the OSI model for networking, it is not entirely accurate but easiest to think of clustering as Layer 4 and collectives as Layer 6. This reflects how the collective is an application-specific path that relies on the transport layer.

Configuration Traffic

The following configuration parameters define the collectives a client is attached to:

```
collectives = mcollective,asia,europe,usa
main_collective = mcollective
```

Place each server only in the relevant, local collectives:

```
collectives = mcollective,asia
main_collective = mcollective
```

You can query the servers to learn which collectives they are part of. You can write the collective structure out to a DOT abstract graph to be read with Graphviz, ZGRViewer, and various conversion utilities:

```
$ mco inventory --list-collectives
   Collective                    Nodes
   ==========                    =====
   asia                          4
   europe                        7
   usa                           3
   mcollective                   14
                   Total nodes: 14

$ mco inventory --collective-graph all_sites.dot
Retrieving collective info....
Graph of 14 nodes has been written to all_sites.dot
```

You can query a given server to learn which collectives it is part of:

```
$ mco rpc rpcutil collective_info -I heliotrope

heliotrope
   All Collectives: ["mcollective","asia"]
   Main Collective: mcollective
```

You can define a `target` for any request you send out, thus limiting a request to the smaller collective. If you don't define a target, the request will be sent to the collective identified in the `main_collective` parameter of your *client.cfg* file:

```
$ mco ping --target asia
```

Only the nodes in the `asia` collective will respond.

Localizing Traffic

The middleware will only send traffic where it knows that someone is listening. This is due to how the topic subscription mechanism works. If only five machines have the Puppet plugin loaded (and are thus subscribed to the `collective.puppet.agent` topic), only those five machines will receive requests sent out from the Puppet client plugin.

Likewise, if all systems on a given collective are attached to certain brokers, the middleware brokers will not replicate the collective's messages to brokers without anyone subscribed to those topics or queues. This will greatly reduce the amount of traffic traveling between the sites.

To gain this benefit, design your collectives as such:

- Use one collective that all hosts are subscribed to for registration and other global messages (e.g., *mcollective*).
- Add one collective for each physical or infrastructure distinct area. You might want to name it the country, city, or airport code, for simplicity.

Configure the middleware to accept the same client and server logins for the new collective names:

```
<authorizationEntry queue="site.>" write="clients" read="clients"
admin="clients" />
<authorizationEntry topic="site.>" write="clients" read="clients"
admin="clients" />
<authorizationEntry topic="site.*.agent" read="servers" admin="servers" />
<authorizationEntry queue="site.reply.>" write="servers" admin="servers" />
```

Configure the servers in that area as follows:

```
collectives = mcollective,site-name
main_collective = mcollective
```

Then configure the clients to have every local site available in their configuration:

```
collectives = mcollective,site #1,site #2,site #3
main_collective = mcollective
```

This configuration will allow the administrators to issue commands only to specific sites, or to all hosts based on how they target their request:

```
$ mco ping --target site #2
...only local site #2 nodes respond

$ mco puppet runall 10 --target mcollective
Puppet runs on every node in any site
```

Limiting Access

Another reason to use multiple collectives is to limit access to local admin teams at each site. To gain this benefit, design your collectives as such:

- Use one collective that all hosts are subscribed to for registration and other global messages (e.g., *mcollective*).
- Add one collective for each set of servers managed by a distinct set of clients.

- Ensure that each collective has a unique group name for access.

Unfortunately, the configuration changes for this grow linear with the number of different groups you have. Each group of admins requires a unique client login and unique group name. In the following example, we will demonstrate a two-group system using administrators and developers. Developers can only take actions in their own collective. Global administrators with the client login can act in every collective:

```
<authenticationUser username="dev-server" password="dev server passwd"
  groups="dev-servers,everyone"
/>
<authenticationUser username="dev" password="dev passwd"
  groups="dev-clients,everyone"
/>

<authorizationEntry queue="dev.>"
  write="clients,dev-clients"
  read="clients,dev-clients"
  admin="clients,dev-clients"
/>
<authorizationEntry topic="dev.>"
  write="clients,dev-clients"
  read="clients,dev-clients"
  admin="clients,dev-clients"
/>
<authorizationEntry topic="dev.*.agent"
  read="servers,dev-servers" admin="servers,dev-servers"
/>
<authorizationEntry queue="dev.reply.>"
  write="servers,dev-servers" admin="servers,dev-servers"
/>
```

This leverages our earlier configuration such that the main client login will continue to have global access to all collectives, while each of these new logins will only be able to send and receive messages on their own collectives.

Configure the servers in the more limited collective as follows:

```
plugin.activemq.pool.1.user = dev-server
plugin.activemq.pool.1.password = dev server password
collectives = mcollective,dev
main_collective = mcollective
```

Configure the clients to have the local collective as their main (default) collective:

```
plugin.activemq.pool.1.user = dev
plugin.activemq.pool.1.password = dev password
collectives = mcollective,dev
main_collective = dev
```

This configuration will allow the dev administrators to issue requests only to dev systems, while the global admins (with the username and password to the client account) will have access to all hosts:

```
$ mco ping --target dev
...only dev nodes respond -- both global and developer admins can do this

$ mco puppet runall 10 --target mcollective
Puppet runs on both operations and dev nodes -- only global admins can do this
```

Conclusion

The use of multiple collectives can assist with handling scale at several different levels. In most situations, you don't need more than the default collective until you are experiencing problems with scale or you need to restrict access for certain groups (customers, dev teams, etc.).

It is good to understand the features available in this chapter, but I wouldn't recommend using multiple collectives until you need them.

## CHAPTER 13

MCollective Security

As you've seen in Chapter 5, MCollective is a powerful tool capable of making significant change in a very short time period. As with any powerful tool, the risk of something going wrong and the damage it can cause are both increased. This chapter describes how to limit that risk and how to control which users can take a given action on a given server.

At this point, your MCollective setup uses a simple security model. You either have rights to issue requests, or you do not. You may want a security model with more granularity than that. Here are some reasons to evaluate alternative security plugins:

Security (authentication) plugin
> The current setup uses a Pre Shared Key to create an MD5 hash of the contents, which the servers use to ensure that the plain-text request was not changed in flight. You may want cryptographic validation stronger than that.

Authorization plugin
> You either have rights to issue requests, or you do not. You may want a security model with granularity to limit some clients to specific hosts or to specific requests.

Auditing plugin
> The basic log files aren't very informative about who issued a given request. You may want a detailed log of accepted and denied requests and who submitted them.

As MCollective has a plugin architecture for security, you'll find considerable flexibility in how to improve that situation. There is no singular *right way* to do security for MCollective; instead, you are provided with tools to make security work exactly as you need. In this chapter, we're going on a tour of options for improving security to meet your needs.

This section describes authentication and authorization between clients (sending requests) and servers (validating the requests). This does not affect security of the middleware transport, which was described in Chapter 11.

As the security is provided by plugins, each organization or even each collective of hosts can use a different security model that meets their needs. We'll compare and contrast the security plugins available for MCollective and document how to enable and use each one of these.

 MCollective documentation refers to the authentication plugin as the security plugin. I don't prefer this term, as there are distinct authorization and auditing plugins that are part of most people's concept of security. I refer to it as the authentication plugin in this section for clarity, but the reader should be aware that the configuration files and Puppet Labs documentation refer to it as the security plugin.

How Authentication Works

When sending a command to a collective, the client embeds a `caller` identification in the request. It works like this:

1. A user invokes an MCollective client request like `mco puppet runonce`.
2. The client authentication/security plugin sets `caller` and adds it as metadata with the command.
3. The client publishes the message to the middleware.
4. The server authentication/security plugin validates the digest on the message.
5. The server authorization plugin validates that the `caller` is authorized to make this request.
6. The server processes the request.

The Pre-Shared Key plugin we have used thus far simply embeds the Unix uid or gid in the request as the caller. Unless every client system is known to have the exact same uid/gid mappings, and no user has local root (e.g., desktops or laptops), the caller information cannot be trusted in this scenario. All you know for certain was that the client had the correct Pre-Shared Key. Is this good enough for your environment?

For more granular access control, you may want to use the SSL, AES, or SSHKey security plugins we describe later. Each of these plugins use public keys to cryptographically validate the identity of the `caller`.

Pre-Shared Key Authentication

The Pre-Shared Key authentication plugin creates an MD5 hash of each request's data with the pre-shared key appended. This hash is verified by each server to ensure that the request was sent from a client with the same key and that the payload had not been modified.

Here's an example configuration that would be put in both the client and server configuration files:

```
# Security provider
securityprovider = psk
plugin.psk = super secret
plugin.psk.callertype = uid
```

With this configuration, the client will insert:

- A *caller* field comprised of the Unix uid into the request
- A *hash* field that is an MD5 digest of the message contents plus the Pre-Shared Key

The server that receives this request will perform a hash of the message contents and their configured key information. If the MD5 hash matches the hash in the request, the server will know the message was sent by an authorized person (i.e., someone who has the same Pre-Shared Key); see Figure 13-1. The *caller* information will be passed to the authorization plugin, if enabled.

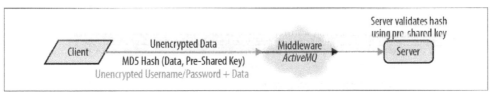

Figure 13-1. The data is passed in the clear with an MD5 hash of the contents and the Pre-Shared Key

 A common misconception is that the Pre-Shared Key is used for encryption of the request. Read the previous paragraph carefully. Examine the packets using Wireshark and you will see the username and password in the clear. The only cryptographic data is the MD5 hash.

The PSK value is *salt* added to the request data before creating the hash. As such, PSK is an authentication mechanism which confirms only that the client has the same secret as the server does and that the payload data has not been changed. It provides no encryption of the request contents.

The Pre-Shared Key plugin is useful for several environments where:

- Small team environments share common passwords.
- All clients are controlled hosts and the uid/gid information is synchronized consistently.
- The protection provided by TLS-encrypted connections to the middleware is sufficient.

Here's a quick determination for whether this model works well for you: do all of you share the same root password among yourselves? If so, this plugin may provide all the security you need. The single shared hash provides the same level of security.

If you do use the PSK model, we do encourage the use of TLS encryption to protect the data (see Figure 13-2).

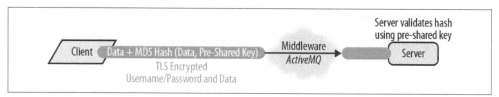

Figure 13-2. The data and a MD5 hash of the contents and the Pre-Shared Key are both encrypted during transit

The PSK plugin has only two options: key and callertype. The callertype can be one of the following:

Callertype	Information included in the request
uid	The UID of the user running client program (default)
gid	The GID of the group running client program
user	The username matching the UID running the client program
group	The group matching the GID running the client program
identity	The identity configuration parameter of the client (configurable, defaults to the hostname)

Which callertype to use depends upon your needs. Your choice will control:

- What value you can compare in the authorization policy
- What information is shown in the audit log

Puppet Setup

If you are using the Puppet module provided with this book, the following Hiera options will enable the Pre-Shared Key authentication plugin in your server and client configuration files:

```
mcollective::security_provider: 'psk'
mcollective::psk_key          : 'super secret'
mcollective::psk_callertype   : [ uid | gid | group | user | identity ]
```

You could of course pass them into the module as parameters if you use declarative Puppet manifests:

```
class { 'mcollective':
  security_provider => 'psk',
  psk_key           => 'super secret',
  psk_callertype    => 'uid',
}
```

SSL Authentication

When using the SSL security plugin, each client issuing commands must have a unique private and public key. All servers will share the same public and private key. This allows for cryptographic assurance of each client request. For this security module to work, the following must be true:

- All servers share a single public/private keypair.
- Each client must have the server public key.
- Each client will sign each request with its own private key.
- Each server must have the client's public key in order to validate the request.

With this configuration, the client will do the following (as illustrated in Figure 13-3):

1. Insert a *caller* field comprised of the client certificate's filename into the request
2. Serialize the message body, the message time, and the time-to-live
3. Insert a *hash* field containing a cryptographic signature of the serialized data

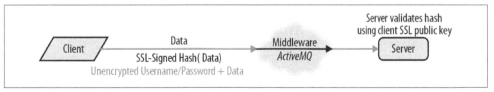

Figure 13-3. The data is passed in the clear with a SSL-signed hash of the contents

When the message is received by the server, it will use the client's public key to validate the signature and confirm that the message is from a valid caller, and that the message time and time-to-live haven't been altered.

If you combine this with TLS encryption on the middleware, then you have both an encrypted tunnel (provided by TLS) and cryptographic validation of the client's request (Figure 13-4). This is Puppet Lab's recommended solution.

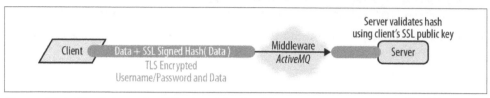

Figure 13-4. The data and a SSL-signed hash of the contents are encrypted by TLS

Server Configuration

With the SSL security model, the server private and public key is common and shared among every server. You can create the server keypair like so:

```
$ mkdir server
$ cd server
$ openssl genrsa -out private.pem 2048
Generating RSA private key, 2048 bit long modulus
....................................................+++
........................................+++
e is 65537 (0x10001)
$ openssl rsa -in private.pem -out public.pem -outform PEM -pubout
writing RSA key
$ cd ..
```

Move these files to mcollective's directory and safeguard them:

```
$ chmod 400 server/private.pem
$ sudo chown -R root:root server/
$ sudo mkdir -p /etc/mcollective/ssl/clients
$ sudo mv server /etc/mcollective/ssl/
```

To use these keys you would remove the two lines referencing the PSK plugin from server.cfg and add the following lines:

```
securityprovider        = ssl
plugin.ssl_server_private = /etc/mcollective/ssl/server/private.pem
plugin.ssl_server_public  = /etc/mcollective/ssl/server/public.pem
plugin.ssl_client_cert_dir = /etc/mcollective/ssl/clients
```

Installing and synchronizing with Puppet

If you are using the Puppet module provided with this book, you would run the following commands to move those keys and files into the Puppet module directory. The Puppet module will distribute the key pair out to all servers automatically:

```
$ chmod 440 server/private.pem
$ sudo mv server/* /etc/puppet/modules]/mcollective/files/ssl/server/
$ sudo chown -R root:puppet /etc/puppet/modules]/mcollective/files/ssl/server
```

The following Hiera options will enable the appropriate configuration in your *server.cfg* file:

```
mcollective::server::security_provider : ssl

# The following are defaults which can be overridden
mcollective::ssl_server_private        : /etc/mcollective/ssl/server/private.pem
mcollective::plugin.ssl_server_public  : /etc/mcollective/ssl/server/public.pem
mcollective::plugin.ssl_client_cert_dir: /etc/mcollective/ssl/clients/
```

Client Configuration

Each client will require a public and private key in order for their requests to be validated. The most common implementation is for all users to generate their own public and private keys and never share them with others.

> Another method is to create certificates for each team, and ensure that only that team has access to the private key. You can likely think of other ways to facilitate access. The important thing to consider is the depth to which you need to authorize and audit. If you authenticate with a shared group key, you won't know which user made the request.

The private key should be kept secure and not shared beyond the people authorized to use it. The public key must be distributed to every MCollective server where this key may be used to sign a request.

Create a client identity

Start out by creating a directory to store the client keys:

```
$ mkdir -p ~/.mcollective.d
$ cd ~/.mcollective.d
$ mkdir -p certs private_keys public_keys
```

If you already generated Puppet keys for a Trusted TLS connector, you can reuse those same keys:

```
$ cd certs
$ ln -s ~/.puppet/ssl/certs/ca.pem
```

```
$ cd ../private_keys
$ ln -s ~/.puppet/ssl/private_keys/user.pem
$ cd ../public_keys
$ ln -s ~/.puppet/ssl/public_keys/user.pem
$ sudo cp user.pem /etc/mcollective/ssl/clients/
```

If you created a new identity with a different CA from "CA-Verified TLS Clients" on page 139, you may have everything except the public key. Create that now using these steps:

```
$ mkdir public_keys
$ openssl rsa -in private_keys/user.pem -out public_keys/user.pem -outform PEM
  -pubout
writing RSA key
```

If you don't have an existing keypair, you can generate a client keypair using Puppet as described in "CA-Verified TLS Clients" on page 139, or you can create a new keypair using openssl:

```
$ openssl genrsa -out private_keys/user.pem 2048
Generating RSA private key, 2048 bit long modulus
.......................................................+++
...................................+++
e is 65537 (0x10001)
$ chmod 0400 private_keys/user.pem
$ openssl rsa -in private_keys/user.pem -out public_keys/user.pem -outform PEM
  -pubout
writing RSA key
$ sudo cp public_keys/user.pem /etc/mcollective/ssl/clients/
```

Create a config file

As each client will need to reference a unique set of keys, you will need to create a unique configuration file per keypair at this time. If a system is used by only one person (personal desktop or laptop), you could add the following lines to the global client configuration */etc/mcollective/client.cfg*. Otherwise you should add these lines to the user's individual client configuration.

The first file check for client configuration is *.mcollective* in the user's home directory. If this file exists, the global client configuration will be ignored. The configuration file must be whole and complete:

```
$ cp /etc/mcollective/client.cfg ~/.mcollective
$ $EDITOR ~/.mcollective
```

 This defies the standard Unix/Linux convention, where *dot-program* would be a directory containing configuration files specific to the program. A prevailing convention for a directory containing files for MCollective is *.mcollective.d*. We used this directory when creating the public and private key files earlier.

To enable SSL authentication, you would change the `securityprovider` line to say `ssl`. Configuration lines referencing the `psk` or another other security connector can be removed. As the client will encrypt the hash for the server, the client configuration needs to reference the server's shared public key. Finally the configuration needs to identify the public and private keys we created. So the changes will look as follows:

```
# security section of /etc/mcollective/client.cfg or ~/.mcollective
securityprovider = ssl
plugin.ssl_server_public = /etc/mcollective/ssl/server/public.pem
plugin.ssl_client_private = /home/user/.mcollective.d/private_keys/user.pem
plugin.ssl_client_public = /home/user/.mcollective.d/public_keys/user.pem
```

Another alternative is for users to specify the key locations in their shell environment:

```
export MCOLLECTIVE_SSL_PRIVATE=/home/user/.mcollective.d/private_keys/user.pem
export MCOLLECTIVE_SSL_PUBLIC=/home/user/.mcollective.d/public_keys/user.pem
```

In the GitHub repo for this book, there is a Puppet class called `mcollective::userconfig` that will autobuild individual user key pairs. Unfortunately it doesn't handle all situations very well, so I didn't include it with the book. You may want to keep an eye on it at *http://bit.ly/1ryhxxe* in case I figure out a way to handle all situations cleanly.

Key Synchronization

SSL authentication requires that three different synchronization issues be solved:

- Every server must have the same public and private key.
- Every server must have the public key of every client.
- Every client must have the shared public key of the servers.

The Puppet module handles all three of the preceding synchronization problems for you. Just store the files as shown and then go grab a beer:

Type	Path on the Puppet server
Server Private Key	*modulepath*/mcollective/files/ssl/server/private.pem
Server Public Key	*modulepath*/mcollective/files/ssl/server/public.pem
Client Public Keys	*modulepath*/mcollective/files/ssl/clients

```
$ sudo cp public_keys/user.pem \
  /etc/puppet/environments/learning_mcollective/modules/mcollective/files/
  ssl/clients/
$ sudo echo "Get me a Beer"
```

If you aren't using the Puppet module, you will need to synchronize the following:

- The client public keys to each server's */etc/mcollective/ssl/clients/* folder
- The server public key to each client as */etc/mcollective/ssl/server/public.pem*:

```
$ sudo cp public_keys/user.pem /etc/mcollective/ssl/clients/
$ rsync -av public_keys/* serverX:/etc/mcollective/ssl/clients/
$ rsync -av public_keys/* serverY:/etc/mcollective/ssl/clients/
...start thinking about how to automate this...
```

RSA Authentication AES Encryption

When using the AES security plugin, each user issuing commands must have a private and public key. Each server will also have a unique public/private keypair. This allows for cryptographic assurance of each client request and cryptographic assurance of both replies from servers as well as data delivery from server to server, such as registration information.

For this security module to work, the following must be true:

- Each server must have a unique public/private keypair.
- Each client must have its own public/private keypair.
- Each server must have the public key for every client.

Each request is encrypted with the client's private key. Only servers with the client's public key can decrypt and process them.

Each reply is encrypted with the client's public key. Only the client with that private key can decrypt and read the replies.

Registration data and other requests from servers are encrypted with the server's private key. Only client's with the server's public key can view the data.

Server Configuration

The server configuration can be made simple by re-using an existing Puppet Certificate Authority.

Puppet module

If you are using the Puppet module provided with this book, you don't need to generate keys for each server. Every Puppet host already has a unique public/private key pair that the server will reuse.

The following Hiera option will enable the appropriate configuration in your *server.cfg* file:

```
mcollective::server::securityprovider: aes_security
```

Manual config

The manual process to create a keypair for the server is as follows:

```
$ cd /etc/ssl
$ openssl genrsa -out private_keys/user.pem 2048
Generating RSA private key, 2048 bit long modulus
.......................................................+++
...................................+++
e is 65537 (0x10001)
$ chmod 0400 private_keys/user.pem
$ openssl rsa -in private_keys/user.pem -out public_keys/user.pem -outform PEM \
  -pubout
writing RSA key
```

Modify the server configuration to use the newly generated keys. Remove the lines referencing the PSK or SSL plugin from *server.cfg* and add the following lines to */etc/mcollective/server.cfg*:

```
securityprovider           = aes_security
plugin.aes.server_public   = /etc/ssl/public_keys/certname.pem
plugin.aes.server_private  = /etc/ssl/private_keys/certname.pem
plugin.aes.client_cert_dir = /etc/mcollective/ssl/clients
plugin.aes.enforce_ttl     = true
```

Client Configuration

Each client will require a public and private key for its requests to be validated. The most common implementation is for all users to generate their own public and private keys and never share them with others.

> Another method is to create certificates for each team and ensure that only that team has access to the private key. You can likely think of other ways of breaking this out. The important thing to consider is the depth to which you need to authorize and audit. If you authenticate with a shared group key, you won't know which specific user made the request.

The private key should be kept secure and not shared beyond the people authorized to use it. The public key must be distributed to every MCollective server where this key may be used to sign a request.

Create a client identity

Start out by creating a directory to store the client keys:

```
$ mkdir -p ~/.mcollective.d
$ cd ~/.mcollective.d
$ mkdir -p certs private_keys public_keys
```

If you already generated Puppet keys for a Trusted TLS connector, you can easily reuse those same keys:

```
$ cd certs
$ ln -s ~/.puppet/ssl/certs/ca.pem
$ cd ../private_keys
$ ln -s ~/.puppet/ssl/private_keys/user.pem
$ cd ../public_keys
$ ln -s ~/.puppet/ssl/public_keys/user.pem
$ sudo cp user.pem /etc/mcollective/ssl/clients/
```

If you created a new identity with a different CA, you may have everything except the public key. Create that now using these steps:

```
$ mkdir public_keys
$ openssl rsa -in private_keys/user.pem -out public_keys/user.pem -outform PEM \
  -pubout
writing RSA key
```

If you don't have an SSL keypair to use, you can create a new keypair from scratch. Generate your own keypair using Puppet as described in "CA-Verified TLS Clients" on page 139, or create a new keypair using openssl:

```
$ openssl genrsa -out private_keys/user.pem 2048
Generating RSA private key, 2048 bit long modulus
.........................................................+++
.......................................+++
e is 65537 (0x10001)
$ chmod 0400 private_keys/user.pem
$ openssl rsa -in private_keys/user.pem -out public_keys/user.pem -outform PEM \
  -pubout
writing RSA key
$ sudo cp public_keys/user.pem /etc/mcollective/ssl/clients/
```

Create a config file

As each client will need to reference a unique set of keys, you will need to create a unique configuration file per keypair at this time. If a system is used by only one person (personal desktop or laptop), you could add the following lines to the global client configuration */etc/mcollective/client.cfg*. Otherwise you should add these lines to the user's individual client configuration.

The first file check for client configuration is *.mcollective* in the user's home directory. If this file exists, the global client configuration will be ignored. The configuration file must be whole and complete:

```
$ cp /etc/mcollective/client.cfg ~/.mcollective
$ $EDITOR ~/.mcollective
```

This defies the standard Unix/Linux convention where *dot-program* would be a directory containing configuration files specific to the program. A prevailing convention for a directory containing files for MCollective is *.mcollective.d*. We used this directory when creating the public and private key files earlier.

To enable AES authentication, you would change the `securityprovider` line to say `aes_security`. Configuration lines referencing `psk`, `ssl`, or another other security connector can be removed. As the client will encrypt the hash for the server, a directory containing server public keys needs to be listed. Finally, the configuration needs to identify the public and private keys we created. So the changes will look as follows:

```
# security section of /etc/mcollective/client.cfg or ~/.mcollective
securityprovider = aes_security
plugin.aes_client_private = /home/user/.mcollective.d/private_keys/user.pem
plugin.aes_client_public = /home/user/.mcollective.d/public_keys/user.pem
```

Another alternative is for users to specify the key locations in their shell environment:

```
export MCOLLECTIVE_AES_PRIVATE=/home/user/.mcollective.d/private_keys/user.pem
export MCOLLECTIVE_AES_PUBLIC=/home/user/.mcollective.d/public_keys/user.pem
```

As mentioned earlier, the GitHub repo for this book contains a Puppet class `mcollective::userconfig` that attempts to autobuild individual user key pairs. Keep an eye on it at *http://bit.ly/1ryhxxe* in case I figure out a way to handle all situations cleanly.

Key Synchronization

RSA/AES Authentication requires that three different synchronization issues be solved:

- Every server must have a unique public and private key.
- Every server must have the public key of every client.
- Every listener (registration, results processor, etc.) must have the public key of every server.

The Puppet module handles all three of the preceding synchronization problems for you. Just store the files as shown and then go grab a beer:

Type	Path on the Puppet server
Server Private Key	*modulepath*/mcollective/files/ssl/server/private.pem
Server Public Key	*modulepath*/mcollective/files/ssl/server/public.pem
Client Public Keys	*modulepath*/mcollective/files/ssl/clients

```
$ cd /etc/puppet/environments/learning_mcollective/modules/mcollective/files
$ sudo cp ~/.mcollective.d/ssl/public_keys/user.pem ssl/clients/
$ sudo echo "Get me a Beer"
```

If you aren't using the Puppet module, you will need to synchronize the following:

- The client public keys to each server's *etc/mcollective/ssl/clients/* folder

- The server public key to each listener as *etc/mcollective/ssl/server/public.pem*:

```
$ sudo cp public_keys/user.pem /etc/mcollective/ssl/clients/
$ rsync -av public_keys/* serverX:/etc/mcollective/ssl/clients/
$ rsync -av public_keys/* serverY:/etc/mcollective/ssl/clients/
...start thinking about how to script this...
```

 If you read the documentation for this module, you will find that there are options to auto-distribute public keys between the systems. In my opinion, this provides equivalent or less security than the SSL security module, and therefore it is extra overhead with a net security loss.

SSHKey Authentication

The SSHKey security plugin utilizes a pre-existing structure of SSH host and user keys. This allows unique identification of all users based on their private SSH keys and validation of the reply from the server against their known public keys.

For this to work, the following must be true:

- Each user has every host's public SSH key in *~/.ssh/known_hosts* or an alternative file specified in the configuration.

- Each host has each user's SSH public key in *~/.ssh/authorized_keys* or an alternative file specified in the configuration.

- Every client and server needs to have the *sshkeyauth* Gem installed.

This is not uncommon in a small environment where every user logs into every host, or where configuration management ensures that *known_hosts* and *authorized_keys* files are kept in sync.

Let's take a look at an example configuration that would be put in both the client and server configuration files. In *mcollective/server.cfg*, use the following:

```
# Security provider
securityprovider = sshkey
plugin.sshkey.server.authorized_keys = /etc/ssh/authorized_keys
# instead of ~/.ssh/authorized_keys
```

In *mcollective/client.cfg*, use the following:

```
# Security provider
securityprovider = sshkey
plugin.sshkey.client.known_hosts = /etc/ssh/known_hosts
# instead of ~/.ssh/known_hosts
```

With this configuration, the client will sign the command using the user's private SSH key from *~/.ssh/id_pub_rsa* as expected. The server will validate the command against public keys stored in */etc/ssh/authorized_keys*. It will sign its reply with its own private key from */etc/ssh/ssh_host_rsa_key*, and the client will validate the reply by checking the signature against */etc/ssh/known_hosts*.

Puppet

If you are using the Puppet module provided with this book, the following Hiera options will enable the appropriate configuration in your server and client configuration files:

```
mcollective::security_provider              : sshkey
mcollective::server::sshkey_authorized_keys : /etc/ssh/authorized_keys
mcollective::client::sshkey_client_known_hosts: /etc/ssh/known_hosts
```

If you read the documentation for this module, you will find that there are options to auto-distribute public keys between the nodes. In my opinion, this provides significantly less security, and depending on the configuration of the server, it actually would open the node up to breach via SSH protocol.

This is the security equivalent of showing up with a badge and handing the security guard the rules for how to validate the badge. The node will keep the new key around, and possibly even replace the existing keys for a user. *Shudder*.

I do not recommend the use of these options.

Authorization

In this section, we will cover *authorization*, the final check before a request is processed by an MCollective server. Authorization provides the strongest and yet the most flexible piece of MCollective security. I believe that authorization is one of the most underused and overlooked features that MCollective provides.

The deployment we have created so far limits who can send requests based on authentication. A person with the right password, the right pre-shared key, or possibly a signed certificate is allowed to submit any request on any system. This is true, unlimited power (*cue demonic laughter*).

This is reasonable and works well for many smaller environments in which a small group of users are the only ones allowed to act. If you have multiple teams, a diverse set of managed systems, or a wide variety of agent plugins, you may wish to limit who can act upon which resources. Utilizing an authorization plugin provides you the ability to limit the possible changes of a given user, on a given host, for a given agent.

Authorization is a topic distinct and yet dependent on our choice of authentication. The authorization plugin uses the caller and request information validated by the security (authentication) plugin and decides whether or not the request is allowed to proceed.

 Be careful when pushing out an authorization policy. You should ensure you have another method to log in to each server to fix any mistake or a safety-net policy that will allow you to regain access.

For any deployment with more than one administrator, I recommend that you deploy the `ActionPolicy` authorization plugin to all servers. `ActionPolicy` uses policy rules for each agent, providing complete flexibility to restrict or allow on a per-agent basis.

Rule Format

The format of an `ActionPolicy` rule is tab-separated with the following fields:

Field #	Name	Description	Values
1	Policy	`allow` or `deny`	
2	Caller	The caller string provided in the request	* (always matches) One `Caller` string (discussed in the next section)
3	Action	An action provided by the agent the policy rule is for	* (always matches) A space-separated list of actions
4	Facts	Facts that must be true about the target server	* (always matches) A space-separated list of fact=value pairs (matches if every listed fact matches) Any valid compound filter string
5	Classes	Puppet classes that apply to the target server	Absent or * (always matches) A space-separated list of class names (matches if every listed class is present) Any valid compound filter string

You can of course create an authorization policy that uses a different file format, and a custom agent could do authorization based on its own criteria. We cover that functionality in Part III.

Caller IDs

No matter what authorization plugin you use, one of the fields available for matching is the `caller` field from the request. This field is set differently based on which `security provider` plugin you are using:

The PSK security plugin sets the caller ID to `uid`=*uid of the user running the client app.*

> This can be modified by setting `plugin.psk.callertype` in the configuration to gid, user, group, or identity. As uids and usernames are not consistent across hosts, these are not considered trustworthy.

The TLS security plugins set the caller ID to `cert`=*client's public key filename without the .pem extension.*

> The server looks in the `ssl_client_cert_dir` or `aes.client_cert_dir` to find a public key with the same name to validate the request.

The SSH security plugin sets the caller ID to `sshkey`=*username invoking the client.*

> The server looks in the user's `authorized_keys` file to find an SSH public key to validate the request.

Defining ActionPolicy with Puppet

The Puppet module provided with this book will install the `ActionPolicy` module and configure it for you. There are two ways to define policies in Puppet:

* Create rules dynamically from Hiera data
* Distribute static policy files

You can mix and match these two approaches, defining some policies in static files and others through Hiera.

Creating a simple policy in Hiera

Here is a simple `ActionPolicy` setup that denies all other requests but allows anyone to run Puppet to update the policy. This is a good safety net in case a mistake is made in the configuration.

If you enable authorization but do not specify a default policy, then authorization will be enabled on your server with `allow_unconfigured` enabled, which effectively enables a default *allow* policy:

```
mcollective::server::authorization_enable: true
mcollective::server::authorization_default_policy: default_deny
mcollective::plugin::actionpolicies:
  default_deny:
```

```
        default: 'deny'
    puppet:
      default: 'deny'
      rules:
        '00 allow puppet to fix policies':
          policy : 'allow'
          caller : '*'
          actions: 'runonce runall'
          facts  : '*'
          classes: '*'
```

This Hiera definition will create a policy file named *default_deny.policy* with a single line specifying the default policy of "deny." This default policy will apply to any agent for which a policy file specific to the agent is not defined.

Next it will create a policy file named *puppet.policy* with two lines: a default of *deny*, and a second line that allows the use of the runonce and runall commands.

When done exactly as specified, the only requests that would succeed would be puppet runonce and puppet runall. All other requests will fail, as shown here:

```
$ mco filemgr --file /etc/hosts status

 * [ ============================================> ] 3 / 3

geode                 : You are not authorized to call this agent or action.
sunstone              : You are not authorized to call this agent or action.
heliotrope            : You are not authorized to call this agent or action.

Finished processing 3 / 3 hosts in 146.81 ms

$ mco puppet runonce

 * [ ============================================> ] 3 / 3

Finished processing 3 / 3 hosts in 662.31 ms
```

Allowing more commands

As just implemented, the policy doesn't allow us to accomplish very much. Let's expand upon this and build some realistic policies.

For each policy, the default attribute defines the default policy for each agent. Any request for that agent that does not match another line in the policy will be be allowed or denied, based on the value defined here.

Each rule requires a unique title. The title should start with a number to indicate its order for evaluation. The MCollective module stores the title in the file as a comment above the rule it defines. This allows you to read the created policy file and understand it.

After the title, there is a dictionary of key/value pairs defining:

- The policy action
- Valid users or the key (e.g., certname) provided by your authentication plugin
- The agent actions that are allowed
- Facts that must match for the rule to apply
- Classes that must match for the rule to apply

Start from this basis to create a distinct policy for each agent. For example, this policy allows most commands but prevents anyone but admins from interacting with files or disabling the Puppet agent. This `callerid` assumes the PSK security provider with `callertype` set to `group`:

```
mcollective::plugin::actionpolicies:
  puppet:
    default: allow rules:
      '01 admins can disable the puppet agent':
        policy : 'allow'
        caller : 'group=admins'
        actions: 'disable'
        facts  : '*'
        classes: '*'
      '02 nobody else can':
        policy : 'deny'
        caller : '*'
        actions: 'disable'
        facts  : '*'
        classes: '*'
```

Here is another policy that allows any developer with the SSL key *jane.doe* to interact with services on development boxes. This `callerid` assumes the SSL or AES security provider:

```
service:
  default: deny
  rules:
    '010 developers':
      policy : 'allow'
      caller : 'cert=jane.doe'
      actions: 'start stop restart status'
      facts  : 'hostgroup=development'
      classes: '*'
```

To allow or deny all requests for a specific agent without any specific rules, simply leave out the rules line. For example, to allow anyone to control packages on the server:

```
package:
  default: 'allow'
```

You can use the same approach to deny all requests for an agent when the global default would allow it. For example, here is a permissive policy that allows everything except shell commands:

```
mcollective::server::authorization_enable: true
mcollective::server::authorization_default_policy: allow_everything
mcollective::plugin::actionpolicies:
  allow_everything:
    default: 'allow'
  shellcmd:
    default: 'deny'
```

Distributing policy files

If you are not using Hiera, the Puppet module can still help you distribute policy files to the nodes.

To manually configure a policy for an agent, create a policy file and place the file in the Puppet module's *files/policies/* directory. You will find example policies in this directory to guide you. This directory will be synchronized to every node with the `mcollective::server` class.

Each file should be named *agentname.policy* except for the default policy, which can be named anything ending with *.policy*. The default policy should be specified with the `authorization_default_policy` class or Hiera parameter, like so:

```
class { 'mcollective::server':
  authorization_enable         => true,
  authorization_default_policy => 'default_deny',
}
```

This specifies that the default rules will be found in a file named *default_deny.policy*. If you enable authorization but do not specify a default policy, then authorization will be enabled on your server with `allow_unconfigured` enabled, which effectively enables a default `allow` policy.

The `allow_psk_root.policy_example` demonstrates a basic default policy. It denies requests from anyone other than root on the client system. It is inherently insecure, given that anyone can be root on their own desktop, but it demonstrates the functionality. There are several other example files included in the *files/policies* directory of the Puppet module.

 Because you will need Puppet to fix any problems created by a new policy, we recommend that you include the first rule listed in the *files/policies/puppet.policy_example* file. This places a Puppet policy that allows any client to run Puppet to fix your authorization setup. Disable this at your own risk and after extensive testing.

Defining ActionPolicy Manually

Download the ActionPolicy agent (*http://bit.ly/1rdgJf8*) and install it as documented in "Installing from Source" on page 25. Then add the following changes to each *server.cfg* file:

```
rpcauthorization = 1
rpcauthprovider = action_policy
plugin.actionpolicy.allow_unconfigured = 0
plugin.actionpolicy.enable_default = 1
plugin.actionpolicy.default_name = default
```

Create a default policy file and a policy for each agent, as documented at the plugin's URL. Install the policy file in */etc/mcollective/policies/* on each server.

Here is an example service policy file:

```
# /etc/mcollective/policies/service.policy
# Admins can do anything
policy default     deny
allow  cert=admin *       *                  *
# devs can do anything to devel boxes
allow cert=devs * customer=startup startup::devsystems
# devs can only do status on production systems
allow  cert=devs  status customer=startup *
```

You can also create a distinct policy for each agent. The file would be named *agent-name.policy* and placed in the same directory. This directory must be synchronized to every server.

If you enable a default policy, then it will apply to any agent for which a specific policy is not available. If you do not have a default policy and allow_unconfigured is enabled, then all requests for that agent will be denied.

Auditing

At this point in the book, you have come to realize that MCollective is a powerful tool capable of making massive changes to thousands of systems in seconds. Hopefully you're asking yourself how to create logs of the requests processed by a server.

You can of course write your own plugin for auditing requests (which we'll discuss in Chapter 20), but MCollective includes a basic audit plugin that may suit your needs. This audit plugin writes out each request that the server receives, and whether it was allowed or denied, to a logfile on disk.

Enable this with the following settings in the server configuration file:

```
rpcaudit = 1
rpcauditprovider = Logfile
plugin.rpcaudit.logfile = /var/log/mcollective-audit.log
```

Unlike the main MCollective log, this plugin doesn't do any rotation of the logfile. You'll need to setup `logrotate` or something similar to handle this.

If you are using the Puppet module included with this book, you need only set the following class parameters and both the logfile and a logrotate script will be set up for you:

```
# Hiera
mcollective::server::audit_logfile: /var/log/mcollective-audit.log

# manifests/site.pp
class { 'mcollective::server':
  audit_logfile => '/var/log/mcollective-audit.log',
}
```

The value logged for who sent the request differs based on which security provider is enabled, as discussed in "Authorization" on page 163. Here are some examples of how your logs might look with each of the security providers we discussed in the book and a client identity of geode:

```
securityprovider = psk, psk.callertype = uid
[2014-02-18 08:10:25 UTC] reqid=addb20797321590db29231f7c782b30f:
reqtime=1392711027
caller=uid=1011@geode agent=service action=status data={:process_results=>true,
:service=>"mcollective"}

securityprovider = psk, psk.callertype = user
[2014-02-18 08:11:26 UTC] reqid=cc3e1168916e5678b78c70ef337afa08:
reqtime=1392711088
caller=user=jrhett@geode agent=service action=status data={:process_results=>true,
:service=>"mcollective"}

securityprovider = ssl or aes, public key file = jorhett.pem
[2014-02-18 08:27:37 UTC] reqid=199d2a3cc16951bab84edba21a75fe71:
reqtime=1392712059
caller=cert=jorhett@geode agent=service action=status
data={:service=>"mcollective", :process_results=>true}

securityprovider = sshkey, username = jrhett
[2014-02-18 08:11:26 UTC] reqid=cc3e1168916e5678b78c70ef337afa08:
reqtime=1392711088
caller=user=jrhett@geode agent=service action=status
data={:process_results=>true, :service=>"mcollective"}
```

The audit log does not contain authentication or authorization failures. Those can only be gathered from the DEBUG loglevel in the main logfile *mcollective.log*.

Conclusion

In this chapter, we have discussed the three types of security plugins you may want to enable or customize for your environment:

Security (authentication) plugin
> A choice of PSK, SSL, AES, or SSHKey security plugins provides a variety of ways to authenticate the requester.

Authorization plugin
> The ActionPolicy plugin can be used to limit which requests a user may send to a server.

Auditing plugin
> The LogFile plugin can be use to write details of every request processed to disk.

MCollective's plugin architecture provides flexibility to tune your MCollective environment to your exact needs.

## CHAPTER 14

Challenges of Worldwide Parallelism

MCollective provides an amazing toolset for orchestrating change in every environment, from small labs all the way up to global enterprises around the world. I'm familiar with a company that manages more than 200 global sites. I've assisted a different company managing more than 6,000 servers in a central site, with hundreds more at remote data centers. MCollective's ability to function well in both environments is unparalleled.

MCollective will likely work in any small environment right out of the box. To make MCollective work in either of the large-scale environments just mentioned required extensive tuning of the server and broker configurations. Much like a database server, file server, or any other major infrastructure service, you'll need to tune it to operate at scale.

Let's review some of the configuration options you'll want to tune:

- Choose an encryption level suitable to protect your middleware, as shown in "Anonymous TLS" on page 129 and "CA-Verified TLS Servers" on page 132.

- Choose a security plugin that meets your needs for authentication and authorization, as discussed in "How Authentication Works" on page 150.

- Define authorization controls to restrict access to specific servers and agents, as shown in "Authorization" on page 163 and Chapter 12.

- Set up a network of brokers or master/slave redundancy to service multiple sites or high-availability needs, as shown in "ActiveMQ Clusters" on page 113.

- Tune the middleware brokers and servers for wide area networking, or density of scale, as shown in "Large-Scale Broker Configurations" on page 118 and Chapter 12.

Soon you'll find yourself building your own custom plugins from Part III, Chapter 21, and Chapter 22 to take advantage of the global infrastructure you've built.

A year from now, you'll wonder how you ever got along without MCollective.

## PART III

Custom Plugins

In this part, we will cover how to create, test, and use custom plugins. The first thing to do is build a custom agent and client. As discussed in Chapter 5, the agent implements server-side functionality that a client can create requests for.

We'll cover how to:

- Provide new, custom requests you can make to your servers
- Make MCollective requests from a script rather than through the mco command line
- Collect registration data from your servers
- Send the results of MCollective requests to a program, instead of returning to your screen

This section is where you'll learn exactly how mutable and adaptable MCollective can be to service your needs.

 I feel that you learn much more by building the agent and applications for yourself. However, if you are having difficulty, you can download the working code using the instructions provided in Chapter 24.

## CHAPTER 15

Building an Agent

In this chapter, you will build a custom agent. You'll start with a basic template useful as a starting point for agent development. Then you'll add more functionality and test it from the mco client application.

We'll expand the basics to provide additional features and discuss different ways to work with the MCollective plugin ecosystem.

After finishing this chapter, you'll be able to take this agent template and replace just a few lines of Ruby to build a different custom agent.

SimpleRPC Framework

As we build MCollective clients and agents, we will be utilizing a set of libraries that comprise the SimpleRPC Framework. These libraries give us useful tools and handlers to simplify the tasks of communicating in the MCollective ecosystem. The SimpleRPC Framework provides conventions and standards that make it easy to work with plugins provided by others as well.

The framework isn't law. You can easily peak beneath the hood using standard Ruby commands. However, it is rarely necessary, and everything we do in this book can be done by someone with little Ruby experience.

In the SimpleRPC Framework, data is passed back and forth in hashes like so:

```
say_goodbye(
  :msg    => "So long...",
  :sender => "Dolphins"
)
```

There are a few simple rules for passing data back and forth:

- Parameters must always be in a hash.

- Parameter names can be anything you want (except `:process_results`, because this has special meaning to the agent and client).

- Parameter values can be any type your authorization plugin (if applicable) understands (e.g., string, array, hash, Boolean, etc.). The default authorization plugin understands all Ruby types.

Thankfully, these are the only rules you must know up front. Let's jump straight in and build an agent.

 If you need some help with Ruby, I've found the books *Learning Ruby* and *Ruby Pocket Reference*, both by Michael Fitzgerald (O'Reilly), to be extremely useful.

Start with a Baseline

Let's create a baseline agent to get started with. If you're a Douglas Adams fan, you might know where I'm going with this one. This is easy to understand even if you haven't read *Hitchhiker's Guide to the Galaxy* (spoiler alert: the book opens with the dolphins leaving Earth):

```
$ mco plugin generate agent thanks actions=say_goodbye
Created plugin directory : thanks
Created DDL file : thanks/agent/thanks.ddl
Created Agent file : thanks/agent/thanks.rb

$ cd thanks/agent
$ $EDITOR thanks.rb
```

You'll find a blank module in the Ruby file. Let's go ahead and flesh this out a bit. Enter in all the bolded sections in the following:

```
module MCollective
  module Agent
    class Thanks<RPC::Agent
      action "say_goodbye" do
        validate :person, String
        person = request.data[:person]

        # This will set statuscode and statusmsg fields in the reply
        reply.fail "Who should I say goodbye to?", 1 unless person != ''
        return unless reply.statuscode == 0

        delicacy = 'fish'

        format = "So long %s, and thanks for all the %s!\n"
```

```
          reply[:message] = sprintf( format, person, delicacy )
        end
      end
    end
  end
```

Here we have created an agent with a single action: say_goodbye.

In the following sections, we'll go through each part of this code and discuss what it does, and how we might have done it differently.

Validate Input

The data from the client is always stored in a Ruby Hash object accessible from re quest.data{}. The keys of the hash are of the Ruby type Symbol.

As you saw in our previous module, we received data from the client. You'll want to use these validators in your code. You always validate your input, right? Here are some of the built-in validators provided by MCollective. You place these in code as shown here, using a colon before the field name to provide the Symbol that is the key in the request object:

```
validate :message, /^[a-zA-Z]+/
validate :message, String
validate :ipaddr, :ipv4address
validate :ipaddr, :ipv6address
validate :enable, :bool
validate :mode, ["all", "packages"]
validate :commmand, :shellsafe  # do this before using data on the command line
```

You cannot pass other variables, even Symbols, into these validators. The code looks directly at the request object. validate can only be used to check input received in the request.

The validate call will throw an exception if the test fails. You should not put a rescue to catch the exception—the SimpleRPC framework will catch these and handle them.

You can create your own input validator plugins for more complex data types. We go over this later in Chapter 20.

The following table lists the fields in the message:

Property	Usage
agent	This will always be your agent's name
action	This will always be the method invoked
time	Timestamp of the message in epoch time
caller	UID/GID for the PSK security provider, cert=TLS Certificate for TLS security providers

Property	Usage
reply-to	Destination response queue. RPC::Util handles this for you
process_results	Not for you to play with

 The request object is an instance of MCollective::RPC::Request. It has some other attributes, but these are not normally useful when building your own agents.

Send Replies

As we inherited from RPC::Agent at the start of our class, we are given a reply object in which to send back our response. This object is an instance of MCollective::RPC::Reply.

In most cases, you'll want to set reply.statuscode to 0 for success or 1 for failure, but there is a complete table of valid response codes in "Results and Exceptions" on page 187.

The following function used in this agent set both the statuscode and statusmsg fields with a single function. If the statuscode was not success, it would immediately return failure:

```
reply.fail "Who should I say goodbye to?", 1 unless person != ''
return unless reply.statuscode == 0
```

If we had known positively that the request had failed, we could use the following variant to bail immediately and raise an exception:

```
reply.fail! "I can't find my towel.", 1
```

For a successful reply, we want to set the statuscode at the data of the reply appropriately:

```
reply[:message] = "So long, and thanks for all the fish!\n"
reply[:statuscode] = 0
end
```

Define an Agent DDL

In the same directory as your agent file, you'll find a very necessary component, *thanks.ddl*, which provides the Data Definition Language for your plugin. DDLs are required documentation for RPC systems, as they document how the agent uses input data and returns output. The client application also uses the DDL to validate the input before submitting the request.

Without a DDL file installed, neither the server agent nor the client application will activate.

For our example plugin, we're going to use the following DDL:

```
metadata :name        => "Thanks",
         :description => "Agent to say thanks, then grab a towel",
         :author      => "Dolphins",
         :license     => "Taken",
         :version     => "1.0",
         :url         => "www.douglasadams.com/creations/hhgg.html",
         :timeout     => 10    # how long before killing off the request

requires :mcollective => "2.5"

action "say_goodbye", :description => "Says Goodbye" do
  display :always    # could be :ok or :failed

  input :person,
        :prompt      => "Person's Name",
        :description => "The name of the person we are saying goodbye to.",
        :type        => :string,
        # could be :number, :integer, :float, :list, or :boolean
        #:list       => ["value1","value2"]  # only for type = :list
        :validation  => '^[a-zA-Z\s]+$',     # only for type = :string
        :maxlength   => 20,                  # only for type = :string
        :optional    => false,
        :default     => "Arthur"

  output :message,
         :description => "The response",
         :display_as  => "Message",
         :default     => "So long, fish, thanks!"
  end
```

The vast majority of this is obvious and easy to read. You'll need to have an action block for each action, an input block for each input desired, and an output block for each value returned. And yeah, it's a lot of typing. The good news is that this DDL is used for data validation by the client application, meaning that you aren't required to do simple input validation in the client.

Both validation and maxlength are required when using type string.

The metadata `:name` field is used by the package plugin to name the package files generated. The package plugin will take every word in the DDL Name field and lowercase and put dashes between them. If you were to put "My New Plugin" in this field and then package your plugin with `mco plugin package`, the packages would be named `mcollective-my-new-plugin-agent`, `mcollective-my-new-plugin-common`, and `mcollective-my-new- plugin-client`.

In most situations, you want only one or two words in the metadata name field.

More information about the DDL file can be found at *http://docs.puppetlabs.com/mcollective/reference/plugins/ddl.html*.

Read Config Files

What if we wanted the plugin to get input from configuration files, rather than from the client?

Within the agent, we could replace this line with the following call:

```
# Retrieve a configuration parameter
#delicacy = 'fish'
delicacy = @config.pluginconf.fetch("thanks.delicacy", 'fish')
```

You can provide configuration data to your plugin by setting key/value pairs in one of the following two files:

```
# /etc/mcollective/server.cfg
plugin.thanks.delicacy = Root Beer

# /etc/mcollective/plugin.d/thanks.cfg
delicacy = Peanuts
```

Either of these files would provide the `delicacy` config option that the dolphins were thanking us for.

You'll have to restart `mcollectived` on the server before any configuration changes are visible. Use either method from "Notify mcollectived" on page 50.

You can make up key names to read from, but both the key name and the value are strings. Due to the way the files are parsed, if you repeat a key name later in the file, the first value will be lost. In my testing, the plugin-specific configuration file always won out over an entry in the main *server.cfg* file.

 There are references on the Puppet Labs website to a *plugins.d* directory. This is a mistype or obsolete. The correct directory name is *plugin.d*.

Install Your Agent

If you are on a platform supported by the plugin packager, you can easily build a package containing your agent. You'll need your platform's package building tools (e.g., rpmbuild, build-essential, etc.) installed. You build the package with the mco plugin package command.

This is how it looks on a RedHat system:

```
$ cd path/to/thanks
$ mco plugin package
Building packages for mcollective-thanks plugin.
Completed building all packages for mcollective-thanks plugin.
$ ls -1 *.rpm
mcollective-thanks-1.0-1.el6.src.rpm
mcollective-thanks-1.0-1.src.rpm
mcollective-thanks-agent-1.0-1.el6.noarch.rpm
mcollective-thanks-agent-1.0-1.noarch.rpm
mcollective-thanks-common-1.0-1.el6.noarch.rpm
mcollective-thanks-common-1.0-1.noarch.rpm
```

If you are on a platform not yet supported by the Plugin Packager, you'll need to follow the instructions in "Installing from Source" on page 25. For most platforms, running the following commands on a server will do the job (adjust for the location of *server.cfg* and *libdir*, of course):

```
$ cd path/to/thanks/agent
$ grep libdir /etc/mcollective/server.cfg
/usr/libexec/mcollective
$ sudo cp -i thanks.rb thanks.ddl /usr/libexec/mcollective/mcollective/agent/
$ sudo service mcollective restart
```

Testing the Agent

Now that you have built and installed the agent, you can invoke the agent directly from the mco command line using direct RPC calls:

```
$ mco rpc thanks say_goodbye --person="Jack"
Determining the amount of hosts matching filter for 2 seconds .... 1
```

```
geode                              : OK
    "So long Arthur, and thanks for all the fish!"
```

You'll notice that only the server on which you installed the new agent will respond. This is implicit filtering—only servers that have a given agent installed will process requests for that agent.

If you recall the ActiveMQ topic setup, you'll understand how this works. Each agent subscribes to a topic named *collective.agent name*.agent. In our test, this would be the mcollective.thanks.agent topic. Only the servers with this custom agent installed will subscribe to this topic; no other server will receive the request.

Now we should test that data validation worked. Our validation setting only allowed letters and spaces, no numbers. Let's see what happens when we give it invalid input:

```
$ mco rpc thanks say_goodbye --person="Jack0" -I geode
 * [ ============================================================> ] 1 / 1

geode                                    Invalid Request Data
    Cannot validate input person: value should match ^[A-Za-z\s]+$

Finished processing 1 / 1 hosts in 85.02 ms
```

What if we don't supply a value at all?

```
$ mco rpc thanks say_goodbye -I geode
 * [ ============================================================> ] 1 / 1

geode
      Message: So long Arthur, and thanks for all the fish!

Finished processing 1 / 1 hosts in 85.02 ms
```

Why did it accept that? Didn't we say that person was required input? This is due to two things:

- We aren't yet using an application to enforce data input.
- The DDL provides a default value.

If you edit the DDL and remove the default value, you'll get this instead:

```
$ mco rpc thanks say_goodbye -I geode
The rpc application failed to run, use -v for full error backtrace
  details: Action say_goodbye needs a person argument
```

## CHAPTER 16

Extending the Agent

Here we'll introduce you to more complex things you can do in your agent. There isn't a use for this functionality in our `thanks` plugin just yet, but it's good to know what is possible.

We'll give it the ability to execute external scripts or command lines; how to send custom log lines; and best of all, we'll review how to blow up tragically, er, I mean error out gracefully. *Of course.*

Executing Scripts

You can call any external script, written in any programming language (including bash) that is capable of writing out the results to a file in JSON format:

```
action "python_script" do
  implemented_by "/lovely/little/python/script.py"
end
```

The script will be given two types of input:

- A path to the file containing the request data in JSON format:
  - The first command-line parameter
  - Environment variable $MCOLLECTIVE_REQUEST_FILE
- A path to the file where the response should be written in JSON format:
  - The second command-line parameter
  - Environment variable $MCOLLECTIVE_REPLY_FILE

The script should write the reply as a JSON hash into the reply file. The return code of your script should be one of the standard result codes from the table in "Results and Exceptions" on page 187.

If you do not specify a full path to the script, it will look for the script in the agent's *plugin* directory. This makes it easy to bundle your scripts in with your agent plugins:

```
action "bundled_script" do
  implemented_by "bundled_script.py"
end

Location:
  $libdir/agent/agentname/bundled_script.py
```

Executing Commands

MCollective provides a `run` function that makes it easy to execute command-line scripts and access their STDOUT and STDERR. It's significantly smarter and more useful than Ruby's basic `system()` call and plays well with `mcollectived`. The simplest form of usage is to run a command and dump the output back in the response:

```
hostinput = shellescape(request[:hostname])
reply[:status] = run(
  "grep " + hostinput + " /etc/hosts",
  :stdout => :out,
  :stderr => :err
)
return reply
```

The `run` command has extensive options to set the working directory, to alter the environment, and to remain trailing whitespace. Shown here is a much more extensive example, which uses a command that will retrieve details from the local keyStore file created in "CA-Verified TLS Servers" on page 132:

```
output = []
errors = ""
rcode = run(
  "sudo keytool -list -keystore keystore.jks",
  :stdout => output, :stderr => errors,
  :chomp => true, :cwd => "/etc/mcollective/ssl",
  :environment => {"MCOLLECTIVE_SSL_PUBLIC" => "/etc/mcollective/ssl"}
)
...from here we can process the output[] array...
```

As `output` is an array, each line of STDOUT will create a new member of the array. Each line of STDERR will be appended to the string `errors`.

Accessing Facts, Agents, and Classes

Your agent may want to access configuration information known to the server already. For example, you may want to access a fact known to the server. You won't need to know how facts are supplied to mcollectived, nor acquire them yourself. You can simply access them in your current namespace:

```
# Access the OS family
os_type = Facts['osfamily']

# Util library provides a library with comparisons
#  supports: '>=', '>=', '>', '>', '!=', '==', and '=~'
if Util.has_fact('osfamily', 'Debian', '==') {
  if Util.has_fact('kernelmajversion', '3.1', '>-') {
    # do things appropriate for modern Debian kernels
  }
}
```

Likewise, the agents plugin provides useful helper methods for determining which agents are installed:

```
# I'd like a list of all agents
array = Agents.agentlist

# These are the same
if Agents.include?("puppet") {
if Util.has_agent?("puppet") {
```

And finally, you can use another Util helper to find out if the Puppet manifest for a server includes a class:

```
if Util.has_cf_class?("webserver") {
  # do spidery things
}
```

Results and Exceptions

The classes and functions within your plugin should always exit with a response code listed in the following table so that the appropriate exception handler can process the result:

Status code	Description	RPCError exception class
0	Success	1
Input was valid, but the action could not be completed	RPCAborted	2
Unknown action	UnknownRPCAction	3
Missing data	MissingRPCData	4
Invalid data	InvalidRPCData	5

When calling functions or classes, you will receive either an exception or a result code. Here is a simple way of handling an error from the agent we built earlier:

```
mc.say_goodbye(:person => "Arthur") do |resp, simpleresp|
   begin
      printrpc simpleresp
   rescue RPCError => e
      puts "Your request resulted in error: #{e}"
   end
end
```

Logging

When you are debugging issues with your agent, you will find it useful to have logs from your agent. As a matter of practice, I sprinkle debugging statements throughout my code to ease the discovery process later. You can call any of the standard logging levels using the Log class:

```
Log.debug("You passed me input:" + )
Log.notice("This value " + input + " isn't valid for the Goodbye function.")
Log.fatal("I blew up!")
```

## CHAPTER 17

Creating a Client Application

We've done a bit of testing with the agent, doing direct RPCUtil queries against it. That's a bit long of a command isn't it? And look at all that messy RPCUtil output.

Why don't we build a proper client plugin to interface with our new agent?

Baseline Client

Unfortunately, there's no easy command to generate a template for us, so we'll just have to do this ourselves. This application will be *thanks/application/thanks.rb*. Assuming you are still inside the *thanks/agent/* directory from earlier:

```
$ mkdir ../application
$ cd ../application
$ $EDITOR thanks.rb
```

Now let's populate the file like so (you can find this file in the source code supplied with the book):

```
class MCollective::Application::Thanks<MCollective::Application
  description "Sends a thanks message."
  usage "mco thanks [OPTIONS]"

  # This options parser updates the help page
  option :person,
       :description => "The person the dolphins say Goodbye to.",
       :arguments   => ["-p NAME", "--person NAME"],
       :type        => String,
       :require     => true

  # another hook where we could throw exceptions if the input isn't valid
  def validate_configuration(configuration)
    # this shouldn't happen since the option is mandatory above
    raise "Need to supply a person to get a reply." \
```

```
      unless configuration.include?(:person)
    end

    # Now we enter main processing
    def main
     client = rpcclient("thanks")
      printrpc client.say_goodbye(
        :person => configuration[:person],
        :options => options
      )

      # Exit using halt and it will pass on the appropriate exit code
      printrpcstats
      halt client.stats
    end
  end
end
```

You may want to disable some of the standard command-line options. If you put one of the following lines inside the class, they will disable the relevant input options:

```
exclude_argument_sections "rpc"                # disables direct rpc calls
exclude_argument_sections "common", "filter" # limits filtering and discovery
```

The application will always have the -help, -verbose, and -config options no matter what you disable.

Client Filters

Your client can be passed filters with the normal command-line clients, or it can define filters itself based on other input. Following are some examples of defining filters for a request that you could put inside the main block of the client code.

Servers named web followed by a digit:

```
client.identity_filter "/web\d/"
```

Servers running Debian Linux or its derivatives (e.g., Ubuntu):

```
client.fact_filter "osfamily=Debian"
```

Servers with the Puppet class apache defined:

```
client.class_filter /apache/
```

Servers with less than four processor cores:

```
client.fact_filter "processorcount", "4", "<"
```

Reset all filters:

```
client.reset_filter
```

If you change filters, you may want to reset so that discovery is re-run:

```
client.class_filter /apache/
client.reset
client.fact_filter "osfamily=Debian"
```

If your script already knows which nodes it wants, you can disable discovery. This obviously won't work in combination with any filters:

```
client.discover(:nodes => ["host1", "host2"])
```

You may also want to limit how many servers execute the command or how many do it concurrently, without making the CLI user specify this. Here's an example that will set limit the targets to 30% of those that match the filter:

```
client.limit_targets = "30%"
client.limit_method = :random
```

This will limit the targets to a random set of 20 servers that match the filter:

```
client.limit_targets = "20"
client.limit_method = :first
```

This will set batch control so that only five process any request from this client at one time:

```
client.batch_size = 5
client.batch_sleep_time = 5
```

This will disable batch control for a single request:

```
client = rpcclient("thanks")
printrpc client.say_goodbye(:person => configuration[:person], :batch_size => 0)
```

Results and Exceptions

The application should exit using the `halt` handler like so:

```
halt client.stats
```

This `halt` handler will output result codes according to the following table:

Status code	Description
0	Nodes were discovered and all passed
0	No discovery was done but responses were received
1	No nodes were discovered
2	Nodes were discovered but some responses failed
3	Nodes were discovered but no responses were received
4	No discovery were done and no responses were received

When calling functions or classes, you will receive either an exception or a result code. Here is a simple way of handling an error from the agent we built earlier:

```
client.say_goodbye(:person => "Arthur") do |resp, simpleresp|
   begin
      printrpc simpleresp
   rescue RPCError => e
      puts "Your request resulted in error: #{e}"
   end
   halt client.stats
end
```

Install Your Client

If you are on a platform supported by the Plugin Packager, you can easily build the packages containing both your agent and the client. This is how it looks on a RedHat system:

```
$ cd path/to/thanks
$ mco plugin package
Building packages for mcollective-thanks plugin.
Completed building all packages for mcollective-thanks plugin.
$ ls -1 *.rpm
mcollective-thanks-1.0-1.src.rpm
mcollective-thanks-agent-1.0-1.noarch.rpm
mcollective-thanks-client-1.0-1.noarch.rpm
mcollective-thanks-common-1.0-1.noarch.rpm
```

If you are on a platform not yet supported by the Plugin Packager, you'll need to follow the instructions in "Installing from Source" on page 25. For most platforms, installing the client involves running the following commands (adjust for the location of *client.cfg* and *libdir*, of course):

```
$ grep libdir
$ cd /usr/libexec/mcollective/mcollective
$ sudo cp -i /path/to/thanks/agent/thanks.ddl agent/
$ sudo cp -i /path/to/thanks/application/thanks.rb application/
```

And finally, we can use the client we have made:

```
$ mco help thanks

Sends a thanks message.
Usage: mco thanks [OPTIONS]

Application Options
    -p, --person NAME                    The person the dolphins say Goodbye to.

all the standard options

$ mco thanks --person=Arthur -I geode
```

```
  * [ ===============================================> ] 1 / 1
geode
    Message: So long Arthur, and thanks for all the fish!

Finished processing 1 / 1 hosts in 60.99 ms
```

## CHAPTER 18

Processing Multiple Actions

In this chapter, we're going to expand our agent and client to handle multiple distinct actions. This adds just one small layer on what you already know, but it provides you great flexibility in how you build and package your agents going forward.

Recalling what you learned in Chapter 15, go back and open up *thanks/agent/ thanks.rb* to add another action. Let's call this new action get_towel. Add it just after the very first end so it will remain inside the Thanks class. You can put anything you want in this new action (just remember to set a message and a statuscode):

```
module MCollective
  module Agent
    class Thanks<RPC::Agent
      action "say_goodbye" do
        blah blah blah
      end
      action "get_towel" do
        something amazing
      end
    end
  end
end
```

Next, we need to update the DDL file to know about the new action. Do yourself a favor and copy/paste the entire action block for *say_goodbye* and then edit the title. Change your input and output for whatever amazing thing you've done with the get_towel action:

```
action "say_goodbye", :description => "Says Goodbye" do
  blah blah blah
end

action "get_towel", :description => "Grabs Towel" do
  display :always   # could be :ok or :failed
```

```
      input :color,
            :prompt      => "Which color towel to grab",
      amazing inputs
    end
```

That was all pretty easy, right? Now let's get dirty with the only nontrivial bit of supporting multiple actions, which is adding multiaction smarts into your application. Open up the *thanks/application/thanks.rb* file and make the following changes:

1. Add documentation of the two distinct actions.

2. Use a post_option_parser to read the action from the arguments.

3. Use Ruby send() method to invoke the correct action.

Update the application file with the bolded lines shown here:

```
class MCollective::Application::Thanks<MCollective::Application
  description "Sends a thanks message before grabbing a towel."
  usage "mco thanks [ACTION] [OPTIONS]"
  usage "ACTION: is one of 'say_goodbye' or 'get_towel'"

  # This options parser updates the help page
  option :person,
         :description => "The person the dolphins say Goodbye to.",
         :arguments   => ["-p NAME", "--person NAME"],
         :type        => String,
         :require     => true

  # this is a hook called right after option parsing
  # values from the options are stored in configuration hash
  def post_option_parser(configuration)
    # action should be the first argument
    if ARGV.length >= 1
      configuration[:action] = ARGV.shift
    end

    raise "Action must be say_goodbye or get_towel" \
      unless ["say_goodbye", "get_towel"].include?(configuration[:action])
  end

  # another hook where we could throw exceptions if the input isn't valid
  def validate_configuration(configuration)
    # this shouldn't happen since the option is mandatory above
    raise "Need to supply a person to get a reply." \
      unless configuration.include?(:person)
  end

  # Now we enter main processing
  def main
   client = rpcclient("thanks")
    printrpc client.send(
```

```
    configuration[:action], # First text string becomes method invoked...
    :person => configuration[:person],
    :options => options
)

# Exit using halt and it will pass on the appropriate exit code
printrpcstats
halt client.stats
  end
end
```

send() is a special Ruby method common to all Ruby objects. It allows you to specify the method to be called by placing a symbol or text string naming the method as the first parameter. This invokes either client.say_goodbye() or client.get_towel() depending on the value of configuration[:action]. I think you can see how easy it will be to add a third or fourth action.

Now we can use the client we have made:

```
$ mco help thanks

Sends a thanks message before grabbing a towel.

Usage: mco thanks [ACTION] [OPTIONS]
Usage: ACTION: is one of 'say_goodbye' or 'get_towel'

Application Options
    -p, --person NAME                 The person the dolphins say Goodbye to.

all the standard options

$ mco thanks

The thanks application failed to run, use -v for full error backtrace
  details: Action must be say_goodbye or get_towel

$ mco thanks thanks get_towel --color=blue -I geode

 * [ ================================================> ] 1 / 1

geode
   Message: I got the blue towel. Seeya Arthur!

Finished processing 1 / 1 hosts in 58.22 ms
```

## CHAPTER 19

Making a Standalone Client

In Chapter 15, we documented how to build an `agent` and in Chapter 17 how to build an `application` to extend the built-in `mco` command. Although that is useful for sending requests interactively or in a small shell script, it may not meet your needs for programatic usage.

Baseline Client Program

You can build stand-alone Ruby scripts that utilize the same client libraries. The structure for these scripts is very similar, and you can use every option shown in the previous sections. Let's walk you through an example here:

```ruby
#!/usr/bin/ruby
require 'mcollective'
include MCollective::RPC

options = rpcoptions do |parser, options|
  parser.define_head "Script for the Thanks agent"
  parser.banner = "Usage: thanks.rb [options] person"

  parser.on('-p', '--person NAME', 'Person to say goodbye to.') do |name|
    options[:person] = name
  end
end

# This is probably covered by the validation in the DDL
unless options.include?(:person)
  puts("You need to specify a person's name with --person")
  exit! 1
end

# Create an MCollective client utilizing our agent
client = rpcclient("thanks", :options => options)
```

```
# Enable to see discovery results
#client.discover :verbose => true

# To disable the progress indicator
#client.progress = false

# Two different ways to get results
# 1. Simple verbose output
printrpc client.say_goodbye(:person => options[:person]), :verbose => true

# 2. Format the output as you like
#client.say_goodbye(:person => options[:person]).each do |resp|
#       printf("%-20s: %s\n", resp[:sender], resp[:data][:message])
#end

## Three different ways to report statistics
# 1. Simple one-command
printrpcstats

# 2. More explicit module methods (same output as #1)
#print client.stats.report + "\n"

# 3. Directly access the RPC results
# read $rubysitelib/mcollective/rpc/stats.rb for more details
#print client.stats.no_response_report # only nodes which didn't respond
#results = client.stats.to_hash        # hash of statistics

# Play nice
client.disconnect
```

Running Your Program

By using the `rpcoptions` function provided by the `MCollective::RPC` library, the program gains a command-line parser and help text.

We can test that it works as shown here:

```
$ ./thanks.rb --help
Usage: thanks.rb [options] --person NAME
Script for the Thanks agent
    -p, --person NAME                  Name of the person to say goodbye to.

$ ./thanks.rb --person=Arthur
Determining the amount of hosts matching filter for 2 seconds...

* [ ================================================> ] 1 / 1

geode                                 : OK
    {:message=>"So long Arthur, and thanks for all the fish!\n"}

Finished processing 1 / 1 hosts in 32.13 ms
```

For greater flexibility in the output display, try any of the normal filters available to you with mco command line:

```
$ ./thanks.rb --person Arthur --target asia
$ ./thanks.rb --person Ford --with-fact osfamily=Debian
$ ./thanks.rb --person Trillian -I heliotrope
```

Try commenting out the printrpc function and use the formatted printf block to output the results instead.

You can read more about SimpleRPC clients at *http://docs.puppetlabs.com/mcollective/simplerpc/clients.html*

## CHAPTER 20

Creating Other Plugins

MCollective allows you to create plugins to replace or enhance much of the built-in functionality. This chapter covers most of the plugin types, where you can find examples to get you started, and the subdirectory where you should place your newly created plugins.

For example, if you are creating an auditing plugin, you would take these steps:

```
$ mco plugin generate agent myagent actions=myfunction
Created plugin directory : myagent
Created DDL file : myagent/agent/myfunction.ddl
Created Agent file : myagent/agent/myfunction.rb

$ cd myagent
$ mkdir audit
$ $EDITOR audit/myaudit.rb
```

Table 20-1 shows a list of all the plugin types, and which directory underneath *myagent/* you should put the file you create. We already discussed the first two (agent and application) in Chapter 5.

Table 20-1. MCollective plugin types

Plugin type	Documentation	Subdirectory
Server agent	*http://docs.puppetlabs.com/mcollective/simplerpc/agents.html*	*agent*
Client	*http://docs.puppetlabs.com/mcollective/reference/plugins/application.html*	*application*
Data plugin	*http://docs.puppetlabs.com/mcollective/reference/plugins/data.html*	*data*
Fact plugin	*http://docs.puppetlabs.com/mcollective/reference/plugins/facts.html*	*facts*
Auditing	*http://docs.puppetlabs.com/mcollective/simplerpc/auditing.html*	*audit*
Validator	*http://docs.puppetlabs.com/mcollective/reference/plugins/validator.html*	*validator*
Discovery	*http://docs.puppetlabs.com/mcollective/reference/plugins/discovery.html*	*discovery*

Plugin type	Documentation	Subdirectory
Connector	*http://docs.puppetlabs.com/mcollective/simplerpc/authorization.html*	*connector*
Registration	*http://docs.puppetlabs.com/mcollective/reference/plugins/registration.html*	*registration*
Aggregate	*http://docs.puppetlabs.com/mcollective/reference/plugins/aggregate.html*	*aggregate*
Authorization	*http://docs.puppetlabs.com/mcollective/simplerpc/authorization.html*	*util*
Security	*http://docs.puppetlabs.com/mcollective/reference/basic/messageformat.html*	*security*
Util	A place to put shared code to be used by other modules	*util*

Authorization Plugins

Notice that authorization plugins don't have their own directory. As they are shared by many applications, they should be installed in the *util* directory.[1]

Because of the special directory needs, `mco plugin package` will not build packages for authorization plugins.

Facts Plugins

If you create a facts plugin, it should be named *myagent*_facts. After installing it on the server, alter the server configuration `param factsource` to the name of your fact plugin in lowercase with the _facts suffix trimmed off:

```
factsource = myagent
fact_cache_time = 300
```

The `fact_cache_time` parameter allows you to tune how often the facts are retrieved from the plugin. If the cost of retrieving the facts is high, you may want to tune this considerably higher. Tuning this lower than five minutes is not generally recommended.

---

1 Puppet bug MCO-86 (*https://tickets.puppetlabs.com/browse/MCO-86*) proposes to give them their own directory.

## CHAPTER 21

Processing Registration Data

Registration is a process where an agent on the server sends out a message on to the `collective.registration.agent` topic every `registerinterval` period. The default registration agent AgentList sends out a list of the MCollective agents installed and running in `mcollectived`.

In a default installation, every server publishes these registration messages, but no listener subscribes to them. I believe the original use was intended to simply keep the TCP connection alive in the presence of connection-tracking firewalls. Now that this is handled by the `heartbeat` support in STOMP 1.1+ protocol, registration ... well, it has found its own reason to live.

Many people have started doing useful things with the registration agent. Let's show you how to build your own agent and your own collector to grab that data and do something with it.

Registration Agent

If you were to look at the default registration agent in your *libdir* directory, you'd be amazed at how simple it is:

```
$ cat /usr/libexec/mcollective/mcollective/registration/agentlist.rb
module MCollective
  module Registration
    # A registration plugin that simply sends in the list of agents we have
    class Agentlist<Base
      def body
        Agents.agentlist
      end
    end
  end
end
```

Yeah, it is simple. The module should subclass `MCollective::Registration::Base`. Define a body method which returns anything you want, and that data is sent out to the *collective*.`registration.agent` topic for you. You can make the data as complex or as simple as meets your needs. Remember that by default, nothing reads what this agent publishes.

If you send the value `nil`, then no message will be sent out.

R.I. Pienaar wrote a registration plugin that supplies not just the installed agents, but also the identity, facts, collectives, and Puppet classes. You can find that at *https:// github.com/puppetlabs/mcollective-plugins/blob/master/registration/meta.rb*.

At one site where we wanted to reduce the registration traffic, we added a registration agent that only sent the hostname:

```
$ cat /usr/libexec/mcollective/mcollective/registration/hostname.rb
module MCollective
  module Registration
    # A registration plugin that simply sends the hostname
    class Hostname<Base
      require 'socket'
      def body
        Socket.gethostname
      end
    end
  end
end
```

Then we changed the server configuration to only send the registration data every hour:

```
registerinterval = 3600
registration = Hostname
registration_collective = mcollective
```

Notice the `registration_collective` parameter there. We haven't talked about this before now. If you have localized traffic, as we have suggested in "Localizing Traffic" on page 145, you may want to put registration traffic on either its own collective or on a global collective distinct from what your primary collective is set to. It depends on what your needs are and where your listeners are expecting to receive this information.

Registration Collector

Collecting responses is nothing more than listening to registration information published on the *collectivename*.`registration.agent` topic. Better yet, you don't have to know how to write a topic subscriber in Ruby. Simply create an MCollective agent named registration. Store the registration collector in the file *libdir/mcollective/agent/*

---

registration.rb. Here is a simple registration agent that logs the sender and the time that the sender sent the message:

```
$ cat /usr/libexec/mcollective/mcollective/registration/registration.rb
module MCollective
  module Agent
    class Registration
      attr_reader :timeout, :meta

      require 'time'
      def initialize
      @timeout = 1

      @config = Config.instance

      @meta = {:license => "GPLv2",
         :author => "Jo Rhett <jrhett@netconsonance.com>",
         :url => "http://shop.oreilly.com/product/0636920032472.do"}
      end

      def handlemsg(message, connection)
        remotetime = Time.at( message[:msgtime] )
        Log.info("server " + message[:senderid] \
             + " sent registration with timestamp " + remotetime.to_s)

        return nil
      end

      def help
        <<-END
LogOnly Registration Agent
==========================

A simple registration agent that writes out one log line for each server
that it receives a registration message from.
END
      end
    end
  end
end
```

How can you tell if your agent is running? Check the debug logs. If the agent has a syntax error, you might get an error:

```
E, [2014-02-26T02:37:06.633580 #18327] ERROR -- : pluginmanager.rb:171:in
  `loadclass' Failed to load MCollective::Agent::Registration:
  /usr/libexec/mcollective/mcollective/agent/registration.rb:19: syntax error,
  unexpected ')', expecting ']'
E, [2014-02-26T02:37:06.633680 #18327] ERROR -- : agents.rb:71:in `loadagent'
  Loading agent registration failed: /usr/libexec/mcollective/mcollective/agent
  /registration.rb:19: syntax error, unexpected ')', expecting ']'
```

But in most circumstances, all the information is at Debug level only:

```
D, [2014-02-26T02:03:40.338394 #14902] DEBUG -- : agents.rb:104:in `findagentfile'
Found registration at /usr/libexec/mcollective/mcollective/agent/registration.rb
D, [2014-02-26T02:03:40.338512 #14902] DEBUG -- : pluginmanager.rb:167:in
`loadclass' Loading MCollective::Agent::Registration from mcollective/agent/
registration.rb D, [2014-02-26T02:03:40.338809 #14902] DEBUG -- : agents.rb:91:in
`activate_agent?' MCollective::Agent::Registration does not have an activate?
method, activating as default D, [2014-02-26T02:03:40.338915 #14902] DEBUG -- :
pluginmanager.rb:44:in `<<' Registering plugin registration_agent with class
MCollective::Agent::Registration single_instance: true D, [2014-02-26T02:03:40.
339014#14902] DEBUG -- : pluginmanager.rb:80:in `[]' Returning new plugin
registration_agent with class MCollective::Agent::Registration D,
[2014-02-26T02:03:40.339281 #14902] DEBUG -- : activemq.rb:373:in `subscribe'
Subscribing to /topic/mcollective.registration.agent with headers {}
```

If you are using the plugin shown earlier, you'll have messages like this in your logs:

```
I, [2014-02-26T02:39:03.832903 #18421]  INFO -- : registration.rb:20:in
`handlemsg' server geode sent us registration with timestamp Wed Feb 26
02:39:03 -0800 2014 I, [2014-02-26T02:39:21.333663 #18421]  INFO -- :
registration.rb:20:in `handlemsg' server sunstone sent us registration with
timestamp Wed Feb 26 02:39:21 -0800 2014
```

As your registration listener must be named `Registration`, you can only have one per system. However, as servers send their registration messages to a topic and not a queue, you can have multiple registration listeners in your collective.

One listener might update a database, for example, while a different listener populates a Memcache or Solr array. As there can be significant amounts of registration traffic, it is best to keep each registration listener small and fast.

Registration and SSL Security

If you are using SSL or AES security plugins, you may have a problem collecting registration data. The registration messages will be encoded with the server's private key. `mcollectived` won't accept the messages because they will fail validation:

```
W, [2014-02-26T02:17:14.203519 #15732]  WARN -- : aes_security.rb:119:in
`decodemsg' Could not decrypt message from client: RuntimeError: Could not find
key /etc/mcollective/ssl/clients/heliotrope.example.net.pem
W, [2014-02-26T02:17:14.203645 #15732]  WARN -- : runner.rb:78:in `run' Failed
to handle message: Could not decrypt message -
MCollective::SecurityValidationFailed
```

What this means is that in addition to synchronizing every valid client's public key out to each server, you will also need to synchronize every server's public key into the */etc/mcollective/ssl/clients* directory on the server listening for registration data.

If you are using the Puppet module provided with this book, you can put the collection of server keys into the *${modulepath}/mcollective/files/ssl/clients* directory and they will be synchronized to every host. However, the method of collecting all the server keys is left as an exercise for the reader.

## CHAPTER 22

Collecting Responses

One of the features that makes MCollective truly unique is the ability to send requests from one client and to process the responses with a different client or listener, as shown in Figure 22-1.

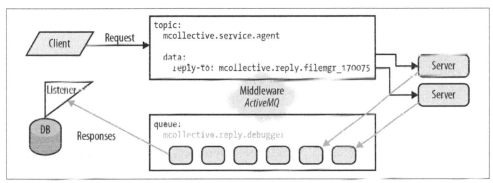

Figure 22-1. A separate listener to process results from requests

Create a Listener

The first thing we'll do here is to create a listener. What I'll introduce to you here is a working listener from which you can debug any problem. You can also copy it and add new functionality. I put my listeners in the *$libdir* directory just like every other plugin, but that's not required:

```
$ cat /usr/libexec/mcollective/mcollective/listener/debugger.rb
# Parse options, load config, and start an MCollective client.
require 'mcollective'
optparser = MCollective::Optionparser.new
options = optparser.parse
config = MCollective::Config.instance
```

```
config.loadconfig(options[:config])
MCollective::PluginManager["security_plugin"].initiated_by = :client
connector = MCollective::PluginManager['connector_plugin']
connector.connect

# Get pretty-print and the Log object
require 'pp'
Log = MCollective::Log

# Get a reply queue name from command line, default to "debugger"
replyqueue = ARGV[0] || 'debugger'
queuename = '/queue/mcollective.reply.' + replyqueue

# Subscribe to the queue
connector.connection.subscribe( queuename, {}, "$$".to_i )

# consume all the items in the queue...
loop do
  # Get an mcollective Message object and configure it as a reply
  message = connector.receive
  message.type = :reply
  message.decode!          # security plugin validates authentication

  # This is the real data, everything else is envelope
  data = message.payload[:body][:data]

  # Debug output showing the data received
  pp data[:text]
end
```

Submit reply-to

Now that we have a listener to process the output, let's send some requests to place responses in the queue:

```
$ mco rpc --agent service --action status --argument service=puppet \
  --reply-to=/queue/mcollective.reply.debugger
Request sent with id: 12afa18ae2105390a73302967edddab8 replies to
/queue/mcollective.reply.debugger
```

 Most applications do not provide the reply-to functionality. You must use the RPC invocation of the agent to get this useful response back from the application.[1]

---

1 Improvement request filed at Puppet Labs BUG MCO-207 (*https://tickets.puppetlabs.com/browse/MCO-207*) for generalized support of this feature.

Using a client application with the --reply-to option often produces the following error message:

```
$ mco puppet status --reply-to /queue/mcollective.reply.debugger

The mco application failed to run, use -v for full error backtrace details:
undefined method 'length' for nil:NilClass

$ mco ping --reply-to /queue/mcollective.reply.debugger

---- ping statistics ----
No responses received
```

You'll notice that ping claims no responses. That's because it's a simple application, and you didn't realize you sent the result elsewhere. Ping also has a different response format, which we will discuss in the next section.

Both of those commands will work—you'll receive the results on your response queue. But mco will produce the error message and return a failure response code. To receive back your request ID as shown earlier, you must invoke the agent using the direct RPC method as shown at the top.

Another way to submit reply-to requests is directly from a standalone Ruby program. In your program, add the following line to have the results sent to a reply queue rather than being processed in your application. To refer back to the example we created in the previous section, you would add the following lines:

```
# Create an MCollective client utilizing our agent
client = rpcclient("thanks", :options => options)

# Optionally send results to a reply queue
if options.include?(:reply_to)
  client.reply_to = options[:reply_to]
end
```

 The standard command-line option is --reply-to, but the option is stored in reply_to.

When reply_to is set, the application won't receive any data back from the client invocation. You'll want to modify the program to deal with that scenario, too:

```
# we don't get any data back if results go to a queue
if options.include?(:reply_to)
  client.say_goodbye(:person => options[:person])
else
  # Format the output
  client.say_goodbye(:person => options[:person]).each do |resp|
```

```
            printf("%-10s: %s\n", resp[:sender], resp[:data][:message])
        end
    end
```

Process Responses

Let's look at the results we receive. We're expecting the hostname, agent, statusmessage, and a pretty-print output of the body:

```
$ ruby debugger.rb
geode/service: OK=0
{:status=>"running"}
sunstone/service: OK=0
{:status=>"running"}
heliotrope/service: OK=0
{:status=>"running"}
```

Yup, that's exactly what we got. Now what about if we send it ping status? Ping is a minimal test that doesn't include status messages. That's the bottom part of the if/then in the previous code block. For this situation, output only the hostname and the body text:

```
$ ruby debugger.rb
ruby listen.rb
geode: "pong"
fireagate: "pong"
heliotrope: "pong"
sunstone: "pong"
```

How about if we do something with more data in the fields, like mco puppet status?

```
geode/puppet: OK=0
{:daemon_present=>true,
 :status=>"idling",
 :enabled=>true,
 :message=>"Currently idling; last completed run 26 minutes 23 seconds ago",
 :idling=>true,
 :applying=>false,
 :lastrun=>1393571918,
 :disable_message=>"",
 :since_lastrun=>1583}
heliotrope/puppet: OK=0
...etc
```

As you can see, there are considerably more fields available to use in your output.

What if you want to see all the gory details? You might want to try adding one of the follow pretty-print commands. Each one of these is a little further inside the reply message, so you only need one of them. Looking at this output is an exercise for the reader: you'll get to see a lot more of how a reply message is structured:

```
# Only use one of these, as each includes the ones beneath it.
# All the gory details
#pp message

# Everything we care about is here
#pp message.payload

# This contains just the data in the response
pp message.payload[:body]
```

How might you use this data? There's no limit, really. Anything you can do in Ruby. Here's a short list:

- Store it in NoSQL like Memcache, Mongo, or Hadoop.
- Store it in a database (better keep that connection open for speed).
- Store it in a file.
- Submit it to another system using a REST API.

I think you get the idea. Even the sky is not the limit—I hear that most satellites support RESTful APIs these days.

## CHAPTER 23

Running MCollective Without Root

It is possible and even recommended to run the MCollective server as a normal user account. The init script installed with the package can't handle this scenario, and some agents won't be able to complete some actions without root privileges. However, if you have a custom agent that manages an application running under a different user ID, this is the best way to ensure all actions are taken as the appropriate user.

Creating a user-specific MCollective server is as easy as this:

```
$ cp /etc/mcollective/server.cfg ~/.mcollective.d/server.cfg
$ echo "identify = special-application" >> ~/.mcollective.d/server.cfg
$ sed -i -e "s/var\/log/homedir\/.mcollective.d/" ~/.mcollective.d/server.cfg
$ /usr/sbin/mcollectived --pid=~/.mcollective.d/pid \
  --config=~/.mcollective.d/server.cfg
```

This mcollectived server will run without difficulties on the same node as the central server running as root. You can safely run dozens or even hundreds of non-root mcollectived servers on the same node.

Obviously this example does not handle every possible scenario:

- You'll need to create a startup script for this user-specific invocation.
- You may need to edit the configuration file to point at user-specific SSL keys used for authentication (depending on which security provider you are configured to use).

I believe this is the easiest way to limit user control to actions appropriate for an account and to ensure that all actions are running under the appropriate user rights. I use nonroot MCollective daemons whenever possible.

## CHAPTER 24

Downloading the Code

In my experience, you learn much more by building the agent and applications for yourself. However, if you are having difficulty, you can download the fully working code for all of my examples from the GitHub repo for the book, at the *Learning MCollective* book reference repository (*https://github.com/jorhett/learning-mcollective*).

You can find the thanks agent and application at *https://github.com/jorhett/learning-mcollective/tree/master/examples/thanks*.

You can find the registration agent and processor at *https://github.com/jorhett/learning-mcollective/tree/master/examples/registration*.

You can find the *debugger* response collector at *https://github.com/jorhett/learning-mcollective/tree/master/examples/listen*.

The code here is in production use at a number of sites. If you find any problems, create an issue in the Github repository with details of your concern.

## PART IV

Putting It All Together

At this point, you have learned about every technical aspect of MCollective. In Part I, you did the following:

- Built a working installation of MCollective you can learn from.
- Installed agent plugins to provide functionality in the MCollective servers.
- Used the mco client application to issue requests to the agents.
- Took control of the Puppet agent using the runonce and runall requests.

In Part II, you learned to do the following:

- Tune parameters on ActiveMQ, which can benefit an MCollective installation.
- Use TLS to encrypt communications between the nodes and the broker.
- Ensure the validity of requests using strong cryptography to prevent tampering.
- Limit the requests which a client can make to specific servers or agents.

In Part III, you built the following:

- A server agent to say "thanks" and "goodbye" based on configurable options.
- A client application to extend the mco command to speak with your agent.
- A standalone Ruby script to utilize the agent.
- A registration agent to supply custom details in the registration messages.
- A debugging tool to listen on reply queues and display the information received.

## CHAPTER 25

Use Best Practices

In the final chapter of the book, I'm going to share some thoughts and recommendations for how to make the best use of MCollective.

Make Use of Configuration Management

It is certainly possible to use MCollective to maintain the configuration of software. I have used MCollective to distribute configuration files for MCollective servers. However, I prefer to use tools for what they are best at.

Configuration management is best done by tools focused on ensuring consistency across nodes. Configuration-management agents like Puppet, Chef, and others are well suited for this effort. You express the desired state of the system through the configuration management tool of your choice, and it will ensure that all nodes are synced. In particular, Puppet has modules and Chef has cookbooks intended to manage the MCollective configuration on nodes.

MCollective is best used for requests to gather information or make a change simultaneously on tens, hundreds, or thousands of nodes. None of the configuration-management systems[1] are designed to make thousands of servers process a simple request in a few seconds.

It requires a lot of coding to make MCollective agents that can effectively manage configurations. Likewise, you'll find it difficult to use configuration management to orchestrate fast action across many systems. MCollective and configuration management are two different tools that extend and enhance each other's abilities.

---

1 Some configuration management plugins can provide orchestration functionality on a limited basis.

Use each tool for what it is best at.

Use Puppet, Chef, or another configuration management tool to maintain the MCollective configuration. You can fix a broken MCollective server with configuration management, and you can fix a broken configuration management agent with MCollective—two great things that play well together.

Choose the Best Discovery Method

The most common complaint of people who claim that MCollective won't meet their needs concerns the use of a broadcast mechanism for discovery. Indeed, the oldest versions of MCollective only supported the mc broadcast discovery method. If a server was offline when a request was issued, it wouldn't respond to discovery and thus wouldn't handle the request.

MCollective has long since grown to include discovery plugins that allow correlation of a wide variety of data. There are plugins to filter the list of servers from flat files, PuppetDB, Chef, Foreman, MongoDB, RiakDB, and Elastic Search. I'm sure there are even more I haven't found or that were created after this book was written.

There is a special message about discovery plugins that I'd like to call attention to: *use the discovery plugin appropriate for your request.*

You must use the same connector and the same security plugin on all nodes in your collective. However, you can use a different discovery plugin for each request. Choose the discovery plugin most appropriate to the request you are making.

For a simple example, in most cases I want requests to be processed only by nodes that are online and functional. If I want all nodes in the San Francisco cluster to restart Apache, I'm not worried about nodes that are currently offline. I will use the mc (default) discovery plugin to handle this request:

```
$ mco service httpd restart --with-class apache --target sf
```

However, if I want to shut down Apache on every node in that cluster, I'd want to ensure that any node that was offline got the message as soon as it came online. I'd use a command like this, which sends the request to all known servers and uses a really long timeout:

```
$ mco service httpd stop --dm flatfile --do sfweb.txt --ttl 3600 --timeout 3610
```

If necessary, I'd use a wrapper to rerun the command with a new list containing only the nodes that didn't respond.

You can find a list of discovery plugins by running a GitHub search for "mcollective discovery" (*https://github.com/search?q=mcollective+discovery&ref=cmdform*).

Authorize and Audit Each Request

Security of your MCollective deployment depends on the tri-part combination of your security (authentication), authorization, and auditing plugins. Each of them provides a necessary function:

- Choose the middleware security model that best protects your resources. Always encrypt if you transit any untrusted networks. If you already use Puppet, you can enable TLS encryption with trivial configuration changes on managed nodes.

- The security (authentication) plugin provides validated `caller` information to the authorization and auditing plugins. A poor choice of authentication mechanisms will reinforce the well-known *garbage in, garbage out* phenomenon.

- Make use of the granular access control provided by the SSL, AES, and SSHKey security plugins. Each of these plugins use public keys to cryptographically validate the identity of the `caller`.

- Don't stop at strong authentication. It is senseless to use strong authentication if you don't authorize each request. This is akin to checking someone's ID card, then handing them your wallet to do with as they please.

- It is better to have an explicit "allow any" rule in the authorization logic than to have none at all. It will be easier to adjust this rule when the time comes than it will be to perform a new installation of authorization rules.

- Always audit MCollective requests. Ensure that the audit data is backed up in the same secure manner that you store the authentication and sudo logs for nodes.

- As security is provided by plugins, each organization or even each collective of hosts can use a different security model that meets its needs.

MCollective's plugin architecture for security provides considerable flexibility in implementation. There is no singular *right way* to do security for MCollective; instead, you are provided with tools to make security work exactly as you need.

You can find detailed instructions for improving MCollective security in Chapter 11 and Chapter 13.

## CHAPTER 26

Grow Your Deployment

Immediately available from our installation of the stock Puppet Labs plugins, you can query and make changes to files, packages, services, and configuration-management daemons. You'll be able to find hundreds of useful plugins at GitHub, too. However, most of my clients found the real value in building plugins that implemented a feature specific to their environment.

There are numerous ways to use MCollective that you may not be aware of yet. After some growth, you may find ways of using MCollective that nobody has thought of. Take time to consider the possibilities.

Consider the Strings Analogy

The marionette metaphor can be a useful spark for creative thought. Consider which aspects of your environment you really wish you had a string attached to. What do you want it to pull? Are you pulling it with a stick in your hand or something more complex? Does a Puppet pull to notify you of something?

Ask yourself questions of this nature:

Where do you want a control knob? Where would you attach a string?

> This is an ideal situation for building a custom agent that can turn that knob or raise that lever. Refer to Chapter 15.

Of what would you like to have more information? What can you feel from the strings?

> This is an ideal situation for building a custom agent that you can query on request. Or perhaps you should create a registration plugin that supplies the information periodically and a listener to collect and process that information. Find more information in Chapter 21.

Do you use a dashboard to issue requests? To what are the strings attached?

> You can issue client commands from any application. Executing a Ruby script that includes the `MCollective::RPC` library client is the easy way, but anything that can issue a properly formatted request to the middleware broker can be a client. Check out Chapter 19.

Do you need to receive information when events occur? Does the Puppet pull on the strings?

> An MCollective agent doesn't have to wait for a request from a client. You could build agents that respond to events on the node and submit data to a client listener. The agent could be slim, and the listener could be a complex program capable of taking action based on the input. This is how you can build self-healing infrastructure. Build a listener from the example in Chapter 22.

This is really just the beginning of questions you can ask yourself. Think about the metaphor and how it could apply to your environment. Consider what you can accomplish.

> Then throw away the metaphor and consider choices that make no sense with a marionette and puppets on a string, too.

Utilize Support Resources

As you go forth with MCollective, I want to remind you of three mechanisms for support with your collectives:

#mcollective channel on Freenode (http://bit.ly/1nwbxPK)

> There is an IRC channel on Freenode for support of open source MCollective. Puppet Labs employees and other developers and users of MCollective provide ad hoc assistance in this channel. You will get the best response if you provide configuration samples and logs using a paste service like Gist (*https://gist.github.com/*) or Pastebin (*http://pastebin.com/*).

mcollective-users@googlegroups.com (http://bit.ly/1nwbzHA)

> Puppet Labs provides a mailing list for support of open source MCollective. This is the best channel for support involving complex questions or significant details. Puppet Labs employees and other developers of MCollective sometimes discuss deployment issues and develop consensus on changes in this mailing list.

Puppet Enterprise (http://puppetlabs.com/puppet/puppet-enterprise)

> Puppet Labs has a commercial product called Puppet Enterprise that contains MCollective and has standard and premium support plans. This is your best path for commercial support with a service-level agreement.
>
> Everything you learn in this book is applicable to the Puppet Enterprise usage of MCollective, but the base path to the configuration files becomes */opt/puppet*.

I personally contribute time to assist people on both the IRC channel and mailing list as much as my day job, tech writing, and need to sleep permit.

You are welcome and encouraged to submit any errors you find in this book using the View/Submit Errata (*http://oreilly.com/catalog/errata.csp?isbn=0636920032472*) link on the O'Reilly page for *Learning MCollective*. We appreciate your comments and intend to publish regular updates to the book.

Read Blogs

I have found the following blogs to be useful for monitoring the development and use of MCollective. Some of these are very active, others not as much. I've always found the content useful:

- R.I. Pienaar (original author of MCollective)

  http://www.devco.net/ and *https://twitter.com/ripienaar*

- Richard Clamp (one of the most active committers on MCollective and a helpful voice on #mcollective)

  http://richardc.unixbeard.net/ and *https://twitter.com/richardclamp*

- Peter Loubser (the other active committer on MCollective and another helpful voice on #mcollective)

  https://twitter.com/pieterloubser

- Jo Rhett (author of this book)

  http://www.netconsonance.com/ and *https://twitter.com/jorhett*

 OK, so I don't read that last blog as much as I should, but I've heard there's MCollective-related stuff posted there :)

There will be plugins and tips on MCollective above and beyond this book available at *http://www.netconsonance.com/tag/mcollective*.

Take the Strings Now

Now we are at the end. I have taught you everything I know about MCollective. You have the strings in your hands now, and you have the knowledge necessary to make your marionettes—er, I mean servers—dance.

You may have skipped through some sections of this book. That's OK; this book was meant to be something you could take a bit from, then come back again later to. I do hope you read about the security considerations of the default installation in Chapter 13. If not, run back and read that right now.

Believe it or not, your journey is just beginning. As you become more familiar and comfortable using MCollective, you will find more and more ways to use it. The people at nearly every site I have installed MCollective at spent time wondering how they would use it. In less than a year, they have all expressed to me that they have no idea how they ever got along without it.

I fully expect you to be one of those advocates. I look forward to hearing how you use MCollective and what unimagined new functionality you've implemented for your team.

Tips and Tools

Useful Commands Reference

Show all configuration data about an MCollective server:

```
$ mco inventory hostname
```

Test connectivity to an MCollective server or list of them:

```
$ mco ping hostname
$ mco ping --nodes /path/to/hostlist
```

Commands for testing host services (nettest agent):

```
$ mco nettest ping activemq.example.net
$ mco nettest connect activemq.example.net 61613
```

Find hosts that match certain criteria:

```
$ mco find --with-identity /web/
$ mco find --with-class webserver
$ mco find --with-fact operatingsystem=CentOS
$ mco find --with-agent package
$ mco find --with "/nameserver/ operatingsystem=CentOS"
$ mco find --select "operatingsystem=Ubuntu and /operatingsystemrelease=13.10/"
$ mco find --select "( operatingsystem=CentOS and !environment=dev )
  and is_virtual=true"
```

Commands for controlling files (filemgr agent):

```
$ mco filemgr --file /tmp/junk touch
$ mco filemgr --file /tmp/junk --detail status
$ mco filemgr --file /tmp/junk remove
```

Commands for controlling packages (`package` agent):

```
$ mco package top status
$ mco package -y top install
$ mco package -y top update
$ mco package -y top uninstall
$ mco package -y top purge
```

Commands for controlling system services (`service` agent):

```
$ mco service ntpd status
$ mco service ntpd restart
$ mco service ntpd stop
$ mco service ntpd start
```

Commands for controlling the Puppet agent:

```
$ mco puppet count
$ mco puppet summary
$ mco puppet disable --with-identity hostname message="Know this..."
$ mco puppet enable --with-identity hostname
$ mco puppet runonce --tags=tags --with-fact fact=value
$ mco puppet runall 5 --no-noop --tags=sudo
```

Using r10k to install Puppet Modules

r10k provides a general purpose toolset for deploying Puppet environments and modules. It implements the Puppetfile format and provides a native implementation of Puppet dynamic environments.

— *https://github.com/adrienthebo/r10k*

To translate that into English, r10k takes all the work out of managing a collection of Puppet modules and their dependencies on GitHub. If you'd like to deploy the *Learning MCollective* test environment (exactly as I used it when writing this book) in a fresh new environment, this is the fastest way to do it.

If you don't have r10k installed yet, let's do this first. Install it directly from the gem:

```
$ sudo gem install r10k
Successfully installed colored-1.2
Successfully installed cri-2.5.0
Successfully installed systemu-2.5.2
Successfully installed log4r-1.1.10
Successfully installed multi_json-1.8.4
Successfully installed json_pure-1.8.1
Successfully installed multipart-post-1.2.0
Successfully installed faraday-0.8.9
Successfully installed faraday_middleware-0.9.1
Successfully installed faraday_middleware-multi_json-0.0.5
Successfully installed r10k-1.2.1
11 gems installed
```

If you are using Ruby 1.8, then you may see errors like this when you run r10k:

```
Faraday: you may want to install system_timer for reliable timeouts
```

If so, install the gem specified:

```
$ sudo gem install system_timer
Building native extensions.  This could take a while...
Successfully installed system_timer-1.2.4
1 gem installed
```

Now that r10k is installed, you can proceed with using it to install the MCollective module. The following command will set up all of the modules in this book:

```
$ wget https://raw.githubusercontent.com/jorhett/learning-mcollective/master/
  r10k.yaml
$ r10k deploy -c r10k.yaml environment learning_mcollective -p
```

This will install files in a *learning_mcollective* environment; it will not affect your *production* environment. You're going to need to make some changes to these files before they will work. Edit the files in */etc/puppet/environments/learning_mcollective/hiera-data/* as follows:

1. Rename the two example.net node-specific YAML files to the names of your middleware broker and a client system.

2. Generate random passwords with openssl rand -base64 32 and put these values in the _password fields in the files.

If you are using a version of Puppet below 3.5.0, you will need changes like the following in the *puppet.conf* file to use dynamic environments:

```
[main]
  modulepath = $confdir/environments/$environment/modules:$confdir/modules

[master]
  hiera_config = $confdir/environments/$environment/hiera/hiera.yaml
  manifest     = $confdir/environments/$environment/manifests/site.pp
```

 More documentation about (pre v3.5) dynamic environments can be found at *http://docs.puppetlabs.com/guides/environment.html*. Documentation for the new directory environments in v3.5 and later can be found at *http://docs.puppetlabs.com/puppet/latest/refer ence/environments.html*.

After you have made these changes, you can test out the module using this Puppet command:

```
$ puppet agent --test --environment learning_mcollective
```

Using the PuppetLabs MCollective Module

Puppet Labs also provides an MCollective module on the Puppet Forge at *https://github.com/puppetlabs/puppetlabs-mcollective*. This module is not covered in this book for the following reasons:

- If you don't override them, the setup will use well-known usernames and passwords. A mistype would make your setup vulnerable to attack.

- It doesn't separate client and server permissions. Using the same authentication creates a security problem—if any server is compromised, it can control all other servers.

- It doesn't separate client permissions and broker link permissions.

- The Puppet Labs module has numerous external dependencies. This can be distracting to set up when trying to follow the book.

The module provided in this book allowed a simple setup to work immediately, and then a way for you to add more as you read each chapter in the book.

The Puppet Labs module does things a little different, and you should take a look. Now that you are proficient with MCollective, you may find this module very useful. Here is a baseline configuration that worked properly and isn't documented as clearly in the module itself:

```
class { '::mcollective::common::setting':
  connector                 => activemq,
  middleware_hosts          => ['activemq.example.net'],
  middleware_user           => 'server',
  middleware_password       => 'IamAServerLaLaLa',
  middleware_admin_user     => 'admin',
  middleware_admin_password => 'IAmAClientHoHoHo',
  securityprovider          => 'psk',
  psk                       => 'DearGnuChangeMe',
}

node 'activemq.example.net' {
  class { '::mcollective':
    middleware => true
  }
}

node 'server.example.net' {
  class { '::mcollective': }
}

node 'client.example.net' {
  class { '::mcollective':
    client => true
```

```
    }
}
```

 You are smart enough to change these passwords, aren't you? Remember that `openssl rand -base64 32` is your friend.

Using RabbitMQ

If you already have RabbitMQ in your environment, or if you need AMQP support (e.g., for `logstash`), then you may want to use RabbitMQ instead of ActiveMQ as the middleware for MCollective. In this section, we'll go over how to setup RabbitMQ and then how to migrate your MCollective environment to it.

Installing RabbitMQ

The process for installing RabbitMQ varies widely depending on your operating system type. In my experience, the versions of RabbitMQ available in your operating system package repositories are generally not the best choice. RabbitMQ has been evolving rapidly, and recent versions work much better with MCollective.

I recommend that you use the packages provided from the RabbitMQ download page (*http://www.rabbitmq.com/download.html*). There are instructions specific to each operating system in the "Installation Guides" section.

The necessary steps are the following:

1. Install Erlang dependencies from your OS packing providers.
2. Install the RabbitMQ package.

On CentOS, the process looks like this:

```
$ sudo rpm --import http://www.rabbitmq.com/rabbitmq-signing-key-public.asc
$ sudo yum install rabbitmq-server-3.3.2-1.noarch.rpm --enablerepo=epel
Loaded plugins: fastestmirror, security
Loading mirror speeds from cached hostfile
 * base: centos.sonn.com
 * epel: mirror.prgmr.com
 * extras: centos.sonn.com
 * updates: centos.sonn.com
Setting up Install Process
Examining rabbitmq-server-3.3.2-1.noarch.rpm: rabbitmq-server-3.3.2-1.noarch
Marking rabbitmq-server-3.3.2-1.noarch.rpm to be installed
Resolving Dependencies
--> Running transaction check
---> Package rabbitmq-server.noarch 0:3.3.2-1 will be installed
```

```
--> Processing Dependency: \
erlang >= R13B-03 for package: rabbitmq-server-3.3.2-1.noarch
--> Running transaction check
---> Package erlang.x86_64 0:R14B-04.3.el6 will be installed
    ...you know this drill

Complete!
```

Enable the STOMP connector and management plugins

If you are using Linux or Unix, the following commands will enable the STOMP connector and the management plugins:

```
$ sudo rabbitmq-plugins enable rabbitmq_stomp
rabbitmq-plugins enable rabbitmq_stomp
The following plugins have been enabled:
  amqp_client
  rabbitmq_stomp
Plugin configuration has changed. Restart RabbitMQ for changes to take effect.
$ sudo rabbitmq-plugins enable rabbitmq_management
The following plugins have been enabled:
  mochiweb
  webmachine
  rabbitmq_web_dispatch
  rabbitmq_management_agent
  rabbitmq_management
Plugin configuration has changed. Restart RabbitMQ for changes to take effect.
```

Start the server

Use the commands appropriate for your architecture:

```
$ sudo chkconfig rabbitmq on
$ service rabbitmq start
Starting rabbitmq-server: SUCCESS
rabbitmq-server.
```

You may see a failure message about *could not start, rabbitmq_stomp*:

```
$ sudo chkconfig rabbitmq on
$ service rabbitmq start
Starting rabbitmq-server: FAILED - check /var/log/rabbitmq/startup_{log, _err}
rabbitmq-server.
$ tail /var/log/rabbitmq/startup_log
Error description:
   {could_not_start,rabbitmq_stomp,
                    {shutdown,{rabbit_stomp,start,[normal,[]]}}}

Log files (may contain more information):
   /var/log/rabbitmq/rabbit@geode.log
   /var/log/rabbitmq/rabbit@geode-sasl.log

{"init terminating in do_boot",{rabbit,failure_during_boot,
```

```
{could_not_start,rabbitmq_stomp,{shutdown,
{rabbit_stomp,start,[normal,[]]}}}}}
```

This means that RabbitMQ can't listen on the default port for STOMP protocol, for example, 61613. This probably means that you are trying to run RabbitMQ and ActiveMQ on the same system.

Install the CLI tool

Download the CLI tool from your new RabbitMQ broker and install it somewhere in your path:

```
$ curl -sS http://rabbitmq.example.net:15672/cli/rabbitmqadmin -o rabbitmqadmin
$ sudo mv rabbitmqadmin /usr/local/sbin/
```

If you'd like to enable bash completion for rabbitmqadmin, run the following command:

```
$ rabbitmqadmin --bash-completion | sudo tee /etc/bash_completion.d/rabbitmqadmin
```

Configuring RabbitMQ with Puppet

The puppet-mcollective module we installed in Chapter 7 can configure a baseline RabbitMQ instance. You would define the middleware node setup and the following Hiera values for the *common.yaml* file:

```
# Common Hiera definitions
classes:
  - mcollective::middleware

mcollective::hosts:
  - 'rabbitmq.example.net'
mcollective::connector: rabbitmq
```

For the *rabbitmq.example.net.yaml* file, use:

```
# Common Hiera definitions
mcollective::middleware::directory   : /etc/rabbitmq
mcollective::middleware::config_file: rabbitmq.config
mcollective::middleware::user        : rabbitmq
mcollective::middleware::service     : rabbitmq-server
```

And declarative Puppet policy statements would look like this:

```
# Declarative policy
node default {
  class { 'mcollective':
    connector => 'rabbitmq',
    hosts     => ['rabbitmq.example.net'],
  }
}
# Declarative policy
  class { 'mcollective::middleware':
```

```
    directory   => '/etc/rabbitmq',
    config_file => 'rabbitmq.conf',
    user        => 'rabbitmq',
    service     => 'rabbitmq-server',
  }
}
```

The RabbitMQ module will perform the queue and topic setup steps documented in the following section.

Configuring RabbitMQ Manually

The final step is to configure the queues and topics for MCollective:

```
$ rabbitmqadmin declare vhost name=/mcollective
vhost declared
$ rabbitmqadmin declare user name=client tags=administrator \
password=Client Password
user declared
$ rabbitmqadmin declare permission vhost=/mcollective \
user=client configure='.*' write='.*' read='.*'
permission declared
$ rabbitmqadmin declare user name=server tags= password=Server Password
user declared
$ rabbitmqadmin declare permission vhost=/mcollective \
user=server configure='.*' write='.*' read='.*'
permission declared

$ for collective in mcollective subcollective1 subcollective2 ...; do
  rabbitmqadmin declare exchange --user=client --password=Client Password \
    --vhost=/mcollective name=${collective}_broadcast type=topic
  rabbitmqadmin declare exchange --user=client --password=Client Password \
    --vhost=/mcollective name=${collective}_directed type=direct
done
exchange declared
exchange declared
exchange declared
exchange declared
exchange declared
exchange declared
```

Using an Exchange with a RabbitMQ Federation

Testing has indicated that RabbitMQ won't support reply delivery using queues in a RabbitMQ federation. If you are using a federation, you will need to configure the clients to receive replies using an exchange instead of a queue:

```
$ rabbitmqadmin declare exchange --user=client --password=password #1 \
    --vhost=/mcollective name=mcollective_reply type=direct
```

Then you would modify the client configuration file as such:

```
plugin.rabbitmq.use_reply_exchange = true
```

You can find more specific information about RabbitMQ collectives at *http://docs.puppetlabs.com/mcollective/reference/plugins/connector_rabbitmq.html* and about RabbitMQ itself at *http://www.rabbitmq.com*.

OS Specifics

Configuring Debian and Ubuntu Firewalls

Debian and Ubuntu systems have `iptables` installed by default, but often without any blocking lines. First check and see if you have configured the firewall. If so, just add a new rule to allow the middleware service to be reached, as follows:

```
$ sudo iptables --list --line-numbers
Chain INPUT (policy ACCEPT)
num  target  prot opt source        destination
1    ACCEPT  all  --  anywhere      anywhere       state RELATED,ESTABLISHED
...etc...
```

Look through the output and find an appropriate line number for this rule:

```
$ sudo iptables -I INPUT 20 -m state --state NEW -p tcp \
  --source 192.168.200.0/24 --dport 61613 -j ACCEPT
```

If you have not confirmed the firewall yet, you can set up a very basic firewall that only allows SSH, ICMP, and ActiveMQ as follows:

```
$ sudo iptables -A 10 INPUT -m state --state RELATED,ESTABLISHED -j ACCEPT
$ sudo iptables -A 20 INPUT -p icmp -j ACCEPT
$ sudo iptables -A 30 INPUT -i lo -j ACCEPT
$ sudo iptables -A 40 INPUT -p tcp -m state --state NEW -m tcp --dport 22 -j
  ACCEPT
$ sudo iptables -A 50 INPUT -m state --state NEW -p tcp \
  --source 192.168.200.0/24 --dport 61613 -j ACCEPT
$ sudo iptables -A 9999 INPUT -j REJECT --reject-with icmp-host-prohibited
```

If all of your servers will fit within a few subnet masks, it is advisable to limit this rule to only allow those subnets. Don't forget to save that rule to your initial rules file. For Debian and Ubuntu systems, you have to manually set up loading and unloading the firewall yourself. Here's a process that will do that for you:

```
$ sudo "iptables-save > /etc/iptables.rules"
iptables: Saving firewall rules to /etc/sysconfig/iptables:[  OK  ]

$ sudo vim /etc/network/if-pre-up.d/iptables
#!/bin/sh
/sbin/iptables-restore < /etc/iptables.rules

$ sudo chmod +x /etc/network/if-pre-up.d/iptables
```

More details can be found at *https://wiki.debian.org/iptables* or *https://help.ubuntu.com/community/IptablesHowTo*.

My apologies, I didn't include IPv6-specific instructions in this section. The commands are nearly identical to the IPv4 counterparts. You can see fully documented IPv6 examples in "Configuring ActiveMQ" on page 17.

FreeBSD

Although Puppet Labs only provides binary packages for Linux systems, I was able to use FreeBSD as a server, client, and middleware broker successfully while writing this book. The configuration steps specific to FreeBSD follow.

Using the Next Generation Package Manager

For FreeBSD 10 and above, use a new package management system. If you are on FreeBSD 9, you will have to make some changes to your system to use the new package manager. I recommend doing this, as it will greatly improve Puppet's ability to manage packages on your systems.

Details on migrating to the new package manager are at *https://wiki.freebsd.org/pkgng*. By the time this book is out, Puppet hopefully will have the new package manager integrated (see bug PUP-1716), but until then, you can install the module from the Forge:

```
$ puppet module install zleslie/pkgng
```

Then add the following to your manifests:

```
if ($::osfamily == 'FreeBSD') {
  include pkgng
  Package {
    provider => pkgng,
  }
}
```

Configuring ActiveMQ

Altering the Java environment parameters is done with the `activemq_javargs` parameter in */etc/rc.conf*. Note that FreeBSD cuts the memory of ActiveMQ in half compared to Linux distributions, such that Java is limited to 256 MB total. You probably want to quadruple this if you have the memory available.

Configuring the Firewall

FreeBSD ships with IPFW installed and available in the base system. Unlike `ipta bles`, one can mix IPv4 and IPv6 statements in the same configuration. You could use the following steps to add a firewall rule to permit inbound connections to a FreeBSD ActiveMQ middleware host:

```
$ sudo ipfw list
00010 allow ip from any to any via lo0
00011 deny ip from any to 127.0.0.0/8
00012 deny ip from any to [::1]/8
00020 check-state
00021 allow tcp from any to any out setup keep-state
...etc...
```

Look through the output and find an appropriate line number for this rule:

```
$ sudo ipfw -q add 31 allow tcp from 2001:DB8:6A:C0::/64 to any 61613 in
$ sudo ipfw -q add 32 allow tcp from 192.168.200.0/24 to any 61613 in
```

If all of your servers will fit within a few subnet masks, it is advisable to limit this rule to only allow those subnets. Don't forget to save that rule to your initial rules file and enable it to be read at boot time:

```
firewall_enable="YES"
firewall_script="/etc/ipfw.rules"

ipfw -q -f flush        # Delete all rules
IPF="ipfw -q add "      # build rule prefix
$IPF 00010 allow ip from any to any via lo0
$IPF 00011 deny ip from any to 127.0.0.0/8
$IPF 00012 deny ip from any to [::1]/8
$IPF 00020 check-state
$IPF 00021 allow tcp from any to any out setup keep-state
$IPF 00022 allow udp from any to any out keep-state
$IPF 00023 allow icmp from any to any
$IPF 31 allow tcp from 2001:DB8:6A:C0::/64 to any 61613 in
$IPF 32 allow tcp from 192.168.200.0/24 to any 61613 in
```

More details can be found at *http://www.freebsd.org/doc/handbook/firewalls-ipfw.html*.

Installing Agents

At the time this book was written, none of the agents was packaged for FreeBSD, and the package tool did not support FreeBSD. To install agents on FreeBSD, follow the instructions in "Installing from Source" on page 25. Here is a short recap with FreeBSD-specific paths:

```
$ git clone http://github.com/puppetlabs/mcollective-filemgr-agent.git
Cloning into 'mcollective-filemgr-agent'...
remote: Reusing existing pack: 49, done.
remote: Total 49 (delta 0), reused 0 (delta 0)
Unpacking objects: 100% (49/49), done.
Checking connectivity... done
$ cd mcollective-filemgr-agent
$ cp agent/filemgr.rb /usr/local/share/mcollective/agent/
$ cp agent/filemgr.dll /usr/local/share/mcollective/agent/
$ cp application/filemgr.rb /usr/local/share/mcollective/application/
$ sudo service mcollectived restart
Stopping mcollectived.
Starting mcollectived.
```

Mac OS X

If you'd like to be able to make MCollective requests from your Mac desktop, or even subscribe as a server from your Mac, the process to set this up is pretty easy.

Installing Ruby

Macs with Mountain Lion (10.8) come with Ruby 1.8.7 installed, which is good. Macs with Mavericks (10.9) or Yosemite (10.10) have Ruby 2.0, which is also good. If your Mac doesn't have an appropriate version of Ruby installed, you want to install Ruby 1.9.3. To do this, install MacPorts and then use the following commands:

```
For Ruby 1.9
$ port install ruby19 +nosuffix
```

The only remaining requirement necessary is to install the STOMP gem:

```
$ gem install stomp
Successfully installed stomp-1.3.2
1 gem installed
Installing ri documentation for stomp-1.3.2...
Installing RDoc documentation for stomp-1.3.2...
```

Installing MCollective

At the time of writing, there were no packages available for MCollective, but the process to build proper Mac OS packages is not difficult.

You will need Xcode installed on one system where you can build the Mac OS package to install on the remaining systems. You can get Xcode from Mac App Store: Xcode (*http://itunes.apple.com/us/app/xcode/id497799835?ls=1&mt=12*).

Next, you should download the latest stable release from GitHub and install it like so:

```
$ curl -sL \
  https://github.com/puppetlabs/marionette-collective/archive/2.5.3.tar.gz \
    -o marionette-collective-2.5.3.tar.gz
$ tar xzf marionette-collective-2.5.3.tar.gz
$ cd marionette-collective-2.5.3
$ bash ext/osx/bldmacpkg .
.................
created: /Users/jorhett/marionette-collective-2.5.3/mcollective-2.5.3.dmg
```

At the time this book was written, the script didn't properly find the version, and you would get packages named *mcollective-@DEVELOPMENT_VERSION@.dmg*. My workaround for that problem was to simply edit one file before building the packages:

```
$ $EDITOR lib/mcollective.rb
    VERSION="2.5.3"
```

At the time this book was written, the installation would incorrectly install the modules in the Ruby 1.8 *site_lib* directory on Mavericks and Yosemite. My workaround for that problem was to simply edit one file before building the packages:

```
$ $EDITOR ext/osx/bldmacpkg
Replace all instances of /Library/Ruby/Site/1.8 with /Library/Ruby/Site/2.0.0
```

You can take these packages and install them on any Mac (Figure B-1). Note that you have to manually install the MCollective-Common package on each machine; the server and client packages won't include it. Configuring MCollective and using it is identical to any other Unix platform. Here's a test from my home iMac to a remote colocation facility:

```
$ sudo $EDITOR /etc/mcollective/client.cfg
Password:
```

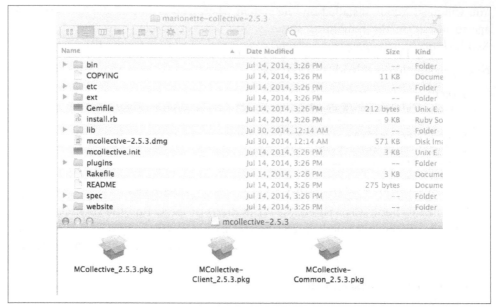

Figure B-1. The Mac OS installer packages

Update the configuration to match your other client systems. Then test just as before:

```
$ mco ping
sunstone                              time=52.14 ms
geode                                 time=52.59 ms
fireagate                             time=52.95 ms
heliotrope                            time=56.69 ms

---- ping statistics ----
4 replies max: 56.69 min: 52.14 avg: 53.59
```

Upgrades Overwrite the Configuration Files

At the time I tested, upgrading the MCollective client on my Mac overwrote the previous client configuration file. So make a backup of your configuration files before you perform an upgrade.[1]

Solaris

At the time I wrote this book, the Solaris MCollective servers and clients had to be compiled from source. The good news is that contributed Makefiles already existed to make the process easy.

---

1 You can track the status of this bug at MCO-244 Bug (*https://tickets.puppetlabs.com/browse/MCO-244*).

Installing on Solaris 11

Installing MCollective on Solaris 11 is quite easy:

```
$ pkg install pkg:/runtime/ruby-18x
$ pkg install system/header
$ pkg install developer/gcc-3
$ gem install stomp
$ gem install json

$ wget -q https://github.com/puppetlabs/marionette-collective/archive/2.5.3 \
  .tar.gz -O marionette-collective-2.5.3.tar.gz
$ tar xzf marionette-collective-2.5.3.tar.gz
$ cd marionette-collective-2.5.3
$ make -f ext/solaris11/Makefile install
```

Updates to this process and instructions on how to build IPS packages are available in the *ext/solaris11/README* file.

Installing on Solaris 10 and Before

Install the following OpenCSW packages to meet the requirements for running MCollective from OpenCSW Solaris packages (*http://www.opencsw.org/*):

- coreuitls (CSWcoreutils)
- gmake (CSWgmake)
- ggrep (CSWggrep)
- ruby (CSWruby)
- rubygems (CSWrubygems)

Install the STOMP and JSON RubyGems. You can do this with the gem command:

```
$ gem install stomp
$ gem install json
```

Or download the RubyGems from *https://rubygems.org/gems/stomp* and *https://ruby gems.org/gems/json* and install them directly:

```
$ gem install --local stomp-1.3.2.gem
$ gem install --local json-1.8.1.gem
```

Now that all the dependencies are installed, build MCollective:

```
$ wget -q https://github.com/puppetlabs/marionette-collective/archive/2.5.3 \
  .tar.gz -O marionette-collective-2.5.3.tar.gz
$ tar xzf marionette-collective-2.5.3.tar.gz
$ cd marionette-collective-2.5.3/ext/solaris
$ ./build
```

Your client and server configuration files will need to reference the OpenCSW-specific plugin path. This will be the same place you will put agent and client plugin files:

```
libdir = /opt/csw/share/mcollective/plugins
```

Updates to this process are available in the *ext/solaris/README* file.

Windows

Windows is not fully supported in the community version of MCollective at this time, but `mcollectived` and various agents all seem to function naturally. Let's take a look at the process for installing MCollective on a Windows server.

Acquiring Ruby

Installing Ruby on Windows is very straightforward:

1. Go to *http://rubyinstaller.org/* (Figure B-2).

Figure B-2. RubyInstaller.org

2. Click Download.
3. Under RubyInstallers, click version 1.9.3.
4. If prompted, choose to run rubyinstaller-1.9.3, as shown in Figure B-3.

Figure B-3. MSIE download prompt

5. Choose your language.

6. Read the license and agree if it suits you.

7. On the Optional Tasks screen, select the following options (as shown in Figure B-4):

   a. Add Ruby executables to your path

   b. Associate *.rb* files with this Ruby installation

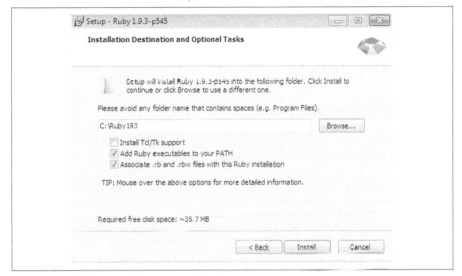

Figure B-4. Ruby Installer optional tasks

8. Click Finish.

Adding the RubyGem Dependencies

Install the RubyGem dependencies by opening the Command Prompt and typing the following three commands. You can find the Command Prompt in the Start Menu under All Programs → Accessories:

```
C:\> gem install --no-rdoc --no-ri stomp win32-service sys-admin windows-api
Fetching: stomp-1.3.2.gem (100%)
Successfully installed stomp-1.3.2
Fetching: win32-service-0.8.4.gem (100%)
Successfully installed win32-service-0.8.4
Fetching: sys-admin-1.6.3.gem (100%)
Successfully installed sys-admin-1.6.3
Fetching: win32-api-1.5.1-universal-mingw32.gem (100%)
Fetching: windows-api-0.4.2.gem (100%)
Successfully installed win32-api-1.5.1-universal-mingw32
Successfully installed windows-api-0.4.2
```

```
5 gems installed

C:\> gem install --no-rdoc --no-ri win32-dir -v 0.3.7
Fetching: windows-pr-1.2.3.gem (100%)
Fetching: win32-dir-0.3.7.gem (100%)
Successfully installed windows-pr-1.2.3
Successfully installed win32-dir-0.3.7
2 gems installed

C:\> gem install --no-rdoc --no-ri win32-process -v 0.5.5
Fetching: win32-process-0.5.5.gem (100%)
Successfully installed win32-process-0.5.5
1 gem installed

C:\> exit
```

Installing MCollective

At the time of writing, there were no Windows packages available for MCollective, but the process to install MCollective is easy:

1. Download the latest stable release from GitHub (*https://github.com/puppetlabs/marionette-collective/archive/2.5.3.tar.gz*).

2. Extract the files into the *C:\mcollective* directory.

3. Fix the version string.

   At the time this book was written, the daemon didn't properly find the version, and you would be told that mcollectived was version @DEVELOPMENT_VERSION@. My workaround for that problem was to simply edit *C:\mcollective\lib\mcollective.rb* before taking any other steps.

   Change: VERSION="2.5.3"

4. Move the binaries into place using the Command Prompt again:

   ```
   C:\> cd \mcollective
   C:\mcollective>copy ext\windows\*.* bin\
   ext\windows\daemon.bat
   ext\windows\environment.bat
   ext\windows\mco.bat
   ext\windows\README.md
   ext\windows\register_service.bat
   ext\windows\service_manager.rb
   ext\windows\unregister_service.bat
           7 file(s) copied.
   ```

5. Make copies of the configuration examples to customize:

   ```
   C:\mcollective>cd etc
   C:\mcollective\etc>copy client.cfg.dist client.cfg
           1 file(s) copied.
   ```

```
C:\mcollective\etc>copy server.cfg.dist server.cfg
       1 file(s) copied.

C:\mcollective\etc>copy facts.yaml.dist facts.yaml
       1 file(s) copied.

C:\mcollective\etc>exit
```

6. Use Notepad++ (or your favorite editor that supports Unix linefeeds) to edit *C:\mcollective\etc\server.cfg* as follows:

```
# ActiveMQ Server
connector = activemq
plugin.activemq.heartbeat_interval = 30
plugin.activemq.pool.size = 1
plugin.activemq.pool.1.host = activemq.example.net
plugin.activemq.pool.1.port = 61613
plugin.activemq.pool.1.user = server
plugin.activemq.pool.1.password = Server Password

# Explicitly indicate puppet agent's location
plugin.puppet.command = C:\Program Files (x86)\Puppet
Labs\Puppet\bin\puppet.exe

# Facts
factsource = yaml
plugin.yaml = /etc/mcollective/facts.yaml

# Security and Connector Plugins
securityprovider = psk
plugin.psk = Pre-Shared Key

# MCollective daemon settings
libdir = C:\mcollective\plugins
logfile = C:\mcollective\mcollective.log
loglevel = info
daemonize = 1
```

7. Use Notepad++ (or your favorite editor) to edit *C:\mcollective\etc\client.cfg* as follows:

```
direct_addressing = 1
main_collective = mcollective
collectives = mcollective

# ActiveMQ Server
connector = activemq
plugin.activemq.heartbeat_interval = 30
plugin.activemq.pool.size = 1
plugin.activemq.pool.1.host = activemq.example.net
plugin.activemq.pool.1.port = 61613
plugin.activemq.pool.1.user = client
plugin.activemq.pool.1.password = Client Password
```

```
# Explicitly indicate puppet agent's location
plugin.puppet.command = C:\Program Files (x86)\Puppet
Labs\Puppet\bin\puppet.exe

# Security and Connector Plugins
securityprovider = psk
plugin.psk = Pre-Shared Key

# MCollective daemon settings
libdir = C:\mcollective\plugins
logger_type = console
loglevel = warn
```

8. Start a Command Prompt as administrator, as shown in Figure B-5.

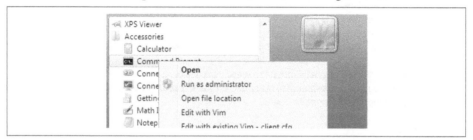

Figure B-5. Command Prompt: Run as administrator

9. Enter the *C:\mcollective\bin* directory and run `register_service.bat`:

```
C:\Windows\system32>cd \mcollective\bin

C:\mcollective\bin>register_service.bat
Service mcollectived installed

C:\mcollective\bin>exit
```

10. Right-click My Computer and select Manage.

    a. Under "Services and Applications," expand Services.

    b. Find "The Marionette Collective" and start the service (Figure B-6).

    c. Click Properties to enable automatic start at boot.

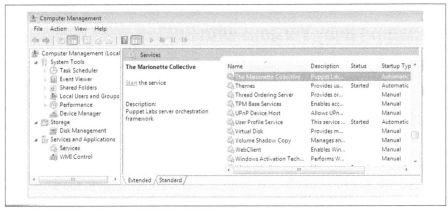

Figure B-6. MCollective Service

11. Add *C:\mcollective\bin* to your *PATH*.

12. Test!

```
C:\mcollective\bin>mco ping
sunstone                              time=1706.05 ms
heliotrope                            time=1721.68 ms
fireagate                             time=1723.63 ms
geode                                 time=1725.59 ms
tanzanite                             time=1727.54 ms
jade                                  time=1930.66 ms

---- ping statistics ----
6 replies max: 1930.66 min: 1706.05 avg: 1755.86
```

If you aren't running Puppet on the Windows box, you may want to add some useful static facts to the *facts.yaml* file. Here's what I used on my test system:

```
---
mcollective: 1
architecture: x86_64
operatingsystem: Windows
operatingsystemrelease: "7 Ultimate SP1"
```

At this point, you have a fully working MCollective daemon and client on your Windows system. Aside from the differences in the installed paths, every configuration option should work identically to the Linux versions.

Managing Ruby Versions with RVM

An easy way to install and manage multiple versions of Ruby on Linux or Unix environments is to use the Ruby Version Manager (RVM).

If your operating system does not include Ruby in the base OS libraries, or you wish to use a different version, RVM is designed to assist you. This large shell script will set up Ruby on your system in one easy step. The only command you need to run is this:

```
$ \curl -L https://get.rvm.io | bash -s stable --ruby=1.9.3
```

The backslash before `curl` is to prevent an alias for curl from being used. The output of this command will walk you through the installation. If you want more than a simple install of Ruby, you can learn more about installing and using RVM at *https://rvm.io/rvm/install*.

Index

About the Author

Jo Rhett is a network architect and DevOps engineer with 20 years of experience conceptualizing and delivering large-scale Internet services. He focuses on creating automation and infrastructure to accelerate deployment and minimize outages.

Jo has been using, promoting, and enhancing configuration management systems for over 20 years. He builds improvements and plugins for CfEngine, Puppet, MCollective, and many other DevOps-related tools.

Colophon

The animal on the cover of *Learning MCollective* is an English Leicester sheep, a breed that is currently found in Australia, New Zealand, Great Britain, and the United States. These sheep can thrive in a wide variety of climactic conditions due to their large frame and heavy fleece: rams average 250 pounds and ewes 180 pounds.

The breed was developed in the 1700s by Robert Bakewell, who was the first to utilize modern animal breeding techniques in the selection of livestock, and even George Washington and Thomas Jefferson brought Leicester rams from England to improve their flocks.

The Leicester fleece is prized for its curl and soft handle, and dyes exceptionally well. The fleece generally weighs from 11 to 15 pounds with some weighing as much as 20 pounds.

These sheep are categorized now as "endangered" since fewer than 500 registered females remain in the United Kindgom. Breeds considered critical have fewer than 200 North American annual registrations and an estimated global population of less than 2,000.

Many of the animals on O'Reilly covers are endangered; all of them are important to the world. To learn more about how you can help, go to animals.oreilly.com.

The cover image is from Meyers Kleines Lexicon. The cover fonts are URW Typewriter and Guardian Sans. The text font is Adobe Minion Pro; the heading font is Adobe Myriad Condensed; and the code font is Dalton Maag's Ubuntu Mono.

Have it your way.

Get even more for your money.

Join the O'Reilly Community, and register the O'Reilly books you own. It's free, and you'll get:

- $4.99 ebook upgrade offer
- 40% upgrade offer on O'Reilly print books
- Membership discounts on books and events
- Free lifetime updates to ebooks and videos
- Multiple ebook formats, DRM FREE
- Participation in the O'Reilly community
- Newsletters
- Account management
- 100% Satisfaction Guarantee

Signing up is easy:

1. Go to: oreilly.com/go/register
2. Create an O'Reilly login.
3. Provide your address.
4. Register your books.

Note: English-language books only

To order books online:
oreilly.com/store

For questions about products or an order:
orders@oreilly.com

To sign up to get topic-specific email announcements and/or news about upcoming books, conferences, special offers, and new technologies:
elists@oreilly.com

For technical questions about book content:
booktech@oreilly.com

To submit new book proposals to our editors:
proposals@oreilly.com

O'Reilly books are available in multiple DRM-free ebook formats. For more information:
oreilly.com/ebooks

O'REILLY®

Lightning Source UK Ltd.
Milton Keynes UK
UKHW031343150419
341049UK00005B/417/P

9 781491 945674